MEALS WITHOUT SQUEALS

Child Care Feeding Guide and Cookbook

SECOND EDITION

Christine Berman, M.P.H., R.D.
Jacki Fromer

A NOTE TO PARENTS THIS BOOK applies as much to your own parenting and child care as it does to professional child care programs. As a bonus, you will learn about important issues facing child care providers as they plan nutrition programs. With this knowledge you can confidently interact with those who care for your children—helping them provide the good nutrition all children deserve.

Bull Publishing Company

Bull Publishing Company
P. O. Box 1377
Boulder, Co. 80306
Phone (800) 676-2855
Fax (303) 545-6354

ISBN 0-923521-39-9

Distributed in the United States by:
Publishers Group West
1700 Fourth Street
Berkeley, CA 94710

Publisher: James Bull
Production: Myrna Engler/Rogue Valley Publications
Cover Design: Robb Pawlak, Pawlak Design
Cover Photo: John Fortunato/Tony Stone Images
Interior Design: Susan Rogin Type+Design
Composition: Susan Rogin Type+Design
Printer: Malloy Lithographing, Inc.

Fourth Printing

Library of Congress Cataloging-in-Publication Data

Berman, Christine.
    Meals without squeals : child care feeding guide and cookbook /
Christine Berman and Jacki Fromer.—2nd ed.
        p.   cm.
    Includes bibliographical references and indexes.
    ISBN 0-923521-39-9
    1. Children—Nutrition.   2. Cookery.   I. Fromer. Jacki.
II. Title.
TX361.C5B47   1997
649'.3—dc21   97–29116
                CIP

Contents

Preface

A walk through the diet/nutrition section of most bookstores may be overwhelming because of the hundreds of books promoting better health or no-fail weight loss through some sort of food regimen. I honestly don't know how people can sort out what's useful from what's a waste of time! My major concern is that useful nutrition and health information—or "the big picture"—is overlooked because of a focus on trendy nutrients and "miracle" foods.

In the 6 years or so since the first edition of this book was published, there have been some noteworthy changes in the nutrition field; many relate to the way information is presented to the public, such as the Food Guide Pyramid or the form of nutrition labels on foods. Some relationships between nutrition and health have been clarified; for example, evidence for the benefits of eating lots of fruits and vegetables grows stronger and stronger. But although there are some very interesting theories regarding foods or nutrients and their effects on our health, at this point they are still just theories, and I will not add to the confusion by including them here. My goal is to present you with solid and practical advice about feeding children, other people's or your own. I have included more checklists to help keep you or your staff organized.

While offering training to parents, teachers, caregivers, and food service workers during the last few years, I have found that there are a few themes I consistently need to emphasize, and I offer them here to you:

1. *Foods are not "bad" or "evil" in themselves (except those that happen to be contaminated or poisonous), but there are eating patterns that may not be especially helpful in keeping us, or our environment, healthy.*

If you avoid making demons or saints out of particular foods, you'll find it easier to keep your perspective when faced with a child who really likes, for example, bologna. Rather than trying to *convert* him to your point of view, you can respect the child's taste and simply realize that his eating bologna occasionally (the definition of which can vary widely) probably won't ruin his health in the long term. Ideally, childhood is the time to experience and learn to enjoy a wide variety of healthful foods, and liking foods that aren't nutritious isn't really at cross purposes with that.

Nutritional balance is in the amounts and frequency of foods eaten. You are in control of how often certain foods are offered to a child and of the amounts that are available to her or him. It is not a sign of your failure if a child dislikes cauliflower or likes candy. So you can relax a little now.

Ask yourself how often you've remarked that you're being "bad" when you eat a chocolate dessert at a party, or that you were really "good" at lunchtime because you had a salad. Do you really think that one piece of chocolate is going to doom you or that one salad will save you? I'm not saying that what you eat or don't eat makes *no* difference (after all, I work as a nutritionist because I think what we eat is important); I'm just hoping people will adopt a more compassionate approach to eating, both in their own case and in dealing with others, children included.

2. *It's important for you to determine what your philosophy and policies regarding feeding are going to be and communicate them to parents, preferably in writing, before their children become part of your classroom or child care site.*

You may set these policies with a group of staff members to make certain they are consistent with the philosophy of your program, you may make decisions on your own, or you may want parents to participate. But trust me, it is better to anticipate problems such as parents who want you to follow a strict schedule in feeding a young baby, or parents who want to bring in special foods because their child doesn't like what's offered in your lunch program, than to face conflicts later that disrupt the environment you are trying to set up for all of the children.

Consider a situation in which some parents don't want you to offer milk or any other animal foods to their child; you are unwilling to cook exclusively, or separate, vegan meals; and not offering milk affects your Child Care Food Program reimbursement. If alternative child care or schooling is available to the family, you might suggest—gently and non-judgmentally—that they seek out a situation more compatible with their beliefs. This way, you avoid disrupting the child's routine later on, after you've bonded with the child and become accustomed to the income.

Parents, when you are seeking a child care or school placement for your child, you should look at foods served, mealtime atmosphere, and food safety practices to make sure you are comfortable with the situation. Inquire about feeding policies and procedures, and make your child's special feeding needs known to all caregivers right away. Look into ways you can be helpful; for example, offer recipes or nutrition information you've collected, provide supplies for nutrition education activities, or volunteer to dig in the school garden.

3. *Because more is discovered about nutrition all the time, it's important to keep yourself well informed so that you can practice good eating habits in your own life and be a reliable source of information about feeding children for the families with whom you are working. This will also help you keep your policies current.*

For general information about nutrition, there are more and better resources now than ever before. Check the appendices in the back of this book for some of my favorites. As positive role models for children and their families, we owe it to them to be well informed about how to reap the benefits of good nutrition in our own lives.

To stay current about child nutrition issues, you may find it useful to cultivate a relationship with your local Child Care Food Program sponsor or Head Start, Special Supplemental Food Program for Women, Infants, and Children (WIC), or Agricultural Extension nutritionist. These people make it their business to inform parents or teachers about feeding children. You might be able to get on the mailing list for a newsletter, attend trainings, or simply find you have someone you can call with questions.

Good luck to you!

C. B.

Acknowledgments

Special thanks to Carol Larson for generosity of time and computer expertise in spite of an incredibly busy schedule, Reed Fromer and Peter White for guidance in editing and organizing, and David Fromer for those invaluable, enthusiastic pep talks.

With loving appreciation . . .

. . . to our family members for their assistance, encouragement, confidence, suggestions, patience, and love: David, Reed, and Rachel Fromer; Mitch Berman; Wynter and Mai Grant; Carol, Brad, Matthew, and Sierra Larson; Ann Spake; Jon Fromer; and Barbara and Art Storeide.

. . . to our dear friends and associates for their ideas, critiques, generosity, enthusiasm, moral support, friendship, and recipes: Barbara Abrams, DR.P.H., R.D.; Rita Abrams; Charlotte Albert; Pat Ayotte; Katy Baer, M.P.H., R.D.; Nina Baker; Judy Bartlett; Linda McKee; Elaine Belle; Georgia Berry; Ruth Bramell; Marek Cepietz; Doris Disbrow, DR.P.H., R.D.; Doris Fredericks, M.ED., R.D.; Elazar Freidman; Diana Goodrow, Robin Goodrow, and Vanilla; Gail Hartman; Geri Henchy, M.P.H., R.D.; Bev Hoffman; Paula James; Sally Jones; Steven Kipperman; Mallory and Kevin Kopple; DeLona Kurtz; Sharon and Chiya Landry; Belinda Laucke; the staff of Marin Head Start; Elizabeth McGrady; Anne Milkie; Hannah Moore; Eileen Nelson; Liisa O'Maley; Katie O'Neill, M.P.H., R.D.; Lloyd Partch; Bayla Penman; Karen Jeffrey Pertschuk, M.P.H., R.D.; Johanne Quinlan; Helen Rossini; Zak Sabry, PH.D.; Ellyn Satter, R.D., A.C.S.W.; Max Shapiro; Jackie Shonerd; Steve Susskind;

Mary Syracuse; The Earth Store; Barbara Taylor; Steve Thompson; Kate Warin; Rona Weintraub; Peter White; Barbara Zeavin; Jill Zwicky; and the Marin Child Care Council staff members: Emilie Albertoli, Lynne Arceneaux, Terry DeMartini, Teresa Leibert, Mary Moore, Susan Sanders, and Hilda Castillo Wilson.

. . . to the wonderful people at Bull Publishing Company for the opportunity to bring our project to fruition, and to those at Rogue Valley Publications for their expert and kind guidance.

. . . in loving memory and admiration of Florence Raskin, Katherine Fromer, Necia "Ida" Fromer, and Arthur Storeide.

. . . and for the continuing inspiration we receive from child care providers and teachers who are dedicated to the well-being of children.

How to Use This Book

Meals Without Squeals is not the sort of book you must read cover to cover, like a novel. We wanted you to have a good place to find easily accessible answers to your questions about food and children, so we addressed very specific topics in one- or two-page sections.

We suggest that you start by reading the first chapter, "What You Should Know About Feeding Children," because that will introduce you to our philosophy and give you an overview of the important issues that come up when you are feeding children. Next, review the table of contents to find the topics that appear to be most useful to you. Briefly, here's what you will find in *Meals Without Squeals:*

Chapter One: **What You Should Know About Feeding Children . . .**
   Your role in good nutrition for children and why it's so important.

Chapter Two: **Feeding and Growth . . .**
   How to handle the feeding issues that arise as children pass through different stages of development.

Chapter Three: **Planning How and What to Feed Children . . .**
   How to plan menus that incorporate the latest guidelines for healthful eating and how to set up mealtimes that everyone can enjoy, including you.

Chapter Four: **The Recipes . . .**
   Dozens of easy, economical, and healthful recipes for foods children love.

*Chapter Five: **Sample Menus Using Our Recipes**...*

*Chapter Six: **Running a Ship-Shape Kitchen**...*
Tips for cutting food costs, choosing ingredients, using
microwave ovens, keeping your kitchen clean and safe,
and more.

*Chapter Seven: **Environmental Concerns**...*
How to run a feeding program that's earth-friendly.

*Appendix A: **A Basic Scheme for Nutrition Education**...*
How to integrate teaching children about food into your
feeding program.

*Appendix B: **Nutrition Basics**...*
A *very* short course in nutrition.

*Appendix C: **Special Topics**...*
Information about subjects that often come up when you're
dealing with children—for example, food allergies, obesity,
or sugar.

*Appendix D: **References**...*

*Appendix E: **Resources**...*
Where to go for supplies or more information.

We hope you will use this book with its companion volume,
Teaching Children About Food, because they really do complement
each other. The foods that you serve and the way that you handle
mealtimes are important in teaching children about food. And a
program of nutrition education can help children accept more
readily the wonderful and healthful foods they're being served.
Dig in and enjoy!

To our children

Wynter and Mai

Reed and Rachel

PART ONE
Feeding and Children

Chapter *One*

What You Should Know About Feeding Children

Why a Child Feeding Guide?

Many factors determine whether we'll enjoy long and healthy lives. Some we don't have much control over, like our heredity and our environment. Others we can do something about, such as developing good eating habits, exercising regularly, managing stress, and not smoking, drinking to excess, or using drugs. Children are in a particularly vulnerable position regarding these lifestyle factors. They depend on adults to provide what they need in order to grow and be healthy, and they look to adults as role models in shaping their behaviors. We think that everyone who works with children, be they parents or caregivers, should be aware of the important connection between nutrition and children's health:

- Children need to consume the right amounts and kinds of nutrients in order to grow well; to avoid overweight, tooth decay, and other problems; and to have good resistance to illness.

- Children who aren't well nourished tend to have more problems in school. They are likely to be tired, inattentive, less curious, and less independent than their well-fed peers. They may also be irritable and less sociable, and in general have more behavior problems.

- During childhood, eating patterns and attitudes develop that may affect health later on. More than two-thirds of the deaths in the United States are caused by diseases that can be related to eating habits: heart disease, some cancers, hypertension, and diabetes.

- The way feeding is handled affects a child's perceptions of what to expect from the world—whether he will see it as a friendly and nurturing place or as a cold and frustrating one.

We have noticed that there is a lot of confusion among parents and caregivers about what to feed children, how to feed children, and how to teach children what they need to know in order to be healthy and happy adults. We wrote this book to make practical information about nutrition available to anyone involved in the care of children.

The Role of the Caregiver in Children's Nutrition

It's 6 P.M. on Wednesday evening. Father has just arrived home from the office. Mother is in the kitchen putting the finishing touches on the evening meal. The cinnamony smell of fresh-baked apple pie permeates the air. Andy and Beth have just finished setting the table. Everyone washes up and sits down to a leisurely family meal. The phone does not ring, for everyone knows it's suppertime. The TV will not be turned on until the table has been cleared.

Sound familiar? Of course not! This scene is likely to be viewed on reruns of a 1960 family sitcom, but is not so typical in a real-life household of today. In fact, a recent survey of American eating habits suggests that if current domestic trends continue, the family meal could be extinct by the year 2000.

In our changing society, the responsibility for seeing that children are well fed is more and more often shifting from mother-in-her-traditional-role-as-homemaker to other caregivers. Whether meals and snacks are made on site or brought from home, providers of child care have the opportunity to make a positive contribution to the nutritional well-being of children and to offer assistance to parents in several ways. These include:

- Helping children feel good about food and eating.
- Helping children learn to enjoy and value healthful foods.
- Protecting children from such hazards as choking on food, food poisoning, and kitchen accidents.
- Establishing feeding policies that respect the beliefs and desires of the parents.
- Providing information to parents interested in improving the eating habits of their families.
- Keeping parents informed about their children's eating behaviors and alerting them to nutrition-related problems that may require professional consultation.

How You Feed Is As Important As What You Feed

You will find that we spend as much time talking about the "hows" of feeding as we do the "whats." This is because we believe that a lot of unhappiness related to food can be prevented by helping children develop a healthy relationship with food, right from the start.

Look at your own feelings about food. Do you feel like you must finish everything on your plate even if you're full already? Do you feel vague pangs of guilt about getting great enjoyment out of eating? Do you find yourself dreading having to eat? These feelings started somewhere, and for most people their origins are in childhood.

Food figures prominently in our lives from day one on, so it's important to feel positive about it and to use it appropriately. Additionally, conflicts over food can do great damage to your relationship with a child, and that's the last thing you want!

Ellyn Satter, in her wonderful books *Child of Mine* and *How to Get Your Kid to Eat . . . But Not Too Much,* describes the "division of responsibility in feeding"* that is central to establishing healthy feelings toward eating. Engrave this on your brain right now! It is one of the most important concepts you will ever learn.

> **Parents** (and caregivers) are responsible for what is presented to eat and the manner in which it is presented.
>
> **Children** are responsible for how much and even whether they eat.

The idea that you don't have to force-feed a finicky eater or restrain a heavy eater may be shocking at first, but it works.

Now, don't get the idea that we're advocating letting children eat *whatever* they want. Contrary to an old belief, children will not intuitively

---

*Source: Satter, Ellyn. *How to Get Your Kid to Eat . . . But Not Too Much.*
Palo Alto: Bull Publishing, 1988.

eat what is good for them, given the choice between a plate of gooey doughnuts and a raw vegetable platter. (The idea that they might was a misinterpretation of some experiments a woman named Clara Davis performed in the 1930s. She confined several orphaned children to a hospital ward for long periods of time and found that they all grew beautifully when allowed to eat as much as they wanted of the foods offered to them, even when they didn't appear to be consuming a "balanced diet." The hitch is, the foods the children were offered were all natural, nutrient-dense foods like plain meats, organ meats, eggs, milk, whole grains, vegetables, fruit, and bone marrow—no heavily sweetened cereals, cookies, or soda pop. Even Miss Davis emphasized the importance of offering nutritious, natural foods to children.)

Of course, you will want to take into consideration the food preferences of your children when planning your menus, but it will be up to you to determine exactly *what* the choices will be and *when* they will be offered. The idea is to set it up so that no matter what a child eats from your offerings, he can't go wrong. Then you've done your job, and you can let the children take it from there. Depending on their age or level of development, you may have to help children with their eating. We'll talk about age-specific issues in their appropriate sections later on.

What Every Child Should Learn About Food and Eating

- When he is hungry, that need will be met.

- His own food preferences will be respected.

- Eating is an enjoyable activity.

- There are ways to deal with uncomfortable feelings, besides eating.

- People in different cultures, and families within those cultures, have different ways of eating and different ways of celebrating special occasions with food.

- Our food choices affect our well-being.

- Food is made available through the efforts of many members of the community.

- To eat, we use up resources, and we create waste that needs to be dealt with responsibly.

The first four concepts are crucial in the development of a child's emotional relationship with food, and the last four in his physical and social relationship with food. Review them often—together they make up the framework for all of the discussions of child feeding and nutrition education in this book.

Children will learn these very important concepts from *you*. How you handle feeding them, how they see you relate to food and eating, the exposure you give them to the world's diversity of food habits, how you dispose of food packaging—all will send clear messages to impressionable young minds.

Children learn that their hunger needs will be met when:

- You feed infants "on demand."

- You set up regular meal and snack times for the older children.

- You help their families find resources for food if they're having problems with it.

Children learn their food preferences will be respected when:

- You let them choose what and how much to eat of what you've offered.

- You ask them what they'd like when you're planning your menus.

Children learn that eating is enjoyable when:

- You make sure that the mealtime environment is pleasant.

- You enforce a code of behavior at the table.

- You make an effort to serve foods they enjoy.

- They see you enjoying eating.

Children learn to deal with feelings in other ways besides overeating when:

- You encourage them to verbalize their feelings.

- You resist the temptation to comfort them with cookies or candy.

- They don't see you running to the cookie jar when *you're* upset.

Children learn to appreciate the foodways of other cultures when:

- You plan meals that have cultural diversity.

- You ask parents to contribute recipes from their own heritage or have potluck dinners with each family contributing a dish that relates to their background.

- You have books and posters that show how people in other cultures eat.

Children learn that our food choices affect our well-being when:

- They see you eating with the intention of providing proper nourishment for your body and you describe to them the benefits of good nutrition.

Children learn about the people who provide food for them when:

- They go on field trips to markets, farms, dairies, and bakeries.
- They spend time in home, child care, or school kitchens.

Children learn to be responsible consumers when:

- They see you making an effort to cut down on waste (food or packaging).
- They participate in gardening and get a feel for the energy that's expended to produce food.
- They help with recycling projects.

Establishing a Nutrition Philosophy Statement and Related Policies for Your Setting

We urge you to spend some time considering what you feel about the importance of nutrition for children and what your commitment to it will be in your program. You may want to do this in a group, with interested parents or staffpersons. When you are done, you should have a *nutrition philosophy statement* unique and relevant to your setting. Here's an example of what one might look like:

> We believe that good nutrition is a basic right of every child. Our nutrition policies reflect our commitment to ensure that the children's nutritional needs are met in a positive, nurturing manner with respect for individual needs and preferences of the children and their families.

Once you have settled on a nutrition philosophy, you have a guide that will help you determine how you will handle food and nutrition issues. Next, you will find it very useful to have some written policies as well. These policies will ensure that parents and/or staff members know what to expect, or what their responsibilities are, in certain situations related to nutrition. There are many such situations, including:

- **Meal schedules and routines** (who will eat with the children, what will be done about reluctant or slow eaters).

- **Infant feeding** (who provides formula, how breast milk will be stored, how feeding will be done and by whom).

- **Allergies** (what substitutions will be made, whether families will be responsible for providing special foods).

- **"Personal" foods** (foods brought from home, whether they are allowed, restrictions as to type).

- **Celebrations** (whether you will have candy at Halloween, sweets for birthday parties).

The staff of the San Anselmo Preschool and Afterschool Program in San Anselmo, California, shared with us the following child care program policy regarding foods brought from home:

> We provide nutritious snacks that are low in fat and sugar, such as fresh fruit and vegetables and water rather than fruit juices.
>
> We encourage the children to bring lunches that emphasize fresh fruits, vegetables, whole-grain breads and low-fat milk, meats, poultry, fish, and cheeses.
>
> We discourage high-sugar foods such as candy, fruit rolls, cookies, cakes, and fruit drinks, and high-fat foods such as potato chips.
>
> If you wish to bring a refreshment for your child's birthday, please make arrangements with the group teacher. Simple birthday finger foods are preferred.

Ten Ways Parents Can Be Involved in Child Care or School Nutrition Programs

Everyone benefits when parents are able to contribute some of their time and ideas to the nutrition component in a child care or school setting. What can they do? Well, here are a few ideas:

- Help to establish or update statements of philosophy or policies.

- Participate in planning the menus (within established guidelines).

- Take turns cooking lunch.

- Contribute recipes for foods their children particularly like.

- Act as chaperones for nutrition-related field trips.

- Work with groups of children on cooking projects.

- Make materials for nutrition learning activities.

- Collect appropriate food packages and other props to be used in role-playing activities.

- Be the supervising adults at meal tables.

- Confer with caregivers or teachers about feeding problems.

Steps to Take Before You Start Feeding Other People's Children

To be successful in promoting good nutrition among the children in your care requires that you plan ahead. We strongly suggest that before you begin to care for other people's children, you:

- ☐ Learn about the basic nutritional needs of children in the age groups you will be serving.

- ☐ Decide which meals, if any, you are going to provide.

- ☐ Decide what your policies will be about which foods, if any, parents are to provide; about what will be done in the case of children with allergies or other special feeding needs; and about what will be served at birthday parties or other celebrations.

- ☐ Call your local Child Care Food Program sponsor and investigate signing up for the program.

- ☐ Practice planning menus that meet meal pattern guidelines required by the Child Care Food Program or licensing authorities, even if you aren't required to do so by a program or regulatory agency. These are good guidelines for everyone!

- ☐ Investigate money-saving sources of food and kitchen supplies in your area. (You may get better prices by linking up with other child-care providers to purchase from wholesalers or in large quantities.)

- ☐ Make sure your kitchen meets standards for safety and sanitation if your local health department has special requirements; otherwise review the section on food safety in this book, and use the "Checklist for a Kid-Ready Kitchen" and the "Food Safety and Sanitation Mini-Inspection."

- ☐ Check your feeding equipment to make sure it's safe and user friendly.

☐ Plan for gathering information about each child's special dietary needs, feeding problems, cultural food patterns, and holiday customs when he or she is enrolled. We have included a form in this book, or you may prefer to design one of your own.

☐ Develop a resource file and list of important phone numbers. (Appendix E in the back of this book may help.)

☐ Learn how to perform the Heimlich Maneuver.

☐ Plan how you will teach the children about nutrition. Look over your books and posters to make sure they give appropriate messages about food; put together a kit of equipment for cooking activities, including some children's cookbooks; find out what resources are available in your community for field trips (farmer's markets, bakeries, cheese factories, recycling centers, and so on); and ideally, plan a garden!

Chapter Two
Feeding and Growth

Feeding children well is both a science and an art. The *science* requires understanding the nutritional needs of children at each stage of their growth. This understanding is the basis of decisions you must make about what kinds of foods to offer, what equipment to buy, and what kinds of feeding structures to set up. The *art* of feeding children involves being sensitive to their responses to foods or your feeding methods and responding appropriately—maintaining a robust sense of humor, creating a spirit of adventure, and keeping respect and kindness ahead of everything else on your agenda. You will certainly enjoy feeding children more when you have refined the "art" of it, and the chances are they will eat better, too.

Growth and the Nutritional Needs of Infants

An infant generally will gain 1 ounce per day (about 2 pounds per month) during her first 5 months, and a half ounce per day (1 pound per month) during the remainder of her first year. By 4 to 5 months, a baby generally will double his birth weight, and by 1 year, he will triple it. The average baby grows in length by 50% during the first year (that means that an infant who was 20 inches long at birth will be 30 inches long at 1 year). Largely because of this rapid growth, infants have a greater need for calories, for each pound of body weight, than adults do.

- Good nutrition is extremely important during this time, not just for general bodily growth, but for the infant's brain as well. The growth of the brain begins prior to birth, continues at a rapid pace into the child's second year, and is essentially complete by age 6. In some cases, but not always, the brain can recover from the effects of poor nutrition if a good diet and stimulating environment are provided later.

- In the first months of life, a baby can only swallow liquids and has an immature digestive system that cannot handle the same foods older children can. *Breast milk or iron-fortified formula provides for essentially all of an infant's nutritional needs during the first 4 to 6 months of life.*

- Infants have small stomach capacities and must eat more frequently than adults or older children. They should be fed "on demand," that is, when they indicate that they're hungry. You can expect some variability in eating patterns; a baby may be able to wait 4 hours for one feeding and then be hungry again 2 hours later.

- Babies usually go through what doctors call "hungry periods." A common time for one of these periods is between 14 and 28 days of age. Follow the baby's lead . . . if he's hungry more often than usual, feed him! He's probably getting ready for a growth spurt.

- Breast milk or formula generally provides enough water for a healthy young infant. If, however, a baby has diarrhea or has been vomiting a lot, or if the weather is very hot, she could become dehydrated if you don't offer her extra water. Once an infant starts eating solid foods, especially protein-rich foods like meats or egg yolks, she will need extra water to help her kidneys eliminate the waste products. Keep in mind that babies sometimes cry because of thirst, not just hunger.

But never try to give an infant extra water by diluting her formula. And don't give a bottle of water as a pacifier; too much water can be as dangerous as too little.

■ Iron deficiency is one of the biggest nutritional problems among young children (read all about it in the section on anemia and iron deficiency, pages 213–214 in Appendix C) later in this book). The most critical time for making sure that a child has adequate iron intake is during the first year. The child will be building up a large blood supply in pace with her rapid growth. Children who do not consume adequate iron at this time are at greater risk for iron deficiency anemia during the toddler and preschool years.

Different Ages, Different Stages . . . Infants

Stages of Infant Development	Related Nutritional Considerations
1. She is attached to her primary caregivers.	1. She needs stable care, and she may refuse to accept feeding from strangers.
2. She will be developing a sense of trust about the world.	2. She is dependent on caregivers for her nourishment. She should be fed when she's hungry and allowed to stop eating when she's full. Weaning (from breast or bottle) should be a gradual process.
3. She uses her mouth to explore her environment.	3. She needs to be protected from hazards associated with choking and from poisonous substances.
4. She will be starting to view herself as a separate person. She needs to feel a sense of control over her environment.	4. She should be allowed to set the pace in feeding. She may refuse food in an attempt to get some sort of response from her caregiver.

Milks for the First Year

Young babies are only equipped to swallow, digest, and obtain proper nourishment from milk. Even after infants are adept at eating solid foods, milk continues to be an important source of nutrients. Breast milk is the ideal first food for infants, but not all mothers want to breastfeed or have favorable circumstances for doing so.

Throughout a large part of human history, animal milks have been used as substitutes for mother's milk. Cow's milk has been used most frequently, but goats, sheep, donkeys, horses, camels, pigs, deer, reindeer, and even dogs have provided milk for human babies! It has been only recently, however, that substitute milks, or formulas, have come close to duplicating the nutritive qualities of breast milk. Thanks to the wonders of modern technology, there are now three major types of commercially prepared formulas that meet the specific needs of infants:

Modified cow's milk formulas

(Similac®, Enfamil®, Gerber Baby Formula®). Most babies who aren't breastfed get these formulas. The milk proteins have been altered to be more digestible, and vegetable oils provide the fat calories. Lactose is added to bring the carbohydrate levels up to that of human milk. Vitamins, minerals, and some other nutrients are added as well. These formulas are made with or without iron; iron-fortified formula is recommended.

Soy formulas

(ProSobee®, Isomil®). These formulas are sometimes used for infants with allergies to cow's milk or infants who are sensitive to lactose after a bout with diarrhea (the carbohydrate in these formulas comes from sucrose or corn syrup).

Hypoallergenic formulas

(Nutramigen®, Alimentum®, Carnation Good Start®). Because some babies can tolerate neither cow's milk nor soy milk, another variety of formula is available. These protein hydrolysate ("predigested") formulas may not smell or taste very good, and they are expensive, but for some infants they are the only option.

Whole cow's milk is absolutely inappropriate as a food for young infants. It is too high in protein and soluble salts, and too low in iron and vitamin C. It also can cause small amounts of gastrointestinal bleeding. Health experts recommend that infants drink breast milk or iron-fortified formula for the entire first year. The American Academy of Pediatrics has reversed its earlier position stating that it was all right to give infants whole cow's milk after the age of 6 months, as long as they were getting at least a third of their calories from cereals, fruits, vegetables, and other foods that contain enough iron and vitamin C. The Academy's latest position is that using breast milk or iron-fortified formula for the first 12 months of life, along with age-appropriate solid foods, best provides balanced nutrition for infants.

Low-fat (2%) and skim milk should not be given to children under the age of 2. They are proportionately too low in fat and too high in protein to provide adequate nourishment for babies. Infants also should not be given nondairy creamers or imitation milks. Soy milk, rice milk, oat milk, nut milks, and other milk substitutes, even when fortified with some vitamins and calcium, do not have the full range of nutrients necessary to make them acceptable substitutes for breast milk or formula.

Some commercial "weaning formulas" have appeared on the market recently. They give the impression that they are somehow advantageous for older babies, but in reality, they aren't. They aren't harmful, but don't feel pressured to buy them.

How to Prepare a Baby's Bottle

Select the Right Feeding

- You should give a baby only formula, breast milk, milk (if he's old enough), and water from a bottle. Juices, cereals, and other solid foods or sweetened liquids do not belong in bottles.

- If you are using formula, get the iron-fortified variety. Babies need the iron, and contrary to popular belief, these formulas are no more likely to cause tummy upset than the varieties without iron.

- If you will be using concentrated liquid or powdered formula, read the directions and measure carefully. It can be very dangerous for a baby to receive formula with too much or too little water in it.

- Check the expiration date on the container of formula, and reject cans that are bulging, badly dented, or rusty.

Make Sure Everything Is Clean

- Wash your hands before preparing bottles.

- For babies up to 3 months of age, boil the water you will be using to mix the formula for 5 minutes.

- Use clean bottles:

  Wash the bottles, nipples, rings, and caps in hot, soapy water, using a brush to scrub all the nooks and crannies. Rinse in hot water, and boil the bottles, nipples, caps, and rings for 5 minutes. Or, after soaking to loosen dried-on formula, run them through the dishwasher.

  If you will be preparing fresh bottles for each feeding, let the clean equipment air-dry, then store it covered in a clean place.

- Wipe the top of the formula can with a clean, damp towel before you open it.

- Add formula for one feeding to each bottle, put the clean nipple in (upside down and with a cap on top if you'll be storing the bottle), and screw the ring on.

- Store prepared bottles for no more than 24 hours in the refrigerator; an open can of formula should be covered and used within 48 hours.

Prepare the Bottle for Feeding Time

- Some babies will take a cold bottle; if you are going to warm the bottle, do it right before giving it to the baby.

- *Never heat a bottle in a microwave oven.* You can set the bottle in a bowl of warm water, hold it under warm running water from the faucet, or use a bottle-warming appliance.

- Before feeding the bottle to a baby, shake the formula or milk gently to mix it, and sprinkle a little onto your wrist to test its temperature.

How to Give a Bottle to a Baby

Feeding a bottle to a baby may seem like a simple task. Don't you just warm it up, stick the nipple in the baby's mouth, and stop when the milk is gone?

Actually, bottlefeeding doesn't always go so smoothly. Some babies are willing to go along with whatever happens; others may fuss, spit up a lot, or drink very little and be hungry again in an hour. When you are feeding a baby, remember that it is important, even at this early stage, for the child to feel relaxed and happy about eating. He will need to do this in order to be able to eat what he needs, as well as to begin a comfortable lifelong relationship with food. It is very easy to think of feeding as the process of making a baby drink a certain number of ounces of formula at a certain time. But what a baby really needs is to have his hunger satisfied when he feels it, and to experience the security of your love at the same time.

- *Feed an infant when she is hungry,* not because the clock says to. Some babies have characteristic cries or wiggles that let you know they're ready to eat; others may be fussier in general, and it may be harder to figure out what these babies want. It's worth checking to see if a baby has a wet diaper, needs to be burped, or just wants company. Once you've explored these possibilities, if she's still fussing, try feeding her.

- Gently get the baby settled down and comfortable for feeding.

- *Always hold a baby when giving a bottle.*

  Hold his head higher than the rest of his body, so the milk doesn't flow into his inner ear and cause an infection.

  Tip the bottle so milk fills the nipple and air doesn't get in.

- Wait for the baby to stop eating before you try to burp her. Then pat or rub her back gently while she rests on your shoulder or sits, supported with your other hand, on your lap.

- Avoid too many disruptions while you're feeding. Babies can get distracted or upset by a lot of burping, wiping, bouncing around, jiggling, and changing of positions.

■ Pay attention to messages from the baby that he's full. He may:

>   Close his lips
>   Stop sucking
>   Spit out the nipple
>   Turn his head away
>   Cover his mouth with his hands
>   Cry
>   Bite the nipple

Sometimes a baby will pause a bit (we all do, don't we?). Maybe he just needs a breather. Offer him the nipple again, but if he refuses it, he's probably had enough.

■ Resist the temptation to make a baby finish the little bit of formula left in a bottle. Assume she knows her needs better than you do, and discard what's left. Rinse out the bottle with cool water to make cleaning easier later on.

How Child Care Providers Can Support Breastfeeding Moms

Because breastfeeding offers an infant so many advantages—just the right balance of nutrients, immune factors, and a special relationship—it is the recommended method of feeding infants today. Many mothers face a challenge: they must return to work but would still like to be able to nurse their babies. There are several ways to manage breastfeeding and child care: an infant can be given breast milk in a bottle; or the mother can nurse the baby in the child care setting during breaks from work; or the baby can be fed formula while in child care and breastfed at home.

If the mother will be nursing in the child care setting:

- Don't feed the baby for 1 to 1-1/2 hours before her mother is due to arrive, so that she will be hungry enough to nurse and keep up her mother's milk supply. Of course, you and the mother will need to have a clear understanding that if for some reason she is late, you will feed the baby as necessary to prevent having a frantically hungry infant on your hands.

- Offer the mother a comfortable chair in a cozy place for nursing.

If you will be feeding the baby breast milk from a bottle, keep the milk safe:

- You can store breast milk in the refrigerator for 48 hours or in the freezer for no more than 2 weeks after it has been expressed.

- Expressed milk should be stored in sterilized bottles or disposable plastic nursing bags.

- Do not allow the milk to sit at room temperature; take it from the refrigerator or freezer right before you use it.

- Thaw the milk, if frozen, by running it under cool, then very warm, water. Shake gently to mix (breast milk separates during storage).

  Do not warm breast milk in a microwave oven! To do so may destroy some of its antiinfective properties.

- Once breast milk has thawed, do not refreeze it.

- Discard unused portions.

When Should a Baby Start Eating Solid Foods?

Breast milk or iron-fortified formula (perhaps with vitamin or mineral supplementation prescribed by a doctor) gives an infant all of the nutrients he needs for the first 4 to 6 months of life.

Some parents and caregivers want babies to eat solid foods as soon as possible. They may believe (mistakenly) that solid foods help young babies sleep through the night, or they may want to prove that their children are truly "advanced." Other parents or caregivers may wait too long to introduce foods with new textures to babies. A time will come when a baby needs the nutrients and the challenges that solids provide; meanwhile, there are good reasons to wait until the infant is developmentally ready to accept them:

- Babies can choke on foods they can't swallow easily.

- Some foods are difficult for young infants to digest.

- Babies can develop food allergies when they're exposed to certain foods too early.

- When babies start eating solid foods, they cut back on breast milk or formula, which is their *ideal* source of nutrients for the first 4 to 6 months.

Suppose a baby is 5 months old and you're wondering if it's time for her to try some infant cereal. How will you know she's ready? In general, she should be able to:

- Hold her neck steady and sit with support.

- Draw in her lower lip when a spoon is removed from her mouth.

- Keep food in her mouth and swallow it.

- Open her mouth when she sees food coming.

It is very important that parents and child care providers communicate with each other and agree on their approach to this transitional time. You need to discuss *what* is to be introduced as well as when to start. Many parents want to be the first to experience these developmental changes with their babies.

A Solid-Food Itinerary for Baby

The solid foods you offer a baby should give her two things: needed nutrients and opportunities to develop her eating skills. Hopefully by the end of her first year, she will be feeding herself soft table food and drinking from a cup. During the transition from exclusive nipple feeding to a more adult eating pattern, she will become accustomed to a wide range of flavors and textures in a relatively short time. It's really quite an accomplishment!

We agree with child-feeding expert Ellyn Satter, who asserts that the best way to get through this time is to start solids late and move quickly into table foods. We recommend that you read *Child of Mine: Feeding with Love and Good Sense* for the finer details of feeding infants. Meanwhile, we've adapted information from her book to give you general guidelines regarding solid foods for babies.

> **Age:** 4–7 months
>
> **Nutritional needs:** Iron
>
> **Feeding skills:** Swallowing smooth, semisolid foods
>
> **New food:** Iron-fortified infant cereal

Start with infant rice cereal, which is the least likely to cause allergies, and mix it with formula, breast milk, or diluted evaporated milk. Wait a week, then try barley, then oats. It is recommended that you wait until a baby is 8 or 9 months old before you give him wheat cereals, because wheat commonly causes allergies.

We don't recommend that you give a young infant regular oatmeal or other adult hot cereals, because they don't have enough available iron. And don't buy jars of fruit mixed with infant cereal; it's hard to tell how much cereal is in them. Please, never add sugar or other sweeteners to a baby's cereal. He doesn't know cereal is supposed to taste sweet, and what he doesn't know will be good for him!

Experiment to find the right consistency for the cereal mixture; some babies like it thin and some like it thick. Eventually, the baby should be eating about a half-cup of cereal mixture, divided between two meals. It is recommended that children continue eating these iron-fortified infant cereals for at least the first year and perhaps up to the age of 18 months.

At this point, you should not be trying to replace milk feedings; rather, cereal should be a supplement to them.

Age: 6–8 months

Nutritional needs: Vitamin A, vitamin C

Feeding skills: Moving tongue from side to side, controlling swallow, beginning up and down munching motion, curving lips around a cup

New foods: Fruits and vegetables, pureed or mashed; later, juice in a *cup*

It doesn't really matter whether you introduce fruits or vegetables first. Very ripe, mashed bananas are often recommended as a first fruit for babies, but they aren't good sources of either vitamin A or C. Be sure to try sweet potatoes, squash, peaches, apricots, spinach, carrots, purple plums, broccoli, cauliflower, cantaloupe, strawberries, and potatoes.

You can puree cooked vegetables or tender fruits in a babyfood grinder or you can mash the foods with a fork, depending on the food and the child's eating skills. Avoid canned vegetables, which are usually high in sodium, and canned or frozen fruits with added sugar. Commercial baby fruits are fortified with vitamin C and may be a convenient option for you. The only problem with them is that they are so smooth and thin that they don't challenge a baby to learn about new textures.

Wait at least 3 days to check for an allergic reaction before introducing the next food. Common reactions are hives, rashes, vomiting, diarrhea, coughing, or excessive gas.

At this time, it's wise to limit fruits and vegetables to 4 tablespoons per day. This is to make sure the baby doesn't fill up on these foods and refuse those with greater nutrient density. It's also a good idea to limit high-nitrate foods like carrots (especially carrot juice), beets, collards, and spinach to a tablespoon or two per serving until the baby is older.

Breast milk or formula should still be providing most of a baby's nutrition at this age. But she is building up experience with tastes and textures, which is important for the next step.

Age: 7–10 months

Nutritional needs: Protein, vitamins, minerals

Feeding skills: Chewing, grasping food in palm of hand and later, fingers; drinking from a cup

New foods: Modified table foods—lumpy fruits and vegetables, finger breads and cereals, milk in a cup, ground meats, flaked fish, cottage cheese, grated cheese, yogurt, cooked dried beans (mashed), tofu, pasta

When an infant has mastered mashed fruits and vegetables, you can let him try to feed himself dry cereals like Cheerios as a snack, or let him gnaw at a breadstick. This is a good time to introduce him to milk in a cup.

Some experts suggest that you wait until a baby is a year old before you give him citrus fruits. If he isn't predisposed to allergies, though, it's probably okay to give him an orange or grapefruit wedge now and see what happens. Many babies enjoy these tart fruits, and they are excellent sources of vitamin C.

By the time a baby is 8 months old, he will be able to eat many table foods, and the real fun begins! Meats are introduced at this point and should be finely ground at first. It helps to moisten the meat with gravy, milk, or some other liquid. Meat is also popular mixed into mashed potatoes or in casseroles with pasta. Later, you can chop the meat finely. Plain commercial baby meats are another option if you are making something for everyone else that would be obviously inappropriate for a baby. Work up to about an ounce of meat or the equivalent of a meat alternative every day.

Meat Equivalents

1 oz. beef, lamb, poultry

1 oz. cheese (1/4 c. grated)

1/2 cup cooked dried beans

1/4 cup cottage cheese

1/4 cup flaked tuna or salmon

4 oz. tofu (does not meet Child Care
Food Program Guidelines)

Babies can easily choke when they try to eat foods that are too advanced in texture for them. Be especially careful not to give babies foods that can form hard plugs in their throats, like raw hard vegetable or fruit chunks, nuts, tough meats, hot dogs, and anything with bones or pits. Hard candies and snack chips are dangerous and have no place in their diet anyway.

These foods should be avoided for children less than a year old:

Salt, sugar, heavy seasonings

Chocolate (allergies)

Egg whites (allergies)

Shellfish (allergies)

Peanut butter (choking)

Honey, even in cooked goods (infant botulism)

How to Feed Solid Foods to a Baby

Don't discourage any method of getting food from plate to mouth. Enthusiasm is what matters. —Penelope Leach

We said earlier that *how* you feed is as important as *what* you feed. Both you and the baby will have an easier time if you keep the following guidelines in mind when feeding solid foods. Call on all your reserves of patience and humor, and realize that even when the baby ends up with more squash in his hair than in his mouth, he will think it's a terrific experience if you do!

- Feed a baby only when he's sitting up; if he can't sit up yet, he's not ready for solid foods.

- When you first offer solids (usually cereals), try them only at one meal a day to get the baby used to the idea of spoon feeding. Serve only a teaspoon or two of a new food at first. You can add more meals and bigger servings later.

- In the beginning, feed the baby a little breast milk or formula first, so he'll be patient but not stuffed. By the time he is 8 to 10 months old and eating table foods, you can skip the milk feeding before the meal entirely.

- Wash your hands and the baby's hands before feeding time.

- Try to keep the atmosphere as tranquil as possible. Sit facing the baby and be friendly but not too entertaining.

- Test the food first to make sure it isn't too hot.

- Offer the food on a small spoon and wait for the baby's mouth to open. Place a small amount of food between the baby's lips; he may force it out of his mouth, in which case it's okay to scoop it up and try again. However, if he doesn't seem to like it, respect his preference.

- Some babies need a lot of exposure to certain foods before they like them. If a baby refuses a food, try it again some other time.

- Stop feeding the baby when he lets you know he's full. He may:

  Close his mouth
  Turn his head away
  Spit out food
  Cover his mouth with his hands
  Play with utensils
  Cry
  Shake his head "no"
  Hand you the bowl or cup

- When a baby grabs the spoon from you and tries to feed himself, or when he wants to eat (or explore) the food with his fingers, stay out of the way and enjoy the show!

- Keep the food safe:

  Don't feed right out of a babyfood jar (unless you're willing to throw out the leftovers).

  Throw out what the baby hasn't eaten if his spoon has touched the food.

  Store opened jars of babyfood in the refrigerator for no longer than 3 days.

How to Prevent Baby Bottle Tooth Decay

We have met young children whose teeth were so rotten that it was painful for them to eat. They were suffering from "baby bottle tooth decay." Cavities formed in their primary ("baby") teeth when these children were put to bed with bottles containing milk, formula, juice, or other sweetened liquids. Such children endure unnecessary discomfort and may require expensive dental work.

Baby bottle tooth decay can be prevented by:

- Using bottles to feed infants breast milk, formula, milk, or water *only*.

- Offering bottles only at feeding times, not before naps or bedtime. If the baby falls asleep anyway, move him around a bit to stimulate swallowing; this will move at least some of the milk out of the mouth.

- Not dipping pacifiers in honey, maple syrup, or corn syrup.

- Putting a baby to bed with stuffed animals, lullabies, or back rubs, not bottles.

- Serving juice to a baby in a cup, not a bottle.

Weaning a Baby from Breast or Bottle

Weaning is ideally a *gradual* transition from milk feeding by nipple to a varied diet with milk drunk from a cup. We aren't going to argue here that one time is better than another for the completion of this process. Some parents are in no particular hurry to see their children off the breast or bottle, some children refuse to give up nipple feeding (and their parents have to endure remarks like "Is he planning to go off to college with that bottle?"), and some children lose interest in breast- or bottlefeeding as soon as they figure out how to drink from a cup.

We believe every family has to find their own best solution to this dilemma. If you are interested in pursuing the topic further, we suggest you read about it in Ellyn Satter's *Child of Mine: Feeding with Love and Good Sense.*

It is important that a child be well established on table foods by the age of 10 or 12 months. She won't receive adequate nutrition if milk remains the major component of her diet past this point. After the age of 1 (and through age 3), two cups of milk a day is plenty; she should be getting the rest of her calories from a variety of other foods selected from the Food Guide Pyramid.

Get the baby used to drinking liquids from a cup by offering small amounts of juice, formula, milk, or water by cup when she's around 7 or 8 months old. She'll need your help at the time, of course, but with the right equipment (plastic cups with two handles are dandy) and lots of practice, in a couple of months she'll be able to drink milk at mealtime by herself. By then, if breastfeeding or a bottle is offered, it should be only at snacks or in the early morning or late evening. Eventually, as the child is eating more and more like the rest of the family or group, these milk feedings can be dropped, one at a time. Usually, the child will scarcely notice what's happened.

Remember, do not let a child of any age go to sleep with a bottle.

Growth and the Nutritional Needs of Toddlers

■ Toddlers don't grow as rapidly as infants. For the next several years, they will be gaining about 3 inches and 4 to 6 pounds a year.

■ By the end of the second year, a child's brain has reached 75% of its adult size.

■ By the age of 2-1/2 years, a child usually has all 20 "baby teeth." Even though these teeth don't have to last a lifetime, they are important for proper chewing. Young children need to learn how to care for their teeth, and they should be offered foods that don't promote cavities. Also, the nutrients taken in during the childhood years will affect the health of the permanent teeth.

■ Iron deficiency and its late stage, anemia, can be problems among toddlers. Especially at risk are children who didn't get enough iron while they were infants, and those who drink too much milk and eat too few iron-rich foods.

■ It is *normal* for toddlers to have erratic appetites or to go on "food jags." An example of a food jag is when a child wants nothing but macaroni and cheese for 2 weeks, then abruptly wants nothing to do with the stuff. Does this sound like anyone you know? Despite these problems, most toddlers manage to grow pretty well.

■ Some children at this age are fond of eating nonfood items like dirt, paint chips, paper, and crayons. Dirt and paint chips can cause lead poisoning, so discourage them from eating these at least.

Different Ages, Different Stages ... Toddlers

How a Toddler Is Developing	Related Nutritional Considerations
1. He has an expanding sense of self, as a separate person.	1. He loves to say "NO" and may refuse to eat even favorite foods as a way of establishing control.
2. He is becoming able to express himself verbally.	2. He can tell you when he's hungry and what he likes to eat.
3. He is involved in intensive exploration of the world around him and needs both the freedom to explore and the security of limits.	3. He may be more interested in playing than in eating. He will play with his food as a way of learning about it. He needs limits in the form of established meals and snack times and expectations regarding behavior at the table.
4. He is refining his fine-motor control, but may be easily frustrated by setbacks.	4. He needs to be set up for success in self-feeding, with the right utensils and seating, and food that's easy to handle. If you are too fussy about tidiness at this point, you could delay the development of his feeding skills.
5. He is neophobic (afraid of anything new). Nature probably installed this tendency in toddlers to protect them!	5. He will almost certainly refuse to try a new food, at least once!
6. He has a short attention span.	6. He may not be able to sit through a long meal.

How to Survive Mealtime with Young Children (and Perhaps Even Enjoy It)

- Allow enough time for an unhurried meal.

- Let the children know in advance what kind of behavior you expect.

- Set aside quiet time before the meal, maybe reading a story or having them listen to some music.

- See that the children are comfortably seated and have the right equipment for eating.

- Respect the children's preferences when planning meals, but don't give in to "short-order cooking."

- Offer new foods in a matter-of-fact way along with some familiar foods, like bread.

- Allow the children to participate in food preparation.

- Don't allow them to fill up on juice or milk throughout the day.

- Help the children to *serve themselves* small portions, and be ready to help them with seconds later.

- Present food in a form that's easy for children to manage (*see* Modifying Foods for Children of Different Ages, page 67).

- Acknowledge desirable behavior and ignore undesirable behavior. Don't, however, praise or reward a child for eating or for trying new foods. Act as though you assume she is able to handle the situation, and she will (eventually).

- Do not make desserts the reward for eating the rest of the meal. Make them *nutritious* and offer them with the other foods. If they're eaten first, so what? Surprise! Fruit is *not* dessert, although many of us were raised to believe it is.

- Eat *with* the children and set a good example by eating a wide variety of foods and being open to trying new ones.

Young Children Eat Better When They Have the Right Equipment (for Feeding)

Picture yourself sitting in a chair that leaves your feet dangling 3 feet from the ground, at a table that reaches to your neck, trying to spear pieces of cauliflower with a fork that's 2 feet long. Would eating be enjoyable?

Well, eating with adult-size utensils at adult-size furniture feels like this to a young child. If children are going to be comfortable enough to sit through meals and successful enough at feeding themselves to feel good about it, they will need utensils they can handle and a thoughtfully set up environment. A bonus for you will be less mess to contend with.

- Chairs should have supports for children's feet or allow the children to have their feet on the floor.

- The table should be at a height that allows children to reach their food easily.

- Plates, bowls, glasses, cups, and flatware should be child-sized and made of unbreakable materials.

- Plates with curved sides are easier for younger children to work with. Glasses should have broad bases and be small enough to allow children to get their hands around them.

- Spoons should have short handles, blunt tips, and rounded bowls. Forks should have short handles and short, blunt tines. Knives should be small and have rounded tips. Disposable flatware isn't recommended except for picnics.

- Children can enjoy pouring their own beverages if you provide small (covered) pitchers with broad handles.

- When you're serving family-style meals, keep the serving spoons small enough for children to manage.

- Children with handicapping conditions may require specialized eating equipment.

Growth and the Nutritional Needs of Preschoolers

■ Preschoolers are growing at much the same rate they did as toddlers—approximately 3 inches and 4 to 6 pounds a year.

■ The nutritional concerns for preschoolers are much the same as for toddlers. Iron deficiency anemia is still a problem, although it becomes less common as children get older. Tooth decay and obesity are significant health problems in this age group.

■ Young preschoolers still display some of the eating behaviors that so worried their parents when they were toddlers: finickiness, erratic appetites, and dawdling at the table. By the time they're 4 or 5, though, most of these children will be eating pretty well and be good company at mealtimes.

Different Ages, Different Stages . . . Preschoolers

How a Preschooler Is Developing	Related Nutritional Considerations
1. Her ability to master skills more easily makes her eager to cooperate and try new experiences. She does need immediate reinforcement of her success to stay interested, however.	1. She will probably be more willing to try new foods. You can still expect some messiness while she eats, but she will be trying hard to imitate grown-up eating. She still needs to be set up for success, with the proper equipment and thoughtful food preparation.
2. She is becoming less attached to her primary caregiver and expands her relationships with peers, family members, and other adults.	2. She will be influenced by the food preferences of her peers and teachers or caregivers.
3. She is learning to feel positively or negatively about herself, depending on her interactions with others.	3. Her own food preferences should be respected. She needs to know that people care enough about her to attend to her basic needs (like food). She feels important when she helps out and will enjoy preparing food for herself and others.

The Most Important Things You Can Do to Help Children Grow Up Having Their Own "Best Bodies"

Foster a Positive Self-Image

- Provide an environment in which children can learn to appreciate the richness of diversity—in body sizes, skin colors, cultural backgrounds, abilities, and the like.

- Remember that children need limits, opportunities to develop self-reliance, and lots of love.

- Be alert to the need for counseling when things aren't going well in the family.

Encourage Lots of Physical Activity

- Set limits on television watching.

- Don't carry a child who can walk.

- Provide a safe play environment outside, with opportunities to use a variety of muscles—pulling, pushing, climbing, jumping, and running.

- Walk with children instead of driving, when you can.

- When it's stormy weather, dance or put on a kids' exercise video.

- Don't just sit there—play along!

Promote Healthful Eating Habits

- Make a variety of foods available, generally avoiding those with excessive sugar and fat, and establish *regular* meal and snack times.

- Allow children to decide whether and how much to eat.

- Don't single out the overweight child with special foods or restrictions.

- Encourage children to eat slowly and appreciatively.

- Never use food as a reward or withhold food as punishment.

- Be a good role model by eating healthfully and staying out of the "dieting" trap.

George Won't Eat His Broccoli?
Melissa Won't Even Look at a Snow Pea?
Here, Try This . . .

- Let him grow it.

- Let her help you pick it out at the grocery store or farmers market.

- Let him help you prepare it for eating (even quite young children can shell peas, pop beans, separate broccoli florets, and wash lettuce).

- Try serving it a different way—raw if you usually cook it, lightly steamed if you usually serve it raw, perhaps even pureed in a soup.

- Let him dip it.

- Put parmesan cheese on top.

- Give it a funny name.

- Serve it when she's hungry, not when she's filled up on other foods.

- Seat him next to a child who *loves* vegetables, and let peer pressure work its magic.

- Tell her she can have it for dessert, but only if she eats all of her cupcake (just kidding . . .).

- Eat it yourself, with obvious enjoyment.

- Don't assume he'll *never* like it. Some children take longer than others to feel comfortable with certain foods, so let it reappear occasionally.

- If a young child still won't eat vegetables, and you are concerned that her health will suffer, offer her fruits that are good sources of vitamins A and C (see lists, pages 79–80).

Calvin and Hobbes   by Bill Watterson

Growth and the Nutritional Needs of School-Age Children

■ Up to about 7 or 8 years of age, children will be gaining their usual 3 inches per year in height and 4 to 6 pounds in weight. Then they'll slow down a bit, gaining about 2 inches a year, until they start their adolescent growth spurts (the spurt can happen as early as age 9 in girls).

■ Between 6 years and puberty, boys are taller and heavier than girls. By the sixth grade, it's not unusual to find classrooms in which most of the girls are bigger than most of the boys (in high school, the boys regain their size advantage).

■ It is *normal* for children to put on some weight before they experience their spurt in height. Tragically, many children, or their parents, become so concerned about this that dieting and weight obsession start at this young age.

■ Feeding problems are uncommon among 6- to 12-year-olds, as children gradually become more accepting of what is served to them. However, as parents lose some of the control over what their children are eating, many children make poor food choices. One study found that school-age children were getting 25% of their calories from *sugar*!

Different Ages, Different Stages...
School-Age Children

How the School-Age Child Is Developing	Related Nutritional Considerations
1. He experiences mastery of physical skills and may become involved in organized sports.	1. He will probably have a hearty appetite.
2. He is increasingly influenced by peers and the school environment.	2. He may start to question his parents' (or caregiver's) credibility. Nutrition education activities may be part of the classroom curriculum.
3. He has more access to money and opportunities for shopping without parents.	3. He can buy foods on his own, some of which may not be acceptable to parents and caregivers.
4. He may have a hectic schedule as he becomes more involved in activities outside the home.	4. He may skip meals, especially breakfast.
5. He may spend large amounts of time watching television.	5. Watching television can contribute to obesity; advertising may encourage children to eat unhealthful foods.

Helping Older Children Make Better Eating Choices

Children become increasingly independent as they progress from kindergarten to junior high. They enjoy learning to make decisions for themselves, and eating behavior is one area over which they can exert some control. As money and opportunities become available, school-age children obtain access to foods their parents and schools or child care settings don't provide. And often the foods they choose to eat are not exactly nutritious!

These "junk" foods aren't going to go away, and so long as they're around, kids will want to eat them. So how can you support a child in thinking for himself, yet keep him from turning into a veritable candy-eating machine?

- Remember that it is still your job to determine what will be served to a child while he is in your home or child care setting, and at what time. It is still the child's job to decide whether to eat or how much to eat. You may not be able to control what a child eats when he's not with you, but at least you can be assured he's getting nutritious food when he is with you. And hopefully, he will enjoy a wide range of healthful foods.

- Include the children in your menu-planning process. Let them know what the guidelines have to be (such as servings from particular food groups or restrictions on sugar, fat, or salt). Explain to them the reasons for the guidelines. Then try to accommodate as many of their suggestions as possible. They will feel very important, and they'll be getting nutrition education at the same time.

■ Involve the children in food preparation. As children get older they usually end up fixing more of their own meals and snacks. Teach them some simple but nutritious recipes (you can make your own laminated recipe cards with pictures); eventually, you'll be able to set out the ingredients and let them do all the work! By the way, it's as important for boys to learn to cook as it is for girls.

■ Teach children to be informed consumers. Discuss how television advertising, prizes, and packaging can lead people to make unwise food choices. Have them read food labels. Make games of finding cereals with the least sugar or the lowest-fat crackers.

Child Feeding History

All Children	Yes	No	Specifics
Is your child allergic to any foods, or are there foods he or she should not eat for any other reason?			
Does your child have any other special dietary needs?			
Does your child need assistance with eating?			
Does your child take any medications that may require consideration in timing or content of meals?			
Do you have any concerns about your child's eating habits?			

What are your child's favorite foods?

Infants

	Yes	No	Specifics
Is your child breast fed?			
Will you bring fresh or frozen breast milk to the site for feeding?			
Does your child drink infant formula?			
What is the usual amount of formula your child takes at one feeding?			
Does your child eat solid foods?			

Special instructions, holiday customs, cultural food patterns:

PART TWO
Your Feeding Program

Chapter *Three*

Planning How and What to Feed Children

Why Bother with a Feeding Program?

We believe that it's beneficial to everyone if a child's meals while in child care are provided by the caregiver. There are many reasons for this:

- Some of the mealtime disturbances that occur when a few children bring "junk" foods, or when food items are traded, can be avoided.

- Children will, in general, get more variety and nutrient balance in their meals. Bag lunches tend to be pretty much the same day after day, in part because they are limited to foods that travel well.

- You can make mealtimes valuable learning experiences when you introduce children to foods they might otherwise never encounter, or when you talk about foods that everyone is eating.

- Parents are usually extremely grateful to be spared the hassle of packing lunches.

Despite the advantages, however, you must look realistically at your situation—that is, the space, equipment, and time you have

available—before you decide whether to offer a full meal program or snacks only. We don't want you to make yourself and everyone else miserable because you've taken on more than you can handle!

You may find that what works best for you is to offer snacks only, but in combination with a specific policy about acceptable bag lunch foods. (For example, some child care providers and schools have policies that forbid sodas, candy, or other sugary foods in lunches brought from home.) It is certainly possible to offer children a wide range of food experiences during snack times, when you're willing to move beyond crackers and juice (we'll show you how later on).

We also suggest that you look into signing up for the Child Care Food Program (CCFP)* if you haven't already. Qualified providers can get CCFP reimbursement for meals and snacks served in child care homes and centers, plus good training opportunities and support. We have followed the meal patterns and serving-size requirements of the program while developing the recipes for this book, to make it easier for you to meet their guidelines.

---

*Check the white pages in your phone directory for "Child Care Food Program."

Scheduling Meals and Snacks

Young children need several opportunities to eat during the course of a day to ensure that their nutritional needs are met. Once past infancy, they begin to appreciate the structure of scheduled meals and snacks, but it's unrealistic to expect them to eat all they require for optimum growth in only 3 meals per day. Plan to feed children at least 2 snacks if you will be with them all day. Some research suggests that this is a healthier way for adults to eat, too. Try it . . . you might like it!

The health and safety guidelines of the American Academy of Pediatrics and American Public Health Association state that:

- Infants should be fed on demand.

- Children in child care for 8 hours or less per day should have at least 1 meal and 2 snacks or 2 meals and 1 snack.

- Children in child care for 9 hours or more should have at least 2 meals and 2 snacks or 3 meals and 1 snack daily.

- Children should be offered midmorning and midafternoon snacks.

- Unless children are asleep, they should be offered food at least every 3 hours.

A few possible meal schedules are:

- Children in day care 7 A.M. to 5:30 P.M.

    | 7:15 | Breakfast |
    | 9:45 | Midmorning snack |
    | 12:30 | Lunch |
    | 3:30 | Afternoon snack |
    | 5:00 | Additional snack for children who will be eating dinner late |

- Children in preschool 9:00 A.M. to 1:30 P.M.

    | 10:00 | Midmorning snack |
    | 12:30 | Lunch |

How to Serve Meals

There are several ways to set up a meal for children, and you may find that it's fun to vary your usual routine now and then. We don't recommend serving children meals already portioned out on plates if you can possibly help it, because it doesn't allow them to decide for themselves how much they want to eat. You may also find that a lot of food is wasted this way. There are better ways to serve meals, and we've outlined them below.

Family Style

Meal tables are set up with plates, flatware, and cups at each place, and the food is passed in small bowls, plates, or baskets from which the children help themselves. Beverages are served in small pitchers so the children can pour for themselves. This is the recommended method for serving most meals to children and can be used even with toddlers; very young children may need more assistance getting the food on their plates, however.

Buffet Style

Foods are placed in serving dishes on one table or counter, and children move along serving themselves from what's offered. This serving method is not recommended for very young children, but you may find it works well with older kids just as a change of pace, for snacks, or for special occasions. Be particularly careful that the children are capable of handling the food and utensils in a hygienic manner.

Picnics

You can serve these meals outside at picnic tables or on blankets, or even inside on a blanket if it's a cold or rainy day. Pack the food items in a basket or insulated chest, being especially careful to keep foods at safe temperatures if you are traveling farther than your back yard.

*Whatever style you choose, remember that
an adult should always eat with the children.*

Mealtime 1-2-3's

- Start with a clean table.

- Designate a helper or two to assist in setting the table, with chores appropriate to each child's stage of development.

- Engage the other children in a transitional activity, such as listening to some mellow music or to a story.

- Turn off the television.

- Make sure everyone has washed hands, is comfortably seated, and has all the proper utensils.

- Allow the children to serve themselves small portions. Be ready to assist children who need help, and offer second helpings when appropriate.

- Model good food safety practices when passing and serving food, and be ready to respond when a child is about to contaminate food or has already done so. (You may need to provide new serving utensils or even replace the contaminated food.)

- Have enough serving pieces so that children don't have to wait too long for food to be passed to them.

- Give the children opportunities to practice skills such as peeling food with their fingers, spreading butter or jam, cutting soft foods with a table knife, and rolling their own burritos.

- Expect children to mop up their own spills, but don't make a fuss about it. (It's easier if you have a small sponge and container of sudsy water standing by.)

- Keep the conversation at the table light. Avoid nagging, criticism, and other unpleasantness, and don't allow fighting or rudeness.

- Please *do* talk about the foods being served (where they come from, what their sensory characteristics are, or why they are healthful to eat).

- Adults should eat meals and snacks with the children (the *same* meals and snacks, unless you have a medical or religious reason for avoiding certain foods, which should then be explained to the children).

- Respect children's food preferences, and resist the temptation to interfere by using such tactics as rewarding children for trying new foods or forcing them to clean their plates.

- Be ready to respond if a child starts choking.

- Allow children who finish early to leave the table and engage in some quiet activity like reading (after they've cleaned up their places, of course).

- Accept that because of variations in children's appetites and food preferences, some food will be wasted. Don't take it personally!

- At the end of the meal, discard food that has been on the plates, as well as food left in serving bowls on the table. Clean the table and wipe it down with a chlorine bleach solution (1 tablespoon bleach in 1 quart of water). Promptly refrigerate leftovers that have not been on the table.

- Finally, have the children clean their faces and hands and brush their teeth before moving on to the next activity.

Adults, your job is to:

Make the meal pleasant

Help the children participate in the meal

Allow eating methods appropriate for the developmental levels of the children

Enforce standards of behavior

Model good manners and enjoyment in eating

How to Plan Menus

A well-planned menu is a time- and money-saving tool for you and a powerful nutrition education message to children and parents. A menu makes it much more likely that the children will get the best nourishment you can provide. Busy families, too, find that planning menus means fewer annoying trips to the store, better meals, and more time to enjoy each other! It seems intimidating at first, but we'll run you through it, step by step.

- Gather all of your tools together: menu form or pad of paper, pencil, cookbooks and recipes, a guide to seasonal fruits and vegetables, information on current prices of various food items, lists of foods high in vitamins A and C and iron, a calendar of holidays or special events, and the menu checklist. Make a list of foods you want to use soon because they are crowding your storage areas or nearing their expiration dates or maximum storage times. Menu forms (like the one on page 134) make it easy to remember to plan servings of all the required food groups.

- Decide the time period of your menu. Some cooks like to plan for a month at a time and then start over; some find that repeating "cycles" of 3 to 4 weeks work best. Families and small child care settings may prefer weekly menu planning.

- Think about the staff, equipment, time, and storage space you have available.

- Figure out how you want to approach planning the meals. You may want to plan breakfasts, lunches, and snacks for one entire day before moving on to the next day. Many people find it helpful to plan all of the main dishes for the time period, then all of the grain items, and so on. It's usually a good idea to plan snacks last, so that you can use them to fill in the nutritional gaps left by the breakfasts and lunches.

- As discussed earlier, you may need to plan adjustments in preparation methods, or even alternative items, in order to accommodate different age groups.

- Consider the time between snacks and meals when you plan snacks. If it will be 3 hours until the next meal, the snack should be more substantial (preferably with a protein-rich food included) than one that precedes a meal by an hour and a half. You want the children hungry at mealtime, but not frantically so.

- Use the menu checklist to see how you did.

- Check which ingredients you have on hand, then make up your shopping list or purchase orders.

Serving-Size Guidelines for Child Care

The most convenient way to ensure that you're providing adequate amounts of nutrients to children is to plan meals that conform to the Child Care Food Program requirements.* **The CCFP guidelines call for a specified number of servings from the five major food groups: milk, meat or meat alternatives, breads and cereals, fruits, and vegetables.** We've printed them for your reference on pages 64–66.

To do the best possible job of planning meals for children, you should become familiar with the Dietary Guidelines for Americans (p. 69) and the good food sources of important nutrients (pp. 79–81). You may also find it helpful to review "Appendix B—Nutrition Basics."

---

*If you participate in the School Lunch Program, you will need to follow its guidelines.

Child Care Food Program
Meal Patterns for Infants

	Food Components		
	Birth through 3 months	**4–7 months**	**8–11 months**
Breakfast	• 4–6 fluid ounces (fl. oz.) breast milk[1] or formula[2]	• 4–8 fl. oz. breast milk[1] or formula[2] • 0–3 T. infant cereal[3] (optional)	• 6–8 fl. oz. breast milk,[1] formula,[2] or whole milk • 2–4 T. infant cereal[3] • 1–4 T. fruit *and/or* vegetable
Lunch or Supper	• 4–6 fl. oz. breast milk[1] or formula[2]	• 4–8 fl. oz. breast milk[1] or formula[2] • 0–3 T. infant cereal[3] (optional) • 0–3 T. fruit *and/or* vegetable (optional)	• 6–8 fl. oz. breast milk,[1] formula,[2] or whole milk • 2–4 T. infant cereal[3] *and/or* 1–4 T. meat, fish, poultry, egg yolk, or cooked dry beans or peas, *or* 1/2–2 oz. cheese, *or* 1–4 oz. cottage cheese, cheese food, or cheese spread • 1–4 T. fruit *and/or* vegetable
Snack	• 4–6 fl. oz. breast milk[1] or formula[2]	• 4–6 fl. oz. breast milk[1] or formula[2]	• 2–4 fl. oz. breast milk,[1] formula,[2] whole milk, or fruit juice[4] • 0–1/2 slice bread *or* 0–2 crackers[5] (optional)

[1] Meals containing only breast milk are not reimbursable
[2] Iron-fortified infant formula
[3] Iron-fortified dry infant cereal
[4] Full-strength fruit juice
[5] Made from whole-grain or enriched meal or flour

Child Care Food Program
Meal Patterns for Children 1–12 Years

	Food Components		
	1–3 years	**3–6 years**	**6–12 years**

Breakfast

1. Milk, fluid — 1/2 cup | 3/4 cup | 1 cup
2. Vegetable, fruit, or full-strength juice — 1/4 cup | 1/2 cup | 1/2 cup
3. Bread and bread alternates (whole grain or enriched):

	1–3 years	3–6 years	6–12 years
Breakfast			
1. Milk, fluid	1/2 cup	3/4 cup	1 cup
2. Vegetable, fruit, or full-strength juice	1/4 cup	1/2 cup	1/2 cup
3. Bread and bread alternates (whole grain or enriched):			
Bread	1/2 slice	1/2 slice	1 slice
or cornbread, rolls, muffins, or biscuits	1/2 serving	1/2 serving	1 serving
or cold dry cereal (volume or weight,	1/4 cup	1/3 cup	3/4 cup
whichever is less)	or 1/3 oz.	or 1/2 oz.	or 1 oz.
or cooked cereal, pasta, noodle products, or cereal grains	1/4 cup	1/4 cup	1/2 cup
Lunch or Supper			
1. Milk, fluid	1/2 cup	3/4 cup	1 cup
2. Vegetable and/or fruit (two or more kinds)	1/4 cup total	1/2 cup total	3/4 cup total
3. Bread and bread alternates (whole grain or enriched):			
Bread	1/2 slice	1/2 slice	1 slice
or cornbread, rolls, muffins, or biscuits	1/2 serving	1/2 serving	1 serving
or cooked cereal, pasta, noodle products, or cereal grains	1/4 cup	1/4 cup	1/2 cup
4. Meat or meat alternates	1 oz.	1-1/2 oz.	2 oz.
Lean meat, fish, poultry (edible portion as served),			
cheese, or cottage cheese	1 oz.	1-1/2 oz.	2 oz.
or egg	1 egg	1 egg	1 egg
or cooked dry beans or peas [1]	1/4 cup	3/8 cup	1/2 cup
or peanut butter, soy nut butter, or other			
nut or seed butters	2 T.	3 T.	4 T.
or peanuts, soy nuts, tree nuts, or seeds [2]	1/2 oz. [3]	3/4 oz. [3]	1 oz. [3]
or yogurt	1/2 cup	3/4 cup	1 cup
or an equivalent quantity of any combination of the			
above meat/meat alternates			

[1] In the same meal service, dried beans or dried peas may be used as a meat alternate or as a vegetable; however, such use does not satisfy the requirement for both components.

[2] Tree nuts and seeds that may be used as meat alternates are listed in Section 1 of the CCFP Guidelines.

[3] No more than 50% of the requirement shall be met with nuts or seeds. Nuts *or* seeds shall be combined with another meat/meat alternate to fulfill the requirement. For the purpose of determining combinations, 1 oz. of nuts or seeds is equal to 1 oz. of cooked lean meat, poultry, or fish.

(continued)

Child Care Food Program
Meal Patterns for Children 1–12 Years, continued

	Food Components		
	1–3 years	**3–6 years**	**6–12 years**

A.M. or P.M. Supplement (Select two of these four components.)[4]

1. Milk, fluid — 1/2 cup | 1/2 cup | 1 cup
2. Vegetable, fruit, or full-strength juice — 1/2 cup | 1/2 cup | 3/4 cup
3. Bread and bread alternates (whole grain or enriched):

	1–3 years	3–6 years	6–12 years
Bread	1/2 slice	1/2 slice	1 slice
or cornbread, rolls, muffins, or biscuits	1/2 serving	1/2 serving	1 serving
or cold dry cereal (volume or weight, whichever is less)	1/4 cup or 1/3 oz.	1/3 cup or 1/2 oz.	3/4 cup or 1 oz.
or cooked cereal, pasta, noodle products, or cereal grains	1/4 cup	1/4 cup	1/2 cup

4. Meat or meat alternates — 1/2 oz. | 1/2 oz. | 1 oz.

	1–3 years	3–6 years	6–12 years
Lean meat, fish, poultry (edible portion as served), or cheese	1/2 oz.	1/2 oz.	1 oz.
or egg	1/2 egg	1/2 egg	1 egg
or cooked dry beans or peas [1]	1/8 cup	1/8 cup	1/4 cup
or peanut butter, soy nut butter, or other nut or seed butters	1 T.	1 T.	2 T.
or peanuts, soy nuts, tree nuts, or seeds [2]	1/2 oz. [3]	1/2 oz. [3]	1 oz. [3]
or yogurt	1/4 cup	1/4 cup	1/2 cup
or an equivalent quantity of any combination of the above meat/meat alternates			

---

[1] In the same meal service, dried beans or dried peas may be used as a meat alternate or as a vegetable; however, such use does not satisfy the requirement for both components.

[2] Tree nuts and seeds that may be used as meat alternates are listed in Section 1 of the CCFP Guidelines.

[3] No more than 50% of the requirement shall be met with nuts or seeds. Nuts *or* seeds shall be combined with another meat/meat alternate to fulfill the requirement. For the purpose of determining combinations, 1 oz. of nuts or seeds is equal to 1 oz. of cooked lean meat, poultry, or fish.

[4] Juice may not be served when milk is served as the only other component.

Modifying Foods for Children of Different Ages

It may be necessary for you to adjust recipes, including those in this book, to make foods suitable for children at different levels of development. You may also need to modify the form of simple foods like apples or toast.

One reason for this is that the texture or shape of a certain food may make it difficult for a very young child to eat it. You want her to be able to get the food into her mouth, chew it, and swallow it without frustration, because, after all, she should feel successful and happy about her eating experiences. You also want her to get the benefit of its nutritional contribution, which she won't if she gives up on it.

Another important reason for modifying some of the foods you serve is that young children are much more likely to choke on foods that are generally safe for older children. Lastly, certain food ingredients are unsuitable for infants.

- Never feed honey to a child less than 1 year of age; this precaution is necessary to avoid the danger of infant botulism.

- Avoid adding salt and sugar to the foods you serve infants.

- Minimize choking hazards for children younger than 4 years old:

     Chop nuts and seeds finely.
     Slice grapes in half lengthwise.
     Slice hot dogs in quarters lengthwise.
     Shred hard raw vegetables and fruits.
     Remove pits from cherries, plums, peaches, and so on.
     Remove bones from fish.
     Spread peanut butter thinly; never serve it right off a spoon.
     Avoid ever giving young children popcorn and hard candies.

     Soft table foods for infants should be cut in pieces no larger than 1/4-inch cubes. A 1/4-inch cube looks like this:

     Soft table foods for toddlers should be cut in pieces no larger than 1/2-inch cubes. A 1/2-inch cube looks like this:

- Depending on an infant's age and eating ability, you can puree, mash, or chop many of the same foods you are feeding to older children (if you will be adding sugar, salt, or heavy seasonings to these foods, remove the infant's portion first).

- Young children prefer meat that is very tender: cooking with moist heat and chopping or shredding the meat finely, or using ground poultry or beef, will make it easier for children to eat.

- Remember that toddlers and preschoolers enjoy "finger foods."

- Some young children prefer foods that are prepared simply and singly. They may balk at tuna salad sandwiches but eat plain flaked tuna and bread wedges eagerly, or they may enjoy plain steamed carrots and reject carrots mixed into a casserole.

Following the Dietary Guidelines the Yummy Way

It's possible to eat the recommended number of servings from each of the basic food groups and still be poorly nourished. This commonly happens when the foods chosen are high in fat, sugar, or salt; when the foods are limited in their variety; or when foods have been stored or prepared in ways that cause losses of nutrients.

To address these concerns, several health organizations have made recommendations for healthful diets. One such set of recommendations is the **Dietary Guidelines for Americans,** issued jointly by the U.S. Department of Agriculture and the U.S. Department of Health and Human Services in 1995. The Dietary Guidelines don't give us hard numbers, but they steer us in the right direction.

> **Dietary Guidelines for Americans**
>
> Eat a variety of foods.
>
> Balance the food you eat with physical activity—maintain or improve your weight.
>
> Choose a diet with plenty of grain products, vegetables, and fruits.
>
> Choose a diet low in fat, saturated fat, and cholesterol.
>
> Choose a diet moderate in sugars.
>
> Choose a diet moderate in salt and sodium.
>
> If you drink alcoholic beverages, do so in moderation.

It's possible to follow the Dietary Guidelines and still have a lot of fun eating (and cooking). Some foods may need to show up on the menu less often or in smaller amounts, or some of your favorite recipes may need adjustments. Be patient, proceed with an attitude of experimentation, and realize that it may take a little while for jaded taste buds to get used to the changes. Some day you may be surprised to find that soups you ate for years now taste too salty. In the next few pages, we show you how to put more variety into your menus; cut down on fat, sugar, and sodium (salt); and add more fiber and complex carbohydrates from fruits, vegetables, and grains.

Get to Know the Great
Food Guide Pyramid!

The Food Guide Pyramid offers us a visual representation of the Dietary Guidelines. It emphasizes complex carbohydrates, fruits, and vegetables as the sources of calories, hence their position at the "base." The number of servings needed depends on one's calorie needs, which vary with age, sex, physical condition, and activity levels. Young children should have the same number of servings as adults, but the portion sizes will be smaller, except for milk.

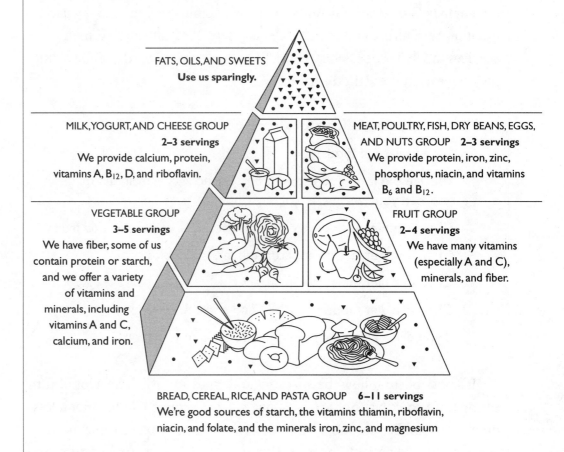

FATS, OILS, AND SWEETS
Use us sparingly.

MILK, YOGURT, AND CHEESE GROUP
2–3 servings
We provide calcium, protein, vitamins A, B$_{12}$, D, and riboflavin.

MEAT, POULTRY, FISH, DRY BEANS, EGGS, AND NUTS GROUP   **2–3 servings**
We provide protein, iron, zinc, phosphorus, niacin, and vitamins B$_6$ and B$_{12}$.

VEGETABLE GROUP
3–5 servings
We have fiber, some of us contain protein or starch, and we offer a variety of vitamins and minerals, including vitamins A and C, calcium, and iron.

FRUIT GROUP
2–4 servings
We have many vitamins (especially A and C), minerals, and fiber.

BREAD, CEREAL, RICE, AND PASTA GROUP   **6–11 servings**
We're good sources of starch, the vitamins thiamin, riboflavin, niacin, and folate, and the minerals iron, zinc, and magnesium

Variety Brings Your Menus to Life

Variety helps make your meals more interesting and more nutritious. A good start is remembering to serve foods from the 5 main food groups every day. The next step is to beware of getting into ruts when planning menus (don't worry, we all get into them). Sometimes we have to curl up with a good cookbook, stroll through the produce department at our local market, or try out a new (perhaps ethnic) restaurant to find inspiration. We love doing that sort of research!

Vary Your Main Dishes

Look at your choices! You needn't serve chicken three times a week when you can choose from dried beans, peas, lentils, peanut butter, cheese, eggs, fish, other seafood, turkey, beef, pork, and lamb.

Balance meat dishes with vegetarian entrees.

Try some ethnic recipes.

Try a main-dish salad.

Tired of Carrot and Celery Sticks?
Try These Vegetables Raw Instead

Tomatoes	Turnips
Cucumbers	Fennel
Sugar-snap peas	Cabbage
Green or red peppers	Sprouts
Jicama	Summer squashes
Cauliflower	Broccoli
Asparagus (best blanched)	Radishes
Snow peas (also best blanched)	Mushrooms

Grain Products Besides Cold Cereal
You Can Serve at Breakfast

Hot cereals (oatmeal, whole-wheat varieties,
   grits, brown rice, polenta, couscous)
Tortillas
Muffins, quick breads
Pancakes, waffles, french toast
Sandwiches
Pizza
Rice cakes, graham crackers
Swiss Breakfast (p. 116)
Bagels, pita bread, cornbread
Noodle kugel

Let's Ditch Some Fat and Saturated Fat

When Shopping

- Choose lean meats; these are generally the leaner cuts:

  Beef: Eye of round, top round steak, top round roast, sirloin steak, top loin steak, tenderloin steak, chuck arm pot roast

  Pork: Tenderloin, top loin roast, top loin chop, center loin chop, sirloin roast, loin rib chop, shoulder blade steak

  Lamb: Leg loin chop, arm chop, foreshanks

  Veal: Cutlet, blade or arm steak, rib roast, rib or loin chop

- Buy "select" or "good" grades of beef rather than "prime," which has more marbled fat.

- Buy ground meat that has the greatest percent lean-to-fat ratio.

- Select fish, poultry, reduced-fat or nonfat cheeses, and, especially, dried beans as protein sources.

- Buy water-packed tuna, not oil-packed.

- Read labels on food packaging and opt for low-fat products.

- Avoid prebreaded meat items.

- Buy plain frozen vegetables, not the varieties with sauces.

- Buy nonfat or low-fat milk for cooking. Evaporated skim milk is a good substitute for light cream.

- Limit your use of butter, cream, whole milk, most cheeses, hard margarine, shortening, lard, coconut and palm oils, and foods containing them.

- Try yogurt as a substitute for mayonnaise or sour cream. Or use the nonfat or reduced-fat versions of these foods.

When Cooking

- Try combining small amounts of high-fat protein foods like ground beef or cheese with cooked dried beans (example: chili with beans).

- Broil, bake, roast, stew, or steam foods rather than frying them.

- Trim the fat from meat and take the skin off poultry. Drain cooked ground beef before adding it to other ingredients (see p. 75).

- Limit your use of whole eggs. Two egg whites can fill in for one whole egg in most recipes.

- Experiment with cutting the amount of fat in your favorite recipes. It's amazing what you can do with a tablespoon of oil rather than a half-cup.

- Use nonstick or seasoned cast-iron skillets.

- Use nonstick spray to prevent foods from sticking to pans.

- Use olive or canola oil in place of butter or margarine where practical. Oil cannot be directly substituted for butter or shortening in baked goods without changing their texture. There are many recipes available for bakery items with a minimum of fat and saturated fat, however (see Appendix E—Resources).

When Serving Foods

- Don't automatically add fat such as butter to breads, grains, and vegetables. Let children get used to the taste of foods without it. Many children enjoy salads more without dressing; that's a nice habit to get into!

- Serve high-fat foods in smaller portions and less often.

Remember: Do not restrict fat in the diets of children under the age of 2!

Helpful Hint: How to Remove More of the Fat from Ground Beef

Method 1

Cook the meat and drain off all the fat you can. Cover with cold water and refrigerate overnight. The next day, skim off the congealed fat, drain the meat, and use it in your recipe.

Method 2

Rinse the cooked meat with very hot water before using it.

High-Fat Foods	Lower-Fat Alternatives
Whole milk	Nonfat or low-fat milk
Sour cream	Yogurt, light sour cream, *Mock Sour Cream* (p. 119)
Hard cheeses—cheddar, swiss, jack, American	Reduced-fat cheeses, low-fat cottage cheese
Cream soups (made with cream or cream sauce)	Clear soups or "cream" soups made with evaporated skim milk or vegetable purees
Mayonnaise	Yogurt, reduced-fat mayonnaise, mustard
Luncheon meats and sausages	Turkey and chicken breast, lean ham, lean roast beef
Oil-packed tuna	Water-packed tuna
Snack chips (potato, corn)	Toast points, *Pita Points* (p. 117), pretzels, rice cakes
Gravies	Broth thickened with a little flour or cornstarch, tomato sauce, catsup
Ground beef	Ground turkey or chicken
Pizza with sausage	Pizza with vegetables or plain cheese
Vegetables frozen with butter sauce	Plain frozen vegetables
Pastries and cakes	Lower-fat muffins and quick breads
Doughnuts	Bagels, raisin bread
Croissants	English muffins
Ice cream	Nonfat frozen yogurt, sorbet
Fried foods	Baked, broiled, or steamed foods
French fried potatoes	*Oven-Fried Potato Sticks* (p. 102)
Fried fish	*Homemade Fish Sticks* (p. 95)
Chicken nuggets	*Chicken Fingers* (p. 97)
Buttered popcorn	Air-popped popcorn
Sugar cookies, sandwich cookies	Graham crackers, animal crackers

Next, Let's Get Rid of Some Sugar

- Watch out for "hidden sugar" in convenience foods. Read labels! Sugar = sucrose, glucose, dextrose, invert sugar, fructose, corn syrup, corn sweeteners, maple syrup, honey, molasses, raw sugar, turbinado sugar, Sucanat.

- Keep the sugar bowl and honey bear off the table.

- Serve fresh fruits, unsweetened frozen fruits, or fruits canned in natural juices or water.

- Serve 100% fruit juices instead of fruit drinks. Read labels carefully!

- Check the breakfast cereals you're using; they should have less than 6 grams of sugar per serving.

- Sweeten cold or hot cereals with fruit, like bananas.

- Try cutting back the sugar (up to 50%) in your recipes.

- Serve muffins instead of cupcakes, graham crackers instead of cookies (or make your own cookies with less sugar).

- Use vanilla, cinnamon, nutmeg, or allspice to enhance sweet flavors.

- Add your own fruit to plain yogurt rather than buying the sweetened variety. Mash it first, and it won't seem so tart.

- When you do serve foods high in sugar, use small portions and serve them less often.

Foods High in Sugar

Chocolate milk	Canned fruits in syrup
Milkshakes	Flavored gelatin desserts
Soft drinks	Candies
Fruit drinks/ades	Sweetened coconut
Jams, jellies	Flavored yogurts
Syrups, sweet sauce	Puddings
Ice cream, sherbet	Sweet pickle relish
Pies, pastries	Many children's cereals
Cakes, cookies	Sweet rolls, doughnuts

Kids Don't Need All That Salt, Either

Foods High in Salt (aka Sodium)

Soy sauce	Bouillon
Gravies	MSG
Pickles	Olives
Sauerkraut	Commercial salad dressings
Bacon	Ham
Frankfurters	Bologna
Canned meats	Sausage
Corned beef	Processed cheeses
Salted nuts/nut butters	Salted crackers
Canned soups	Miso
Snack chips	Many prepared foods

- Don't add salt to pasta, rice, cereals, and vegetable cooking water.

- Leave the salt shaker and soy sauce bottle off the table.

- *Gradually* reduce the amount of salt in your recipes. *Never* add salt to baby foods.

- Use chicken or vegetable stock or water instead of bouillon.

- Use herbs, spices, and lemon juice to enhance the flavors of foods.

- Use unsalted nut butters and crackers with less salt.

- Serve high-sodium foods less often and in smaller quantities.

- Make homemade versions of foods you usually buy ready to serve or as mixes.

- Read labels! Check the nutrition information for the milligrams of sodium in a serving.

Now There's Room for More Starch and Fiber

■ Serve more bread, potatoes, tortillas, rice, pasta, and unsweetened cereals, and fewer cookies, pastries, doughnuts, and sweetened cereals.

■ Look for *whole-grain* cereal products, breads, and tortillas.

■ Serve lots of fruits and vegetables, *unpeeled*.

■ Serve *raw* fruits and vegetables often.

■ Serve (cooked) dried beans and peas often.

■ Serve dried fruits like prunes, raisins, or dried apricots occasionally; they are sticky, however, so make sure children brush their teeth afterward.

■ Make sure children drink plenty of water so the fiber can move through their intestines.

■ Don't depend on bran products to add fiber to children's diets; they generally don't need them.

High-Fiber Foods

Whole-grain breads	Nuts and seeds
Shredded wheat cereals	Popcorn
Nutrigrain® cereals	Dried beans, lentils
Oatmeal	Fresh fruits with skins
Barley	Berries
Brown rice	Bananas
Bulgur wheat	Dried fruits
Millet	Raw vegetables

Foods Chock-Full of Vitamin A

Vitamin A is found in enormous quantities in fish liver oils and in animal livers in general. Milk products, eggs, butter, and margarine are also good sources of vitamin A. The most significant sources of vitamin A in our diets, however, are fruits and vegetables. Actually, they contain substances called *carotenes* (of which beta carotene is the best known), which the body can convert to vitamin A. Carotenes appear to be safe even when consumed in very large amounts *in foods*. So plan to serve some of these carotene-rich fruits and vegetables at least every other day!

Vegetables

Asparagus

Broccoli

Carrots

Chard

Chili peppers

Collard greens

Dandelion greens

Kale

Mixed vegetables (frozen)

Mustard greens

Peppers (sweet red)

Pumpkin

Romaine lettuce

Spinach

Squash, winter

Sweet potatoes

Tomatoes

Turnip greens

Fruits

Apricots

Cantaloupe

Cherries (red sour)

Mangoes

Nectarines

Papayas

Peaches (except canned)

Plums (canned purple)

Prunes

Foods Bursting with Vitamin C

Foods containing vitamin C should be included in meals every day. Because vitamin C can be destroyed by cooking and exposure to air, you must take special care with these foods. Serve fruits and vegetables raw or lightly cooked to get the most vitamin C from them.

Vegetables

Asparagus	Mustard greens
Broccoli	Okra
Brussels sprouts	Peppers, red and green
Cabbage	Potatoes
Cauliflower	Spinach
Chili peppers	Sweet potatoes
Collards	Tomatoes
Cress, garden	Turnip greens
Dandelion greens	Turnips
Kale	

Fruits

Cantaloupe	Orange juice
Grapefruit	Oranges
Grapefruit juice	Papayas
Guavas	Raspberries
Honeydew melon	Strawberries
Kiwi	Tangelos
Lemons	Tangerines
Mangoes	

Good Sources of Iron

Iron is one nutrient that often comes up short in children's diets. The iron found in meats ("heme" iron) is absorbed much more efficiently than that from nonmeat sources ("nonheme" iron), but nonmeat foods can and do make important contributions to the iron intake of children. Nonheme iron is absorbed better if vitamin C-containing foods are eaten along with it. Include several sources of iron in your menus daily.

Meat and Meat Alternatives Group

Dried beans and peas

Eggs

Meats, especially liver

Peanut butter

Shellfish

Turkey

Vegetables

Asparagus (canned)

Beans (green, lima, canned)

Beet greens

Beets (canned)

Broccoli

Brussels sprouts

Chard

Collards

Kale

Mustard greens

Parsley

Parsnips

Peas

Spinach

Squash, winter

Sweet potatoes

Tomato juice

Tomato paste

Tomato puree

Tomatoes (canned)

Turnip greens

Fruits

Apples (dried)

Apricots (canned or dried)

Cherries (canned)

Dates

Figs (dried)

Grapes (canned)

Peaches (dried)

Prunes

Raisins

Strawberries

Watermelon

Breads and Grain Products   Any enriched or whole-grain breads and cereals

Your Faithful Lunchbox Guide

Protein-Rich Foods

Roasted chicken breast (1–2 oz.)
Lean roast beef (1–2 oz.)
Roasted turkey (1–2 oz.)
Tuna or leftover fish (1–2 oz.)
Hard-boiled egg (1) or egg salad
Peanut butter (2 T.)
Low-fat cheese (1–2 oz.)
"String" cheese
Low-fat cottage cheese (3/8 cup)
Tofu cubes (3–4 oz.), tofu salad
Tempeh "fingers" (2 oz.)
Beans, bean soups (1/2 cup)
Salmon loaf/patty (2 oz.)
Veggie-burger

Starchy Foods

Bread (1 slice, small roll)
Bagel (1/2)
Flour or corn tortilla (1)
Rice or pasta (1/3–1/2 cup)
Crackers (3–4)
Rice cakes (2, or 6–8 mini)
Unsweetened cereal (1/2 cup)
Muffin, small
Tabouli (1/2 cup)
Bread sticks

Calcium-Rich Foods

Low-fat or nonfat milk (6 oz.)
Yogurt (3/4 cup)
Low-fat cheeses (1 oz.)
Tofu* (5 oz.)
Cottage cheese (3/4 cup)
Corn tortillas (2)

Fruits and Vegetables

Carrot sticks
Celery "boats"
Zucchini sticks
Turnip rounds
Jicama slices
Broccoli "trees"
Sprouts
Tomatoes
Lettuce
Pepper rings or sticks
Apples, oranges, pears,
    berries, bananas,
    kiwi slices, pineapple . . .
Unsweetened juices

---

*Must contain calcium sulfate, not nigari.

DO use leftovers and combination foods: casseroles, salads, dips made from cottage cheese or yogurt, and soups. See how your child likes cold leftover enchiladas at home first, though!

It's best for lunches to be refrigerated until serving time; frozen "juice boxes" or freezer packs will work if no refrigerator is available.

Snacks Are Important

Snacks can make important contributions to good nutrition. Children often can't eat enough to satisfy all of their needs at the standard three meals, and they may feel tired and miserable when opportunities to eat are spaced too far apart (so can adults, actually). The keys to making snacks work are *timing* and *food choices*.

- Establish regular snacktimes. Don't give handouts all day long, and don't let the children fill up on juice when they're thirsty.

- Schedule snacks a few hours before the next meal (so the children will be hungry enough at mealtime to eat, but not so hungry they are frantic), and a few hours after the last meal (so the children don't get the idea that they can refuse a meal and be rescued shortly thereafter).

- Snacks can be fairly substantial if it will be a long time before the children will eat again—lighter if you just need to hold off the hunger for a little while. When children are in child care for long afternoons, they may need a second, light snack around five o'clock. Parents facing the ride home and preparing late dinners are usually very appreciative when their children are fortified and reasonably cheerful!

- Be creative! Snacktime is a wonderful opportunity to use up leftovers, serve foods that are new and unusual, and have the kids participate in food preparation.

- Avoid serving foods that are highly sweetened or salted; make what you offer as nutritious as possible.

Snacktime Mix and Match

Plan snacks to include a serving from at least *two* food groups. Be creative! Here are some ideas to get you started.

Breads and Cereals

Pita Points (p. 117)
Rice cakes
Bagels
Graham crackers
Quick breads and muffins
Savory Scrambled Cereals (p. 121)
Nori-Maki Rolls (p. 118)
Tortillas
Toast fingers
Pancakes
Bread sticks
Hot or cold cereal
English muffins

Fruits and Vegetables

Micro-Fruit (p. 109)
Any fresh fruit
Any raw vegetable
Vegetable soups
Soft-Serve Fruit (p. 110)
Wiggly Fruit (p. 109)
Unsweetened canned or frozen fruit
Baked potatoes or *Oven-Fried Potato Sticks* (p. 102)
Unsweetened fruit juice

Meat and Meat Alternatives

Vegetarian Chili (canned or homemade, p. 94)
Bean or lentil soups
Hummus (p. 121)
Cheese (preferably reduced-fat varieties)
Cottage cheese
Turkey loaf cubes
Yogurt
Peanut butter
Mock Sour Cream (p. 119) as a dip or topping
Tuna salad
Bean Dip (p. 120)

Milk*

Fluid milk
Milk in "shakes" or smoothies

---

*Only fluid milk is in this group for Child Care Food Program reimbursement purposes, although cheese, cottage cheese, and yogurt are also considered dairy foods.

How Does Your Menu Measure Up?

A good menu does more than meet the basic requirements for servings from the 5 basic food groups of the Food Guide Pyramid. With proper planning, you can make sure that the foods you serve are appealing, emphasize critical nutrients, and teach healthful eating habits. You also will be able to manage your costs and workflow better. Check your menu against the criteria below:

- ☐ Menu has some variety in:
    - Color
    - Texture
    - Shape
    - Temperature
    - Flavors
    - Preparation methods

- ☐ Whole-grain bread/cereal products are served often.

- ☐ Raw fruits and vegetables are served often.

- ☐ Good source of vitamin C is served daily.

- ☐ Good source of vitamin A is served at least three times/week.

- ☐ Good source of iron is served daily.

- ☐ Most of the foods are familiar to and enjoyed by most of the children.

- ☐ Some of the foods are new; some are familiar foods prepared in a different way.

- ☐ Higher-fat foods are balanced with lower-fat foods.

- ☐ Snacks fill in nutritional gaps in the main meals.

- ☐ Cultural, ethnic, and religious preferences are considered.

- ☐ Substitutions are planned for children with allergies.

- ☐ Holidays, birthdays, field trips, and special events have been planned for.

- ☐ Expensive foods are balanced with less expensive foods.

Computers and Your Kitchen

What do computers have to do with feeding kids? Well, you can use a computer to plan menus, adjust and store recipes, generate a shopping list, and perform various accounting functions. You can also use a computer to determine what levels of nutrients your menus are providing.

Many computer programs will analyze individual foods, recipes, or a day's menus for nutrient content. They also will compare a given menu with the Recommended Dietary Allowances (RDAs) for persons of a specified age, sex, and size. They can compute the percentage of fat and the amounts of sugar, cholesterol, and fiber in foods and meals. A program we like is DINE HEALTHY® (for both Macintosh and IBM/Windows). It's simple to use and available from:

> DINE Systems, Inc.
> 586 North French Rd.
> Amherst, NY 14228
> 1-800-688-1848
> $129.00 plus $7.95 shipping and handling

If you aren't inclined to use the computer yourself, perhaps you have a friend who would love an excuse to work with a new program. You can also seek out a registered dietitian (check your yellow pages) who may be willing to perform menu analyses for you.

Chapter *Four*

The Recipes

About the Recipes...

In developing these recipes, we kept in mind that people who take care of children generally don't have a lot of time to cook. Even people who cook for children as a full-time job enjoy saving time! What we are promoting is the use of simple foods, made "from scratch." These foods are usually cheaper and taste fresher than processed foods. And very important, they give us more control over the amounts of fat, sugar, salt, and additives we serve.

Most of the recipes have been tested in very large quantities as well as very small ones. We aimed for testers in a variety of situations and in different parts of the country to make sure that we got a good picture of taste preferences and that ingredients would be readily available. Some recipes will obviously be unworkable due to time, transportation, or storage problems if you are running a centralized kitchen serving 500 children. They may, however, be useful as cooking projects in classrooms.

We have cut the fat, salt, and sugar in these recipes as much as possible, while still pleasing our obliging "taste testers," both children and adults. You may find at first that these recipes don't taste salty or sweet enough, but eventually your (and the children's) taste buds will get used to less salt and sugar. We also made the foods less spicy than we would ordinarily serve to adults. If you know that the children you're cooking for are very sensitive to spicy foods, you may want to cut the seasoning even further. On the other hand, some children have quite adventuresome palates, and you can be a little freer with the chili powder and such.

The serving sizes listed are the minimum amounts that must be served to count for reimbursement through the Child Care Food Program or the School Lunch Program.* You will want to make large enough quantities to allow for second helpings, and you are probably aware, by now, of which items are likely to be especially popular with the children you're cooking for. In the interest of the children's health and of your budget, however, we don't suggest that you feel obliged to serve huge amounts of the meat or meat substitutes. Protein-rich foods (except dried beans) are usually the most expensive, and children don't need as much as you may think. If the children are still hungry, they can eat more vegetables, fruits, and grains instead. It's a habit that will serve them well when they grow up!

Bon Appetit!

---

*Unless otherwise specified, one serving
of vegetables or fruit = 1/4 cup.

Recipe Table of Contents

Main Dishes

Lentil Soup
"Gentle Lentil Soup"

2-1/2 cups lentils, rinsed and drained
7 cups water or stock
2 medium onions, chopped
3 cloves garlic, minced
Juice of one lemon
Salt and pepper to taste

2 stalks celery, chopped
2 T. olive oil
1 or 2 bunches spinach,
**   chard, or collards, washed**
**   and chopped coarsely**

1. Sauté onions, garlic, and celery in the olive oil, 5–10 minutes.
2. Add lentils and water or stock, and simmer until lentils are very soft. If necessary, add more water to get soup to desired consistency.
3. Add greens, salt, and pepper. Simmer for 10 more minutes or until greens are tender.
4. Stir in lemon juice right before serving.

Serves 16 preschool or 12 school-age children • 1 meat alternative

Garbo-Burgers
"Beanie Burgers"

1 15-1/2 oz. can garbanzo beans, drained
1-1/3 cup rolled oats
1 cup water
1 t. Italian seasoning
1 small onion, minced OR 1 t. onion powder

1/8 t. garlic powder
1-1/2 T. soy sauce OR
**   2 t. Worcestershire sauce**
1 T. olive oil

1. Run beans through food processor until they have a texture like ground meat.
2. Add remaining ingredients (except for oil) and allow to sit for 10–15 minutes so water is absorbed.
3. Heat olive oil in skillet.
4. Spoon large or small patties into the skillet; press down into burger shapes.
5. Cook on both sides until browned.

Note: Use as burgers or to fill in for the veal in a vegetarian version of "Veal Parmesan." Small patties can be eaten as finger food and/or dipped into sauces, too.

Serves 4–5 preschool or 3 school-age children • 1 meat alternative

White Bean Soup*
"Speckled Soup"

1-1/2 cups white beans
4 cups water or stock
2 cloves garlic, minced
2 stalks celery, chopped
2 carrots, chopped
1 onion, chopped
2 T. olive oil

2 t. dried basil
1/2 lb. green beans in 1″ pieces OR
   1/2 lb. zucchini, sliced in half-moons
2 T. lemon juice
3/4 t. salt
Pepper to taste

1. Soak beans in water to cover by 2" overnight. Drain in the morning.
2. Sauté garlic, onion, celery, and carrots in oil for about 10 minutes.
3. Add soaked beans and the 4 cups of water or stock.
4. Simmer until beans are tender, about 45 minutes.
5. Add basil and green beans or zucchini and simmer another 30 minutes or so, until tender.
6. Before serving, stir in lemon juice, salt, and pepper.

Serves 8 preschool or 6 school-age children • 1 meat alternative

---

*Adapted from *Still Life with Menu* © 1988 by Mollie Katzen. Reprinted by permission of Ten Speed Press, Berkeley, California.

Easier-Than-Lasagna

8 oz. macaroni or spiral pasta
1 onion, chopped
4 cloves garlic, chopped
2 T. olive oil
2 t. oregano
1 t. basil
1 bay leaf

1 28-oz. can (3-3/4 cups) crushed tomatoes
1 t. salt
1/2 cup water
2 cups cottage or ricotta cheese
1/2 cup Parmesan cheese
9 oz. brick or jack cheese, grated

1. Sauté onion and garlic in the oil.
2. Add tomatoes, herbs, salt, and water and simmer 30 minutes.
3. Cook pasta until just tender.
4. Stir all ingredients together except the brick or jack cheese to sprinkle on top.
   Bake for 20 minutes at 375°.

Serves 12 preschool or 8 school-age children • 1 meat alternative + 1 bread/grain + 1 vegetable

Chilaquiles*

1 dozen corn tortillas, several days old
1 cup onions, chopped
2 cloves garlic, pressed *OR*
   1/4 t. garlic powder
2 t. chili powder
1 t. cumin powder

1-1/2 cups low-fat cottage cheese
1-1/2 cups canned crushed
   tomatoes
6 oz. grated jack or cheddar cheese
Salt to taste
1 T. oil

1. Cut tortillas into wedges or tear into strips.
2. Sauté onions in oil for 5 minutes. (A nonstick or cast-iron skillet that's ovenproof is ideal for this.)
3. Add tortilla pieces, chili powder, garlic, cumin, and salt.
4. Toss until the tortilla pieces are wilted.
5. Purée cottage cheese and tomatoes in blender until smooth.
6. Stir gently into tortilla pieces.
7. Sprinkle with grated cheese.
8. Bake at 350° for about 20 minutes.

Serves 8 preschool or 6 school-age children • 1 meat alternative + 1 bread/grain

*Adapted from *Laurel's Kitchen* by Laurel Robertson, Carol Flinders, and Bronwen Godfrey. Petaluma, CA: Nilgiri Press, 1976.

One-Pot Macaroni and Cheese

8 oz. dry macaroni or other pasta
2 cups low-fat milk
1-1/2 T. cornstarch
3/4 t. salt
1/4 t. fresh-ground pepper

1/2 t. dry mustard
1/4 t. paprika
12 oz. sharp cheddar cheese, grated
2 scallions, green part only, thinly sliced
   OR 2 T. minced chives (optional)

1. Cook macaroni.
2. While macaroni is cooking, combine milk and dry ingredients in a jar and shake very well.
3. When macaroni is tender, drain it and return to pan.
4. Add milk mixture and stir gently over medium heat until sauce thickens.
5. Add cheese and optional scallions or chives, stir until melted, and serve.

Serves 8 preschool or 6 school-age children • 1 meat alternative + 1 bread/grain

Vegetarian Chili

"Jack and Jilli Chili"

3 I-lb. cans pinto or black beans, drained
   (save liquid)
I T. oil
I large onion, chopped
I bell pepper, chopped

3 garlic cloves, chopped
I t. cumin
2 t. chili powder
I I-lb. can tomatoes
1/2 t. salt

1. Sauté onion and green pepper in oil for about 5 minutes.
2. Add garlic and sauté another minute.
3. Add remaining ingredients and simmer about 20–30 minutes. Add bean liquid if necessary to retain moist consistency.

Variation: **Chili-Mac.** Toss with 6–8 oz. of macaroni, cooked.

Serves 12 preschool or 9 school-age children • I meat alternative (+ I bread/grain if macaroni is added)

Tuna Salad

"Looney Tooney Salad"

2 6-1/2-oz. cans water-packed tuna,
   drained and flaked
1/2 cup plain yogurt *OR* a mixture of
   1/2 yogurt and 1/2 mayonnaise
2 minced scallions

2 minced celery ribs
1/2 t. curry powder
1/4 t. salt
4 T. water chestnuts, chopped
   (optional)

1. Mix all ingredients together.
2. Eat as salad or sandwich spread.

Serves 7 preschool or 5 school-age children • I meat

Yummy-for-the-Tummy
Baked Fish

1 lb. fish filets (flounder, sole, perch,
   orange roughy)
2-1/2 cups fresh whole-wheat
   bread crumbs
1/3 cup chopped onion
1-1/2 T. lemon juice
1/2 t. Italian seasoning

1 t. parsley flakes
1/4 t. salt
1/8 t. pepper
1 T. olive oil
3 T. Parmesan cheese
1/8 t. garlic powder

1. Spread out fish filets in oiled baking pan.

2. Combine remaining ingredients and spread over fish.

3. Bake at 400° for about 15 minutes or at 375° for 20 minutes.

Serves 7 preschool or 5 school-age children • 1 meat

Homemade Fish Sticks
"Sea Sticks"

1 lb. snapper or cod, cut into sticks
1 egg white, beaten
1-1/2 T. oil
3/4 cup cornflake crumbs

1/2 t. onion powder
1/16 t. garlic powder
Salt and pepper to taste

1. Mix together beaten egg white and oil.

2. Combine cereal crumbs, onion powder, garlic powder, salt, and pepper.

3. Dip fish sticks into egg white mixture, then roll in seasoned flakes.

4. Bake at 400°, 10–15 minutes, turning once.

Serves 7 preschool or 5 school-age children • 1 meat

Chow Mein Salad

1/2 lb. Napa (Chinese) cabbage, shredded
1/3 lb. mung bean sprouts
1/4 lb. snow peas
1 or 2 scallions, tops only, thinly sliced
1 rib celery, thinly sliced
1 8-oz. can water chestnuts, sliced
9 oz. cooked chicken meat, shredded
1 5-oz. can chow mein noodles (crispy type)

Dressing:
2 T. plain rice vinegar
2 T. toasted sesame oil
1 T. vegetable oil
2 T. soy sauce
1 garlic clove, pressed
  OR 1/8 t. garlic powder
1/2 t. powdered ginger
1/2 t. sugar

1. Blanch bean sprouts and snow peas separately, about 2 minutes, in boiling water. Let cool in refrigerator.

2. Combine all salad ingredients in large bowl.

3. Combine dressing ingredients and toss with salad.

Variations: Romaine lettuce can be used instead of Napa cabbage. You can substitute 9 oz. cooked shrimp for the chicken.

Serves 6 preschool or 4 school-age children • 1 meat + 2 vegetables

Marek's Chicken

4 lbs. chicken pieces
2 cloves garlic, pressed
Juice of one lemon
1″ piece ginger root, peeled and chopped fine

2 bunches scallions, cut into 1″ pieces
1 T. curry powder
2 T. oil
Salt to taste

1. Remove skin from chicken pieces.

2. Brown chicken and ginger in oil, about 5 minutes.

3. Add scallions, garlic, and curry powder, and sauté about another 5 minutes.

4. Add lemon juice, about 1/4 cup water, and salt. Cover the pan and simmer until chicken is thoroughly cooked, adding more water if necessary to keep the mixture very moist. Serve with rice.

Note: Chris's friend, Marek, learned to cook this dish in Nepal.

Serves 16 preschool or 12 school-age children • 1 meat

Chicken Fingers
"Slim Pickin' Chicken Fingers"

**1 lb. boneless, skinless chicken breasts
  sliced across the "grain" in 3/4" strips**
**1 cup cornflake crumbs (ready-made
  crumbs are cheaper than the cereal!)**

1-1/4 t. Spike seasoning
1/8 t. garlic powder
1/8 t. pepper
2 egg whites
1 T. oil

1. Combine cereal crumbs and seasonings.
2. Beat oil into egg whites.
3. Roll chicken pieces in egg mixture, then in crumbs.
4. Spread out on a greased baking sheet.
5. Bake at 400° for 15 minutes.

Variation: For eggless version, roll chicken pieces in 1/2 cup yogurt
thinned with 1 T. milk, then in crumbs.

Serves 6 preschool or 4 school-age children • 1 meat

Three Marinades for Chicken
Each is enough for about 2 lbs. chicken pieces
or strips of chicken breast

Mustard-Honey Marinade
1/4 cup honey
2 T. Dijon-type mustard
**1 clove garlic, pressed
  OR 1/8 t. garlic powder**
2 T. rice vinegar
1-1/2 t. dark sesame oil
1-1/2 T. soy sauce

Mint-Garlic Marinade
1 cup plain yogurt
2 T. chopped onion
1 t. dried mint
**2 cloves garlic, pressed
  OR 1/4 t. garlic powder**
1/2 t. salt

Teriyaki Marinade
1/4 cup soy sauce
1/4 cup orange juice
1 T. brown sugar
2 cloves fresh garlic, pressed *OR* 1/4 t. garlic powder
1 t. fresh grated ginger *OR* 1/2 t. powdered ginger

Sloppy Josephines

1 lb. ground turkey
3/4 cup onion, chopped
1 cup tomato sauce
2 T. prepared mustard
1 T. Worcestershire sauce

1 t. brown sugar
1/8 t. garlic powder
Salt and pepper to taste
Whole-grain hot dog or
   hamburger buns

1. Sauté onion and turkey gently until turkey is cooked through, breaking up large clumps. Add small amount of oil if necessary to prevent sticking.
2. Add remaining ingredients and simmer 15 minutes.
3. Serve on hot dog or hamburger buns.

Serves 7 preschool or 5 school-age children • 1 meat + 1 bread/grain

Turkey Loaf
"Loafin' Turkey"

1 lb. ground turkey
1 10-oz. package frozen broccoli
1 cup sharp cheddar cheese, grated
1 cup soft bread crumbs
1 egg

1/3 cup milk
1/2 cup chopped onion
1 t. fines herbes
2 t. prepared mustard
1/2 t. salt
1/8 t. pepper

1. Steam broccoli until just barely cooked.
2. Mix with all other ingredients in a large bowl.
3. Pack into a loaf pan and bake about 1 hour at 350°.

Serves 9 preschool or 6 school-age children • 1 meat

Taco Salad

8 cups shredded lettuce
1 lb. fresh tomatoes, diced
6 oz. cooked chicken or turkey, shredded or diced
   OR **6 oz. cooked ground beef**
   OR **1-1/2 cups cooked dried beans**
   (kidney, pinto, or black beans)
6 oz. grated cheddar or jack cheese
1 cup crumbled tortilla chips

Dressing:
3 T. oil
1-1/2 T. red wine vinegar
2 T. water
1/8 t. garlic powder
1/2 t. oregano
1/2 t. chili powder
1/4 t. cumin powder
1/4 t. salt

1. Combine dressing ingredients.
2. Toss lettuce and tomatoes with dressing.
3. Spread meat or beans and cheese over top.
4. Sprinkle crumbled tortilla chips over all.

Optional additions: Fresh raw corn cut from the cob, scallions, cilantro, avocado.

Serves 8 preschool or 6 school-age children • 1 meat + 2 vegetables

Salmon Cakes or Muffins

1 1-lb. can of salmon, flaked
1/2 cup chopped onion
2 T. lemon juice
1-1/2 t. dill weed
1/4 t. tabasco
   OR **dash of cayenne pepper**

3/4 cup cracker meal
2 egg whites
1/2 cup milk
1/4 t. salt
1/4 t. pepper

1. Mix all ingredients well.
2. Shape into patties and place on a greased baking sheet or portion into greased muffin cups.
3. Bake at 400° for about 20 minutes.

Serves 7 preschool or 5 school-age children • 1 meat

Green Eggs and Ham

8 eggs
1/2 cup minced fresh parsley (chives are
    also nice, but optional)
1/2 cup milk

Oil
4 oz. cooked turkey ham
   OR Canadian bacon
Salt and pepper to taste

1. Beat eggs, parsley, and milk together.
2. Scramble egg mixture in a heavy or nonstick pan in a small amount of oil.
3. Serve with small amounts of turkey ham or Canadian bacon on the side.

Serves 8 preschool or school-age children • 1 meat

Vegetables

Sweet Potato Fries

2 lbs. sweet potatoes or yams   **1–2 t. vegetable oil**

1. Peel sweet potatoes or yams and cut into sticks or wedges.
2. Toss with oil in a bowl.
3. Spread out on baking sheet.
4. Bake about 1/2 hour at 375°, or until browned and tender.
5. Sprinkle with a little salt and lemon juice, if desired.

16 vegetable servings

Homemade Potato Chips
"Tato Pips"

1 lb. russet potatoes   **Vegetable oil**

1. Preheat oven to 400°.
2. Slice potatoes paper-thin. (A food processor will make this easier.)
3. Spread the slices out in a single layer on a foil-lined or lightly oiled cookie sheet.
4. Bake for 15 or 20 minutes.
5. Remove when cooked to a crisp, golden brown.

8 vegetable servings

Oven-Fried Potato Sticks
"Fiddlesticks"

4 baking potatoes, scrubbed and dried (about 2 lbs.)
1 T. oil
1/4 t. paprika

1. Cut each potato into 8–12 wedges.
2. Toss with oil and paprika.
3. Spread in shallow pan.
4. Bake until tender, 20–30 minutes at 450° *OR* 35–40 minutes at 400°.

16 vegetable servings

Mashed Potatoes and Carrots
"Monster Mash"

1 lb. raw potatoes (russet)   **Salt and pepper to taste**
1 lb. raw carrots   **1/2 t. soy sauce (optional)**
2 t. butter or olive oil

1. Wash potatoes and cut into eighths.
2. Scrub carrots and cut into 1" chunks.
3. Cook potatoes and carrots gently in about 1 cup water. If they get too dry, add a little more water. If it looks too runny, let some of the water evaporate.
4. Mash, or put in food processor, with butter, salt, pepper, and the soy sauce (if desired).

Note: Thanks to Barbara Zeavin for this recipe.

16 vegetable servings

Senegalese Veggie Stew

1 onion, chopped
1 T. oil
2 cups winter squash or sweet potato,
    peeled and cut into chunks
2 medium potatoes, cut into chunks
1 large carrot, cut into chunks
1 small bunch of greens (collards or turnip
    greens) OR 1 10-oz. pkg. frozen greens

1/4 t. cayenne
1 cup tomato sauce
1 to 1-1/2 cups water
3/8 cup peanut butter (6 T.)
Salt to taste

1. Sauté onion in oil for a few minutes.
2. Add remaining vegetables one at a time, sautéeing each for a few moments before adding the next.
3. Add cayenne, tomato sauce, and water.
4. Simmer until vegetables are tender.
5. Mix some of the broth with the peanut butter.
6. Add to the vegetables and cook another 10 minutes.
7. Taste for seasoning and add salt if desired.
8. Serve over rice or millet.

16 vegetable servings

Winter Salad

1/2 head butter lettuce
1 large carrot, grated
2 medium-sized raw beets, grated
1 package radish sprouts OR 1 piece of daikon (white) radish
    about the same size as the carrot, grated*
Seasoned rice vinegar to taste (the seasoned vinegar has some sugar
    and salt in it, which is important for the flavor of this salad)

1. Arrange lettuce leaves on a platter.
2. Arrange carrot, radish sprouts or radish, and beets in separate piles on top of the lettuce. It's fun to play around with decorative patterns.
3. Sprinkle some of the vinegar over each salad before eating.

8 vegetable servings

*Alfalfa sprouts can be substituted for radish or radish sprouts.

Far East Slaw

6 cups finely shredded cabbage (1-1/2 lb.)
1 red or green pepper, chopped fine
1 8-oz. can sliced water chestnuts
1/4 cup chopped peanuts
Seasoned rice vinegar *OR* **Buttermilk Dressing to taste**

1. Combine ingredients in a large bowl.
2. Dress with seasoned rice vinegar or Buttermilk Dressing (p. 120).

24 vegetable servings

Shred-That-Salad!
"Confetti"

Salad Mix:
3/4 lb. green cabbage
1/2 lb. red cabbage
2 carrots
2 green peppers

1. Shred in food processor and place in large bowl.
2. Toss with either Oil and Vinegar *OR* Curry-Yogurt Dressing.

Oil and Vinegar Dressing:
3 T. olive oil
3 T. vinegar
Salt and pepper

Curry-Yogurt Dressing:
6 T. yogurt
6 T. reduced-calorie mayonnaise
2 t. curry powder
Salt

20 vegetable servings

A Different Potato Salad

4 medium potatoes, scrubbed
1 10-oz. pkg. peas and carrots
1/2 large dill pickle, chopped
1/4 cup chopped onion
2 T. plain low-fat or nonfat yogurt

2 T. reduced-fat mayonnaise
2 T. lime juice
1 t. olive oil
Salt and pepper to taste

1. Steam the potatoes until tender. When cool enough to handle, cut them into cubes.
2. Steam the peas and carrots until cooked. Then cool.
3. Mix remaining ingredients in a large bowl.
4. Add the cooled potatoes, peas, and carrots.
5. Chill and serve.

12 vegetable servings

Corn Soup
"Uni-corn Soup"

1 medium onion, chopped
2 t. oil
2 10-oz. pkg. frozen corn OR
  fresh corn cut from 6 ears
2-1/4 cups chicken or vegetable broth
  OR **water**

2 cups milk
1 red pepper, chopped (optional)
3/4 t. salt
1–3 cloves garlic, chopped
1/2 t. sugar

1. Sauté onion in oil until transparent.
2. Add corn, cover, and cook 15 minutes.
3. Add broth, 1 cup milk, salt, garlic, and sugar.
4. Simmer for 15 more minutes.
5. Take out about 1 cup of the corn; add 1 cup milk to the pot.
6. Purée in batches in blender until smooth.
7. Return to pot, add the reserved whole corn kernels and red pepper, and heat gently.
8. Season to taste with pepper.

12 vegetable servings

Vegetables

Creamy Winter Squash Soup

2 lbs. winter squash (butternut, acorn),
   peeled and cubed
1 onion, chopped
1 red pepper, diced
10 oz. frozen corn OR fresh corn
   cut from 2 ears

1 T. oil
2–3 t. mild curry powder
Salt to taste

1. Lightly sauté onion and curry powder in oil.
2. Add squash and 3 cups water, and simmer until squash is very tender.
3. Purée mixture in batches in blender.
4. Return to pot and add enough water or milk for desired consistency.
5. Add red pepper and corn, and cook gently until they are tender.
6. Add salt to taste.

16 vegetable servings

Cream of Broccoli Soup
"Swamp Soup"

1-1/2 lb. broccoli,
   chopped (include most
   of the stems)
1/2 medium onion, chopped
1 T. oil

1 potato, scrubbed
   and cut into chunks
1 rib celery, sliced
1 carrot, chopped
2 cups water
2 cups milk

1/2 t. nutmeg
3/4 t. salt
1/2 t. pepper
   (preferably
   fresh ground)

1. Sauté onion in oil.
2. Add carrot and celery and sauté for 2–3 minutes.
3. Add broccoli, potato, and water, and simmer until vegetables are quite tender.
4. Stir in 1 cup of the milk, and purée the mixture in a blender or food processor.
5. Return to pan and add the other cup of milk and seasonings.
6. If too liquid, thicken with 1 T. cornstarch mixed into 2 T. cold milk and heat.

Note: Nice with Parmesan cheese on top!

12 vegetable servings

Harvest Squash Bake
"Harvest Moon Squash"

**1-1/2 lb. winter squash (butternut, acorn, banana),
    peeled, seeded, and cut into chunks**
1 apple, cored and cut into chunks
2 T. raisins or currants
1/2 cup orange juice
1 T. butter, cut into pieces

1. Stir all ingredients together.
2. Put into greased shallow baking dish.
3. Bake covered at 375° for about 45 minutes, stirring occasionally.

10 vegetable servings

Pumpkin "Custard"
"Jack O'Lantern Pudding"
(no milk, no eggs)

1 15-oz. can pumpkin purée (2 cups)
8 oz. tofu (regular or firm)
6 T. brown sugar
1 T. molasses

1 t. cinnamon
1/4 t. ginger
1/4 t. cloves

1. Blend all ingredients in food processor until very smooth.
2. Pour into oiled casserole.
3. Bake at 350° for 35–40 minutes.
4. Chill and serve.

Note: This can also be used as a dairyless pie filling.

7 vegetable servings

Vegetables

Fruits

Wiggly Fruit

2 t. (1 envelope) unflavored gelatin
2 cups unsweetened fruit juice (not fresh pineapple)
2–3 cups sliced fruit

1. Mix gelatin with 1/4 cup juice in a bowl.
2. Measure another 1/2 cup juice and bring to a boil.
3. Add hot juice to gelatin mixture, stirring until all of the gelatin is dissolved.
4. Add remaining juice and chill until it begins to set.
5. Add fruit, stir, and chill until firm.

Note: Strong-flavored juices like grape, cherry, or raspberry work best.
Apple-raspberry juice with peach slices is great!

8 fruit servings

Fruits

Micro-Fruit

1 lb. apples, halved and cored
  OR
1 lb. pears, halved and cored
  OR
1 lb. bananas, halved lengthwise

Cinnamon, ginger,
OR **cinnamon sugar**

1. Sprinkle fruit with cinnamon, ginger, or cinnamon sugar.
2. Place on microwave-safe dish.
3. Bake in microwave oven: pears—about 1-1/2 minutes
  apples—about 3 minutes
  bananas—about 45 seconds to 1 minute

Note: This is even yummier with a spoonful of plain yogurt on top!

6 fruit servings

Soft-Serve Fruit

"Frosty Fruit"

2 lbs. bananas, peeled and cut into chunks
   OR
2 lbs. mangoes, peeled and cut into chunks

1. Freeze fruit (but not rock hard).
2. Run frozen fruit through food processor. (You may need to soften it up a bit first. Let it run long enough to whip a lot of air into the mixture, but not long enough to completely thaw the fruit.)
3. Serve right away.

Note: Cantaloupe, peaches, or strawberries may also be used, but you will need to use a little fruit juice to get the right consistency.

12 fruit servings

Grains & Breads

Pancake Mixtures
"Flying Saucers"

The following dry mixtures can be prepared in advance. When you wish to make pancakes, mix wet ingredients together, combine with dry mixture of your choice, and cook pancakes on a lightly greased griddle.

Basic:

4 cups unbleached flour	**4 t. baking powder**	Combine **1-1/4** cups dry mixture with
4 cups whole-wheat flour	**4 t. baking soda**	**1 cup water, 1 egg,**
2 cups buttermilk powder	**2 t. salt**	and **2 T. oil.**
1/4 cup sugar		

Multigrain:

1 cup unbleached flour	**2 T. sugar**	Combine **1-1/2** cups dry mixture with
1 cup whole-wheat flour	**2 t. baking powder**	**1 cup water, 1 egg,**
1 cup cornmeal	**2 t. baking soda**	and **2 T. oil.**
1 cup oat bran	**1 t. salt**	
1 cup buttermilk powder		

Wheatless:

1 cup rice flour	**1-1/2 t. baking powder**	Combine **1** cup dry mixture with
1 cup oat bran	**1 t. soda**	**1 cup buttermilk,**
1 T. sugar	**3/4 t. salt**	**1 egg,** and **2 T. oil.**

Eggless: Replace egg with egg substitute.

Each batch makes about 12 3" pancakes

Chris's Pancakes

I cup whole-wheat flour	I-I/2 cup buttermilk
I cup unbleached flour	I/2 cup orange juice
I T. sugar	2 eggs
I t. baking soda	2 T. oil
I t. baking powder	I t. vanilla
I/2 t. salt	
I t. cinnamon	
I t. nutmeg	

1. Mix dry ingredients together.
2. Mix wet ingredients together.
3. Mix wet and dry ingredients together.
4. Cook on lightly greased griddle.

Makes about 24 3" pancakes

Gingerbread Pancakes
"Gingerbread Frisbees"

I cup whole-wheat flour	3 T. molasses
I cup white flour	I t. ginger
I/2 t. salt	I/2 t. cinnamon
I t. soda	I/2 t. ground cloves
I-I/2 to 2 cups buttermilk	I T. oil
2 eggs	

1. Mix dry ingredients together.
2. Mix wet ingredients together.
3. Mix wet and dry ingredients together.
4. Cook on lightly greased griddle.

Makes about 24 3" pancakes

Banana Bread

"Banana Gorilla Bread"

1 cup regular tofu, mashed
1/3 cup oil
1-1/4 cups sugar
2 eggs, slightly beaten
2 t. vanilla
2 cups very ripe mashed bananas
   (4 large or 5 small)
2 T. lemon juice

3-1/2 cups flour (can use
   1-1/2 cups whole wheat)
2 t. soda
1 t. baking powder
1 t. salt
1 cup chopped walnuts or
   pecans (optional)

1. Blend tofu and oil in food processor or blender until very smooth.
2. Add sugar, egg, and vanilla and blend very well.
3. Add bananas and lemon juice and process briefly.
4. Combine flour, soda, baking powder, and salt.
5. Gently combine liquid and dry ingredients. Fold in nuts (optional).
6. Put batter into 2 greased loaf pans.
7. Bake at 350° for 50–60 minutes or until done.

Each loaf serves 32 preschoolers or 16 school-age children • 1 bread/grain

Pumpkin Bread

1 cup regular tofu, mashed
1/4 cup oil
1-1/2 cups brown sugar
4 eggs
2/3 cup orange juice
1 15-1/2-oz. can pumpkin (2 cups)

3-1/2 cups flour
1 t. baking powder
2 t. baking soda
1 t. salt
2 t. cinnamon
2 t. ground cloves
1 cup currants or raisins

1. Blend oil and tofu in blender or food processor until very smooth.
2. Add sugar, eggs, orange juice, and pumpkin, and blend again.
3. Stir together dry ingredients.
4. Add to pumpkin mixture.
5. Stir in currants or raisins.
6. Pour into 2 greased loaf pans.
7. Bake at 350° for about 1 hour or until toothpick comes out clean.

Each loaf serves 32 preschoolers or 16 school-age children • 1 bread/grain

Grains & Breads

Tropical Bread

1 cup whole-wheat flour	1/2 cup oil
2-1/2 cups unbleached flour	2 eggs
2 t. baking soda	2 very ripe bananas, mashed
1/2 t. salt	1 cup crushed pineapple, drained (1 8-oz. can)
1 cup sugar	2 t. vanilla

1. Combine flours, salt, and soda.
2. Cream together sugar, oil, and egg.
3. Stir in bananas and pineapple.
4. Add flour mixture, stirring gently.
5. Stir in vanilla.
6. Bake in 2 greased loaf pans at 350° for 45 minutes.

Each loaf serves 24 preschoolers or 12 school-age children • 1 bread/grain

"Bikini Bread"

1 cup whole-wheat flour	1/2 t. salt
1 cup unbleached flour	1/3 cup oil
1-1/2 t. baking powder	1/2 cup sugar
1 t. cinnamon	2 eggs
1 t. ground cloves	1 t. vanilla
1/4 t. baking soda	2 cups grated zucchini
1/2 cup chopped walnuts	

1. Sift or stir dry ingredients together.
2. Beat oil, sugar, eggs, and vanilla until fluffy.
3. Add dry ingredients to wet mixture.
4. Fold in zucchini and nuts.
5. Bake in greased loaf pan at 350° for 45 minutes.

Serves 32 preschoolers or 16 school-age children • 1 bread/grain

Lemon Blueberry Muffins

2 eggs
1/2 cup sugar
1/4 cup oil
7/8 cup milk
rind and juice of 1 lemon
2 cups flour (whole-wheat pastry
   OR 1/2 whole-wheat, 1/2 white)

1 T. baking powder
1/2 t. baking soda
1/2 t. salt
1-1/2 cups blueberries
   (dredged in 1 T. flour)

1. Mix eggs, sugar, and oil, and beat until foamy.
2. Add milk and lemon.
3. Stir together flour, baking powder, soda, and salt.
4. Stir into liquid ingredients until just blended.
5. Gently fold in blueberries.
6. Spoon batter into muffin cups.
7. Bake at 425° for 20 minutes.

Makes 12 muffins • 1 bread/grain

Crunchy Apricot Bread

1-1/4 cups dried apricots, chopped
1 cup boiling water
1/3 cup oil
1/2 cup sugar
2 eggs

2-1/4 cups unbleached flour
1 T. baking powder
1/2 t. salt
3/4 cup Grapenuts cereal
2/3 cup milk

1. Pour boiling water over apricots. Let sit for 10 minutes. Drain.
2. Beat oil, sugar, and eggs until fluffy.
3. Stir together flour, baking powder, salt, and Grapenuts.
4. Add flour mixture to oil-sugar-egg mixture alternately with milk.
5. Fold in apricots.
6. Bake in greased loaf pan at 350° for 1 hour.

Note: This can also be made with dried peaches, which are cheaper and less tart.

Each loaf serves 32 preschoolers or 16 school-age children • 1 bread/grain

Grains & Breads

Bulgur Pilaf

1/2 cup onion, chopped
1 T. oil
1 cup bulgur wheat
2 T. sesame seeds

2 cups water or stock
3/4 t. salt
2 t. parsley flakes
1 clove garlic, whole

1. Sauté onion in oil for 5 minutes.
2. Add bulgur and sesame seeds. Sauté for 2 minutes.
3. Add remaining ingredients.
4. Bring to a boil, then simmer for about 15 minutes or until liquid is absorbed.
5. Remove garlic clove before serving.

Serves 12 preschool or 6 school-age children • 1 bread/grain

Swiss Breakfast

1-1/4 cups raw oats
1 cup water
2 T. wheat germ
2 T. honey or brown sugar

3–4 cups fresh fruit (bananas, peaches, blueberries, grated apples, etc.)
1 cup plain yogurt
1 T. orange juice

1. Stir oats and water together.
2. Let sit overnight in refrigerator.
3. In the morning, stir all ingredients together and serve.

Note: Chopped toasted almonds and/or hazelnuts may be added.

Serves 8 preschool or 4 school-age children • 1 bread/grain + 1 fruit

Cereal Hash

Equal amounts of a variety of low-sugar cereals, which can include naturally multicolored cereal rounds (available at health food stores)

Mix up a variety of cereals and store in an airtight container. Aim for an interesting mix of shapes and sizes.

Preschool: 1/3 cup = 1 bread/grain

School-age: 3/4 cup = 1 bread/grain

Assorted Chips for Dips
"The Big Dippers"

Won Ton Chips:

1 lb. won ton wrappers

1. Cut won ton wrappers into triangles.
2. Place in a single layer on lightly oiled baking sheet.
3. Bake for 4–7 minutes at 400°, until lightly browned and crisp.

Serves 32 preschool or 16 school-age children

Pita Points:

1 lb. pita bread

1. Cut pita breads in half and separate pieces where joined at the edges.
2. Stack and cut pieces into wedges.
3. Place in a single layer on a lightly oiled baking sheet.
4. Bake for 6–10 minutes at 400°, until brown and crisp.

Serves 32 preschool or 16 school-age children

Grains & Breads

Nori-Maki Rolls

You may think kids won't like sushi,
but you might be surprised!

2 cups medium-grain white rice
2-1/2 cups water
3 T. rice vinegar (not the seasoned variety)

2 t. sugar
1 t. salt
5–6 sheets toasted
    seaweed (sushi nori)

Fillings: About 2 cups altogether (Use your imagination!
This is a good way to use up little bits of leftovers):

Carrots, cut into thin strips and
    steamed lightly
Cucumber, cut into thin strips
Spinach or chard, steamed and sprinkled
    with toasted sesame seeds and
    a little soy sauce

Green onions, cut into
    thin strips
Avocado
Cooked shrimp or crab
Canned or smoked
    salmon (lox)

1. Rinse the rice and let it drain.
2. Place rice in saucepan with water. Bring to a boil, cover, turn heat way down, and cook for 20 minutes.
3. At the end of the cooking time, let the rice sit for 10–15 minutes. Resist the urge to remove the lid from the pot!
4. Turn rice out into a large bowl or roasting pan. Sprinkle the vinegar, salt, and sugar over it and mix well.
5. Allow rice to cool to room temperature.
6. Place a sheet of the seaweed (shiny side down) on a cutting board. The short side should be top-to-bottom.
7. Wet your hands and spread with 3/4–1 cup rice, leaving about 1/2-inch border at the bottom and 1 inch at the top.
8. Make an indentation in the rice horizontally along the middle. Arrange your choice of fillings over this. (It's okay if it's humped up.)
9. Start rolling from the bottom, squeezing with both hands as you go. Moisten the top border of the seaweed with some water, and keep rolling until the end.
10. Cover rolls tightly with plastic wrap and refrigerate until ready to serve (up to 48 hours, depending on the fillings).
11. At serving time, cut each roll with a sharp knife into 8 pieces and arrange on a platter. Mustard and pickled ginger are good accompaniments.

Serves 20 preschool or 10 school-age children • 1 bread/grain

Snacks & Such

Mock Sour Cream
"Make Believe Sour Cream"

2 cups cottage cheese
2 T. lemon juice
2 T. low-fat milk

Run ingredients through food processor or blender until absolutely silky smooth. Makes about 2 cups.

Serves 16 preschool or 8 school-age children for snack • 1 meat alternative

Creamy Dill Dip
"Dippity Doo Dah Dip"

2 t. parsley flakes
2 small garlic cloves, pressed
1 t. dill weed

Add to 2 cups Mock Sour Cream.

Serves 16 preschool or 8 school-age children for snack • 1 meat alternative

Toasted Onion Dip

2 T. dry minced onion, toasted lightly
  3–5 minutes at 350°
2 t. soy sauce
Dash of garlic powder

Add to 2 cups Mock Sour Cream.

Serves 16 preschool or 8 school-age children for snack • 1 meat alternative

Buttermilk Dressing
"Brontosaurus Milk Dressing"

1 cup buttermilk
1/2 cup mayonnaise
1/2 t. pepper
2 t. dried minced onion

1/2 t. garlic powder
1/4 t. salt
1 t. parsley flakes
1/4 t. dill weed

1. Whisk ingredients together.
2. Let sit for at least 1 hour to blend flavors before using.

Makes 1-1/2 cups

Bean Dip
"Mud Dip"

1-1/2 cups cooked (or canned) pinto beans
1 T. Mexican spice mix (below)
6 oz. grated jack or cheddar cheese

1. Mash beans with a fork or potato masher.
2. Stir in spice mix and grated cheese.
3. Heat until cheese melts, on the stove or in the microwave.

Mexican Spice Mix:
1/4 t. garlic powder
1 T. onion powder
1 T. cumin
2 T. chili powder

Serves 24 preschool or 12 school-age children for snack • 1 meat alternative

Hummus
"Quicksand"

2 cups chickpeas (16-oz. can)
1 T. tahini
1 T. lemon juice
1 clove garlic, pressed
1/2 t. cumin

1/4 t. paprika
1/4 t. salt
1 t. olive oil
1/4 cup water

1. Blend all ingredients except water in food processor.
2. Add water 1 T. at a time, until you have the right consistency (a fairly thick purée).
3. Process until very smooth.
4. Use as spread with crackers or pita bread.

Serves 12 preschool or 6 school-age children for snack • 1 meat alternative

Savory Scrambled Cereals

5 cups unsweetened or low-sugar
   cereals, mixed (e.g., Cheerios, Wheat
   Chex, Rice Chex, Corn Chex, Crispix,
   Kix, Shredded Wheat)
1 cup small pretzel rings*
1 cup unsalted, roasted peanuts*

2 T. margarine
1 T. Worcestershire sauce
1 t. Spike seasoning
1/8 t. garlic powder

1. Melt margarine in a roasting pan in 250° oven.
2. Stir Worcestershire and seasonings into the melted margarine.
3. Toss in cereals, pretzels (optional), and peanuts (optional), stirring gently to coat.
4. Bake at 250° for 30–45 minutes, stirring about every 15 minutes, until toasty.

_____
*Omit for children under 5 years old.

Serves (approximately) 15 preschool or 7 school-age children • 1 bread/grain

Snacks & Such

Rice Cake Snacks
"Saucy Cheese Cake"

1 rice cake
2 T. grated cheddar or jack cheese
salsa

1. Spread cheese on rice cake.
2. Bake at 350° until cheese melts.
3. Top with salsa.

Serve 1 per preschool or 2 per school-age child for snack • 1 bread + 1 meat alternative

"Pizza Cake"

1 rice cake
2 T. "Instant" Pizza Sauce (p. 124)
2 T. grated mozzarella cheese

1. Spread sauce, then cheese, on rice cake.
2. Bake at 350° until cheese melts.

Note: Can be microwaved, but they get soft.

Serve 1 per preschool or 2 per school-age child for snack • 1 bread + 1 meat alternative

Peanut Butter Ping Pong Balls

Version 1:

1/2 cup peanut butter　　　　**1/2 t. vanilla**
1/4 cup honey　　　　**2–3 cups Rice Krispies or crispy brown rice cereal**

1. Stir together peanut butter, honey, and vanilla.
2. Stir in cereal.
3. Wet hands and form the mixture into balls.
4. Place on waxed paper and chill. Store in covered container in refrigerator.

Version 2:

1/2 cup peanut butter　　　　**1/2 t. cinnamon**
1/4 cup molasses　　　　**2–3 cups Rice Krispies or crispy brown rice cereal**

Repeat directions as above.

Serves 6 preschool or 4 school-age children for snack • 1 meat alternative + 1 bread/grain

Build-a-Sundae

1-1/2 cups yogurt *OR*　　　　**Optional toppings:**
　　cottage cheese　　　　　　　**Nuts**
1 lb. chopped fruits　　　　　　**Unsweetened cereals**
　　　　　　　　　　　　　　　　Honey or maple syrup

1. Put yogurt or cottage cheese in individual bowls.
2. Add fruits (applesauce, raisins, chopped dates, berries, bananas, etc.).
3. Top with nuts, cereals, and/or honey or maple syrup (optional).

Serves 6 preschool or 3 school-age children for snack • 1 meat alternative + 1 fruit

Snacks & Such

"Instant" Pizza Sauce

2 cups canned crushed tomatoes
3/4 t. garlic powder
1 t. basil

1-1/2 t. oregano
1/2 t. salt
1/4 t. pepper

1. Stir all ingredients together.
2. Let sit at least 1 hour.
3. Use as sauce for pizzas.

Makes 2 cups

Quick Pizzas
"Road Runner Pizza"

For each child:
Base: **English muffin half, or flour tortilla, or pita bread, split,
     or slice of french bread**

2 T. "Instant" Pizza Sauce *(recipe above)*
**2–4 T. (1/2–1 oz.) cheese—mozzarella, cheddar, jack, provolone, or a mixture,
     grated or sliced**

1. Spread "Instant" Pizza Sauce over base.
2. Cover with cheese and any other toppings you fancy.
3. Bake at 425° until bubbly.

Toppings: Sliced mushrooms, green peppers, onions, olives, artichoke hearts, and so on.

1 meat alternative + 1 bread per serving for snack

Sunshine Dip

2 cups plain nonfat or low-fat yogurt   **2 T. orange juice concentrate**

1. Mix together.
2. You can experiment with concentrates of other juices, too! Try grapefruit, tangerine,
   lemonade, or limeade.
3. Use as a dip for pieces of raw fruit—peaches, strawberries, kiwi, bananas, and so on.

Serves 8 preschool or 4 school-age children for snack • 1 meat alternative

Frosty Fruit Shakes

Peanut Butter Banana:	**2 cups milk OR 1-1/2 cups plain yogurt** **2–3 bananas, frozen (about 1 lb.)** **3 T. peanut butter**
Liquid Sunshine:	**2 cups milk OR 1-1/2 cups plain yogurt** **1 cup crushed pineapple** **2–3 bananas, frozen (about 1 lb.)** **1/2 t. vanilla**
Bananaberry:	**2 cups milk OR 1-1/2 cups plain yogurt** **2–3 bananas, frozen (about 1 lb.)** **1 cup strawberries or blueberries (may be frozen)** **1/2 t. vanilla**
Spicy Apple:	**1-1/2 cups plain yogurt** **2 cups chunky applesauce** **1/2 t. cinnamon** **Ice cubes or crushed ice**

Purée in blender and serve immediately.

Each recipe serves 4 preschool or 2 school-age children
1 milk (or 1 meat alternative if yogurt is used) + 1 fruit

Hot Chocolate

4 cups milk
1-1/2 T. cocoa powder
1-1/2 T. sugar

1. Combine cocoa powder and sugar with about 1/4 cup milk.
2. Whisk in the remaining milk.
3. Cook over medium heat, stirring constantly, until milk is hot but not boiling.
   OR heat in microwave 2–3 minutes, or until milk is hot.

Serves 8 preschool or 4 school-age children • 1 milk

Beverages

Chapter *Five*

Sample Menus Using Our Recipes

In spite of many, many years of experience planning menus for children and adults (for our own families, too), inevitably an afternoon comes when we face a menu-planning form littered with blank spaces. Sometimes we need to get out of a rut, for example, serving the same vegetable with the same meat and grain combination for years. Sometimes we're trying a new recipe and aren't sure what flavors, colors, and textures will go well with it, and sometimes a menu-planning session comes at the end of a day that has already been 'way too long. Whatever the reason, all of us need inspiration now and then, and sample menus offer just that.

The following menus feature recipes from this book and aim for nutritional balance, fun for the children, and ease for the cook!

Ten Breezy Breakfasts

It's easy to help children get a good start on the day when you have health-ful make-ahead foods on hand. Quick breads and muffins can be made in large batches and frozen until needed. The dry ingredients for pancakes can be measured out the night before or made up in large quantities as a "mix." You can cook hot cereals and stew fruit very successfully in a micro-wave oven. And you needn't restrict your thinking to traditional "breakfast foods." Sandwiches and even pasta can taste great in the morning!

Banana Gorilla Bread
Sliced apples
Hot chocolate

Multigrain Pancakes
Applesauce
Milk

Pumpkin Bread
Orange slices
Milk

English muffins
Micro-Fruit
Yogurt topping
Milk

Bikini Bread
Orange juice
Milk

Bagels
Sliced turkey and low-fat cheese
Tomatoes
Milk

Cereal Hash
Strawberries
Milk

Swiss Breakfast
Milk

Lemon-Blueberry Muffins
Banana chunk
Milk

Crunchy Apricot Bread
Orange slices
Milk

Fine Finger Feasts

Most children love eating with their hands. Although we certainly think that they should get lots of practice with flatware, we know that meals that can be eaten entirely with the fingers are a fun change of pace. They're also easy on the cook.

—————

Cold sliced omelets
Nori-Maki rolls
Sliced cucumbers
Tangerines
Milk

—————

Chicken Fingers
Bread sticks
Assorted raw vegetables
Apple wedges
Milk

—————

Cold **Turkey Loaf** cubes
Oven-Fried Potato Sticks
Broccoli and carrot sticks
Crackers
Milk

—————

Bean Dip
Tortillas (corn or flour), heated and
cut into strips or wedges
Jicama sticks
Fresh pineapple spears
Milk

—————

Quick Pizzas
Assorted raw vegetables
Apples
Milk

—————

Homemade Fish Sticks
Sweet Potato Fries
Zucchini and green pepper strips
Bread
Milk

Teddy Bear Tea Parties

Tea parties, complete with teddy bears or other favorite stuffed animals, are a delightful and relaxing ritual for snacktime. The "tea" can actually be warmed apple cider, hot cocoa, or basic herbal tea, such as peppermint (chamomile, although mild, can cause problems for children with ragweed allergies). If you have some sturdy teacups, by all means use them. Lots of foods are appropriate for teatime—as long as they are dainty.

—————
Assortment of crackers
Slices of cheese (preferably
reduced-fat varieties)
Assorted fruits
"Tea"

—————
Bikini Bread
Strawberries with
Sunshine Dip
"Tea"

—————
Peanut butter and honey sandwiches,
cut into triangles
Sliced peaches with milk
"Tea"

—————
Peanut Butter Ping Pong Balls
Banana
"Tea"

—————
Open-faced **Tuna Salad**
sandwiches on toast points
Apples and raisins
"Tea"

Lunch Around the World

Few of the ethnic recipes in this book are authentic. That's because we found that traditional preparation methods were too lengthy, ingredients were difficult to find, or the authentic versions contained too much fat or salt. Similarly, the menus listed below are not truly representative of meals eaten in certain cultures. However, these menus do illustrate typical flavor principles of a variety of cuisines and include foods that might be eaten together in a meal. If you're interested in presenting truly ethnic meals to the children, ask friends or the children's parents for family recipes and menu outlines.

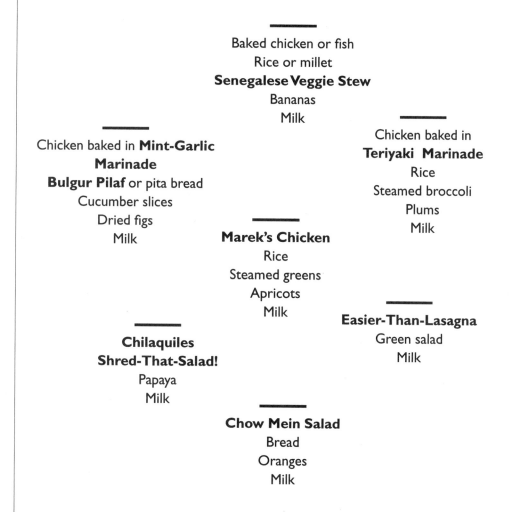

———

Baked chicken or fish
Rice or millet
Senegalese Veggie Stew
Bananas
Milk

———

Chicken baked in **Mint-Garlic Marinade**
Bulgur Pilaf or pita bread
Cucumber slices
Dried figs
Milk

———

Chicken baked in
Teriyaki Marinade
Rice
Steamed broccoli
Plums
Milk

———

Marek's Chicken
Rice
Steamed greens
Apricots
Milk

———

Easier-Than-Lasagna
Green salad
Milk

———

Chilaquiles
Shred-That-Salad!
Papaya
Milk

———

Chow Mein Salad
Bread
Oranges
Milk

Vegetarian Menus

One-Pot Macaroni and Cheese
Steamed broccoli
Apple wedges
Milk

White Bean Soup
Whole-wheat bread
Assorted raw vegetables
Pears
Milk

Chilaquiles
Cabbage salad
Pineapple chunks
Milk

Vegetarian baked beans
Cornbread or crackers
Shred-That Salad!
Oranges
Milk

Red beans
Rice
Sweet Potato Fries
Far East Slaw
Milk

Lentil Soup
Bread sticks
Green salad
Apples
Milk

Garbo-Burgers in pita bread
with lettuce, tomato, and sprouts
Melon wedges
Milk

Scrambled eggs
English muffins
Oven-Fried Potato Sticks
Fresh fruit salad
Milk

Taco Salad with Beans and Cheese
Crackers
Milk

Quick Pizzas
Spinach salad
Pears
Milk

Easier-Than-Lasagna
Carrot and zucchini sticks
Milk

Peanut butter or cheese
toast points
Creamy Winter Squash Soup
Apples
Milk

Are You Feeling Firmly Stuck in a Meal-Planning Rut? Have a Little Fun with These Ideas!

- Serve "breakfast" foods for lunch.

- For a fun change, serve any kind of sandwich filling in an ice-cream cone (sorry, not reimbursable on the Child Care Food Program) or a whole-wheat hot dog bun.

- Make a "dip-it" lunch with a serving of protein-rich dip (examples: hummus, cottage cheese, nut butter, or Bean Dip), an assortment of vegetables and/or fruit, and crackers, soft tortillas, or bread strips.

- Plan a "shapes" week: Monday all square-shaped food, Tuesday all rounds, Wednesday all sticks, Thursday all triangles, Friday all stars (use small cookie cutters, usually available at cake-decorating shops).

- Plan a "colors" week: Monday all yellow food, Tuesday all red, Wednesday all green, Thursday all orange, Friday all white (if you're feeling really adventurous, try blue!).

- Plan a meal with foods that begin with the same letter (examples: chicken, crackers, corn, cantaloupe).

- Fill a flour tortilla with unconventional fillings and take advantage of children's enthusiasm for burritos: scrambled eggs, cheese, and potatoes or broccoli; peanut butter and bananas; Yummy-for-the-Tummy Baked Fish, lettuce, and tomato or tartar sauce; Tuna Salad, sprouts, and tomatoes; teriyaki chicken and Far East Slaw; shredded chicken in barbeque sauce and coleslaw . . . you get the idea!

- Set up stuffed baked potato bars and let the children put together their own "personal potatoes." Here are some possibilities: broccoli, cheese, and ham or turkey ham; spinach, ricotta and mozzarella cheeses, and marinara sauce; chili with beans, cheese, lettuce, tomato, and olives; chicken in barbeque sauce and corn. Some light sour cream (thinned with milk if desired) or Buttermilk Dressing may be appreciated to moisten the mixture.

Meal Planner

Week of: _____

Meals	Monday	Tuesday	Wednesday	Thursday	Friday
Breakfast Bread or Grain Fruit or Veggie Milk					
Snack Choose from 2 groups					
Lunch Bread or Grain "Meat" Vegetable Fruit or Veggie Milk					
Snack Choose from 2 groups					
Supper Bread or Grain "Meat" Vegetable Fruit or Veggie Milk					

Shopping List

Week of: _____

☐ **Fresh Fruits**
- ☐ _____
- ☐ _____
- ☐ _____
- ☐ _____
- ☐ _____
- ☐ _____
- ☐ _____
- ☐ _____
- ☐ _____
- ☐ _____

☐ **Fresh Vegetables**
- ☐ _____
- ☐ _____
- ☐ _____
- ☐ _____
- ☐ _____
- ☐ _____
- ☐ _____
- ☐ _____
- ☐ _____
- ☐ _____

☐ **Frozen Foods**
- ☐ _____
- ☐ _____
- ☐ _____
- ☐ _____
- ☐ _____
- ☐ _____
- ☐ _____
- ☐ _____

☐ **Poultry/Fish/Meat**
- ☐ _____
- ☐ _____
- ☐ _____
- ☐ _____
- ☐ _____
- ☐ _____

☐ **Dairy Products**
- ☐ _____
- ☐ _____
- ☐ _____
- ☐ _____
- ☐ _____
- ☐ _____
- ☐ _____
- ☐ _____

☐ **Staples**
- ☐ _____
- ☐ _____
- ☐ _____
- ☐ _____
- ☐ _____
- ☐ _____
- ☐ _____
- ☐ _____
- ☐ _____
- ☐ _____

☐ **Breads/Cereals/Grains**
- ☐ _____
- ☐ _____
- ☐ _____
- ☐ _____
- ☐ _____
- ☐ _____
- ☐ _____
- ☐ _____
- ☐ _____
- ☐ _____

☐ **Canned Goods**
- ☐ _____
- ☐ _____
- ☐ _____
- ☐ _____
- ☐ _____
- ☐ _____
- ☐ _____
- ☐ _____
- ☐ _____
- ☐ _____

☐ **Baking Supplies**
- ☐ _____
- ☐ _____
- ☐ _____
- ☐ _____
- ☐ _____
- ☐ _____
- ☐ _____

☐ **Beverages**
- ☐ _____
- ☐ _____
- ☐ _____
- ☐ _____

☐ **Spices/Condiments**
- ☐ _____
- ☐ _____
- ☐ _____
- ☐ _____
- ☐ _____
- ☐ _____
- ☐ _____
- ☐ _____

☐ **Other Items**
- ☐ _____
- ☐ _____
- ☐ _____
- ☐ _____
- ☐ _____
- ☐ _____
- ☐ _____
- ☐ _____
- ☐ _____
- ☐ _____

☐ **Paper Products**
- ☐ _____
- ☐ _____
- ☐ _____
- ☐ _____
- ☐ _____
- ☐ _____

☐ **Cleaning Supplies**
- ☐ _____
- ☐ _____
- ☐ _____
- ☐ _____
- ☐ _____
- ☐ _____

☐ **Household Items**
- ☐ _____
- ☐ _____
- ☐ _____
- ☐ _____
- ☐ _____
- ☐ _____
- ☐ _____
- ☐ _____

Chapter *Six*

Running a Ship-Shape Kitchen

Many of us find ourselves in the position of cooking for 6 children, or 60, without the benefit of professional cooking training or even a high-school home economics course! Managing a kitchen, even at home, requires shopping with budget *and* nutrition in mind, impeccable hygiene and safety practices, efficient setup and techniques, a well-organized food storage system, and a good working knowledge of ingredients and food preparation techniques. It's not as hard as it sounds, though. Tracking down information like cooking temperatures for meat or substitutes for buttermilk in a recipe used to take hours, but not any longer. We put it all in one place for you, and you might even be able to teach your mom a thing or two.

How to Save Money on Food

You don't have to spend a lot of money to provide good nutrition. Some of the most nutritious foods are very inexpensive, and some expensive foods aren't very healthful. So go ahead, save some money—you aren't being cheap, you're being smart!

- Decide how much money you can spend on food.

- Plan menus ahead of time. Make a shopping list and stick to it!

- Shop no more than once a week. The more often you walk into a store, the more you'll be tempted by impulse items.

- Serve less meat and more beans, grains, fruits, and vegetables.

- Have children drink water instead of juice or milk when they're thirsty between meals.

- Be very careful to transport and store foods properly so they don't spoil before you can use them.

- Use leftovers, but handle them carefully!

- Have a garden and grow your own (or let the children do it).

- Shop smart . . .

    Eat before you go shopping.

    Leave children at home, unless you can say "no" and mean it!

    Read labels—know what you're buying.

    Compare unit ("per pound") prices to decide which size and brand of an item is the better buy. See *Anatomy of a Shelf Pricing Label* (page 139).

    Compare the price of convenience foods with their "from scratch" counterparts.

    Be aware of the high cost of packaging. Buy in bulk when you can.

Take advantage of seasonal specials on produce, meats, and groceries.

Buy house brands rather than name brands when their quality suits you as well.

Don't run all over town to save ten cents; you'll spend more on gas!

Use coupons *when they're for items you would use anyway.*

Look into opportunities for cooperative food buying with other families, child care providers, or feeding programs.

Buy only what you can use.

Anatomy of a Shelf Pricing Label

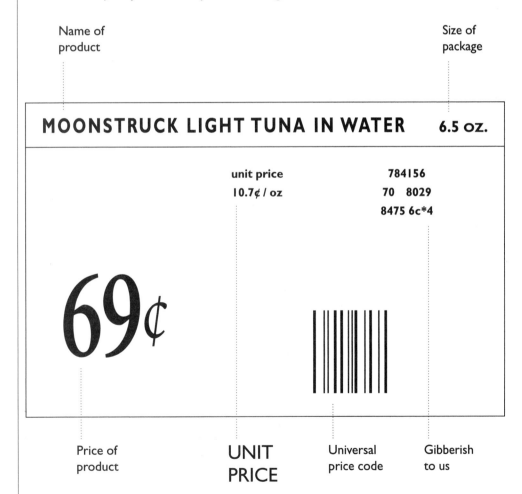

Name of product

Size of package

MOONSTRUCK LIGHT TUNA IN WATER 6.5 OZ.

unit price 784156
10.7¢ / oz 70 8029
  8475 6c*4

69¢

Price of product

UNIT PRICE

Universal price code

Gibberish to us

How Much Am I Spending on Protein?

Meats and meat substitutes can be the most expensive items on your menu. If you are interested in saving money on food, you have several options. You can serve the less expensive protein foods more often. You can combine inexpensive and more costly protein foods at the same meal (for example, bean chili with cheese on top). You can avoid overloading children with high-protein foods (you should offer at least the minimum serving size, of course, but you don't need to offer a child 9 ounces of meat at one meal). And if you would like your children to experience the taste of shrimp or other expensive food, serve it as a snack, in small portions.

We walked through a national-chain supermarket and noted the prices for various meats and meat substitutes. Then we calculated the cost of a lunchtime serving for a preschooler. Some of our results surprised us!

Food Item	Cost per serving (1-1/2 oz./equiv.)*
Lentils, dried	$ .04
Pinto beans, dried	.05
Turkey franks	.13
Canned chickpeas	.17
Turkey, from whole roasted bird	.18
Eggs	.21
Canned tuna, water packed	.21
Peanut butter, natural	.22
Cheddar cheese, store brand	.25
Cottage cheese	.27
Chicken drumsticks	.32
Frozen fish sticks	.32
Ground turkey	.35
Chicken breasts (bone in)	.39
Lean ground beef	.44
Parmesan cheese, store brand	.45
Fresh snapper fillets	.67
Pork chops	.75

*Depending on where you get your food, of course, your actual costs will differ.

Price isn't everything, and you should consider whether a food has much to offer nutritionally, as well. For example, turkey franks are relatively cheap, but they are also high in fat and sodium.

How to Calculate the Price Per Serving of Any Food

Divide the price for the purchase unit (pound, piece, package) by the number of servings you will get from the unit. You can refer to "How Much to Buy?" on page 152 for information on servings per unit for some foods. Your local Child Care Food Program office can give you information about purchasing their buying guides.

For example, on the day of our survey, chicken drumsticks were $1.39/lb. According to our buying guide for the Child Care Food Program, a pound of drumsticks yields 4.3 servings (1-1/2 oz.):

$$\$1.39 \div 4.3 = \$0.32 \text{ per serving}$$

Don't Let Those Nutrients Get Away!

Nutrients can be destroyed when foods aren't handled properly. Long storage times, exposure to air and light, and prolonged cooking are notorious nutrient-robbers. Make the foods you serve as nutritious as possible by following these basic guidelines:

Buy it right

- Avoid food that looks wilted, bruised, or spoiled.

- Check expiration dates on packages.

- Fresh produce is generally preferable. However, fruits and vegetables that have been sitting in storage or in produce bins for a long time will gradually lose their advantage. In that case, frozen foods will be better. Some foods that don't freeze well, like tomatoes and pineapple, are okay canned.

Store it right

- When you're taking food home from the store, or if you've received a delivery of perishable foods, don't delay putting them away.

- Keep foods at the proper temperature:

    65° or below for canned foods
    40° or below in the refrigerator
    0° or below in the freezer

- Use foods within their recommended storage times (see *How Long Will It Keep?*, pages 144–145).

Cook it right

■ Don't overcook foods.

■ Serve raw fruits and vegetables often.

■ Wash produce before cooking or serving, but don't soak it.

■ Cut fruits and vegetables as close to serving time as possible. If you must prepare them ahead of time, seal in air-tight bags and refrigerate.

■ Cook vegetables in a minimum of water and only until tender-crisp. Steaming, microwaving, and pressure-cooking are better than boiling.

How Long Will It Keep?

	Canned/Pantry (months)	Refrigerator (days)	Freezer (months)
Produce			
Asparagus	6	4–6	8–10
Broccoli	—	3–5	10–12
Carrots	12	7–14	10–12
Corn	12	1	10–12
Green peppers	—	4–5	10–12
Greens	12	1–2	10–12
Lettuce	—	7–10	—
Onions	1–3 weeks	—	—
Potatoes	1–2 weeks	—	—
Sweet potatoes	5–7 days	—	—
Tomatoes	6	1–2	2
Apples	12	2–4 weeks	10–12
Bananas	—	7	3
Grapefruit	6	10–14	10–12
Oranges	6	10–14	10–12
Peaches	12	3–5	10–12
Strawberries	—	3–5	10–12
Watermelon	—	7	10–12
Dairy Products			
Butter	—	1–3 months	6–9
Cheese, cheddar	—	1–2 months	6
Cheese, cottage	—	7	—
Cheese, mozzarella	—	2–4 weeks	6
Cheese, Parmesan	—	12 months	—
Fluid milk (opened)	—	1–5	3
Infant formula	12–18	2 (opened)	—
Nonfat milk powder	12	2–3 months	—
Puddings, etc., with milk	—	2–3	1
Yogurt	—	7–14	1

	Canned/Pantry (months)	Refrigerator (days)	Freezer (months)
Meats/Meat Substitutes			
Beans, dried	12	—	—
Beef, roast	—	3–5	6–12
Beef, ground	—	1–2	3–4
Beef, cooked in casserole	—	3	2–3
Beef, cooked in gravy	—	1–2	2–3
Chicken parts	—	1–2	9
Chicken, cooked, plain	—	3–4	4
Chicken, cooked, in sauce	—	1–2	6
Eggs, fresh	—	3 weeks	—
Eggs, hard-boiled, in shell	—	7	—
Eggs, hard-boiled, peeled	—	7	—
Fish, fatty	—	1	3
Fish, lean	—	1	6
Frankfurters	—	4–7	1–2
Frozen prepared entrees	—	—	3–4
Peanut butter	12	3–4 months	—
Turkey parts	—	1–2	3–6
Grain Products			
Breads, tortillas	2–4 days	4–7	4
Cereal, cooked	—	2–3	—
Cereal, ready-to-eat			
Opened	3	—	—
Unopened	12	—	—
Pancakes, waffles	—	1	2–3
Oats, rolled	12	—	—
Wheat flour, unbleached	6–12	12 months	12
Whole-wheat flour	1	12 months	12

Sources: Bailey, Janice, *Keeping Food Fresh.* New York: Harper & Row, 1989.

Duyff, Roberta, *The American Dietetic Association's Complete Food & Nutrition Guide.*
Minneapolis: Chronimed Publishing, 1996.

Know Your Ingredients

- **Bulgur** is cracked parboiled wheat. It cooks very quickly and is terrific in pilafs and salads.

- Look for whole-grain or enriched **cornmeal,** not the degerminated variety, for baking. **Polenta,** or coarsely ground cornmeal, is cooked like a hot cereal.

- **Couscous** is a tiny round pasta made from semolina wheat; it comes in whole-grain and refined varieties and is great as a breakfast cereal and in pilafs.

- The flavors of **fresh garlic, fresh ginger,** and **fresh onion** are far superior to their dehydrated, powdered, frozen, and paste versions. However, when saving time is a consideration, you can get good results with the processed forms of these seasonings.

- **Honey, brown sugar,** and **turbinado ("raw") sugar** are not much more nutritious than white table sugar. In the case of honey and "raw" sugar, you pay a lot more for trace amounts of vitamins and minerals. Honey and brown sugar can lend a unique taste to a recipe, however. We urge you to exercise moderation in the use of *all* sweeteners.

- Our preferred vegetable oils for cooking are **olive oil** and **canola oil,** both of which are low in saturated fat and high in monounsaturated fat. Both are high in fat and calories, though (about 2,000 calories per cup!), so use as little as you can to get the job done.

- **Peanut butter** often has shortening and sugar added, which contribute nothing worthwhile nutritionally. Buy "natural" peanut butter made only from peanuts. It tends to separate, so stir it up after you open the jar and refrigerate it.

- We suggest that you use **reduced-sodium soy sauce** in place of regular soy sauce—same rich flavor, less sodium.

- **Spike** and its low-sodium counterpart **Vegit** are seasoning blends available in most health food stores and some supermarkets. They happen to be our favorites, but there are other blends you can try as well: **Parsley Patch** and **Mrs. Dash** are two of them.

Some low-sodium seasonings are quite peppery and may be too "hot" for children, so shop around until you find one everybody likes. We suggest that you avoid any seasoning mixtures containing monosodium glutamate (MSG).

Foods labeled **"sugar free"** may contain artificial sweeteners. Check the ingredients, and if the food is artificially sweetened, avoid serving it to children. Artificial sweeteners can cause diarrhea in susceptible children. They can also train children to expect a very sweet taste in foods.

Toasted sesame oil, which you may also see as "oriental sesame oil," is a very dark and richly flavored oil that is added sparingly to some Asian dishes. Light-colored sesame oil won't do the trick.

Tofu is sometimes called "soy cheese" or "soy bean curd." It is made from soy milk and, though rather bland by itself, is much appreciated by vegetarian (and nonvegetarian) cooks for its ability to accept a wide variety of seasonings. It is a good source of protein, is low in saturated fat, and can be a good source of calcium if it is made with calcium sulfate. As this book goes to press, tofu is not yet acceptable for reimbursement under child-feeding program guidelines. However, we believe that because it is a healthful food that many children like, it may be worth your while to serve a little of it along with other reimbursable items. If you are not concerned with meal program reimbursement, go ahead and use this wonderful food frequently! We have found that it makes a nice replacement for some of the fat in quick breads and muffins, so you will see it as an ingredient in some of our recipes. Check the Resources (Appendix E) in the back of the book for information about tofu and other soy foods.

Ground **turkey** can be used in place of ground beef in most recipes, or even substituted for half the beef, and is lower in fat. You have to be careful when you cook it, as it can get dry and tough when cooked too long; cook just until no pink remains.

Whole-wheat pastry flour is best for making muffins and quick breads; regular **whole-wheat flour** is used in making yeasted breads.

How to Get the Most Information from a Product Label

The nutrition label on a food product can help you decide whether it would be a good choice for a healthful diet. Today's food labels contain ingredient listings; *Nutrition Facts,* which give specific information on calories and nutrients; and occasionally a *nutrition description,* for example, "reduced fat" or a health claim describing the relationship between a particular food and health.

- Nutrition labeling is *required* on most packaged foods. Some fresh fruits and vegetables, meat, poultry, and seafood are labeled as well.

- A nutrition label *must* list the total calories, calories from fat, total fat, saturated fat, cholesterol, sodium, total carbohydrate, dietary fiber, sugars, protein, iron, vitamins A and C, and calcium content of the product. Labels on foods specifically for children ages 4 and under are somewhat different because their dietary needs don't fit neatly into the recommendations of the Dietary Guidelines for Americans. A label may list the calories from saturated fat, stearic acid, polyunsaturated fat, monounsaturated fat, potassium, soluble fiber, insoluble fiber, sugar alcohol, other carbohydrate, percent of vitamin A as beta carotene, and other vitamins and minerals. If a food is enriched with one of these voluntary components or if a health claim is made regarding one of them, its content must be listed on the label.

- Check the serving size carefully. Although serving sizes on the present labels are more realistic than in years past, they still might not reflect what you actually eat or serve.

- The ingredients in a food product are listed in order by weight, from the most to the least. For example, if butter is the first ingredient on the list, there is more butter in the product than any other ingredient.

■ You will need to know alternative names for certain food components in order to get a clear picture of how much of them a product contains.

Sugar:

brown sugar	dextrose
honey	fructose
corn syrup	sucrose
corn syrup solids	maltose
invert sugar	molasses
maple syrup	

Sodium:

salt	monosodium glutamate
baking soda	sodium benzoate
sodium caseinate	sodium nitrate
sodium nitrite	sodium phosphate
sodium propionate	

■ Know what the various terms on labels *really* mean:

Sodium free = less than 5 mg sodium/serving

Very low sodium = 35 mg or less sodium/serving

Low sodium = 140 mg or less sodium/serving

Reduced sodium = at least 25% less sodium compared with the usual product

Unsalted, no salt added = no salt added during processing of a food usually made with salt

Sugar free = less than 0.5 g per serving

No added sugar, without added sugar, no sugar added = no sugars added during processing

Reduced sugar = at least 25% less sugar per serving than the usual product

Calorie free = fewer than 5 calories per serving

Low calorie = 40 calories or less per serving

Reduced or **fewer calories** = at least 25% fewer calories than the usual food product

Cholesterol free = 2 mg or less cholesterol and 2 g or less saturated fat per serving

Low cholesterol = 20 mg or less cholesterol and 2 g or less saturated fat per serving

Reduced or **less cholesterol** = 25% or more reduction in cholesterol from the usual product and at least 2 g less saturated fat

Fat free = less than 0.5 g fat per serving

Saturated fat free = less than 0.5 g and less than 0.5 g *trans* fatty acids per serving

Low fat = 3 g or less fat per serving

Low saturated fat = 1 g or less per serving and not more than 15% of calories in the food

Reduced or **less fat** = 25% or less than the usual food product

Reduced or **less saturated fat** = 25% or less than the usual food product

Extra lean = meat or poultry contains no more than 5 g total fat, 2 g saturated fat, and 95 mg cholesterol per 3-oz. serving

Lean = meat or poultry contains no more than 10 g fat, 4.5 g or less saturated fat, and 95 mg cholesterol per 3-oz. serving

Light, lite = contains 1/3 fewer calories or 1/2 the fat of the reference food

High fiber = 5 g or more per serving

Good source of fiber = 2.5 to 4.9 g per serving

More or **added fiber** = at least 2.5 g more than the reference food

Cook's Tour of a Nutrition Facts Label

This heading indicates that you're about to learn specifics about the nutrient content of the food!

This section tells you how the calories from fat compare to the total calories in a serving. It does not tell you the *percent* calories from fat.

These nutrients are the biggest concerns for most consumers today. *In general,* we need to be alert to getting too much of certain items like fat rather than too little of most vitamins and minerals.

This conversion guide helps you learn the caloric value of the energy-producing nutrients.

Nutrition Facts

Serving Size 2 Waffles (78 g)
Servings Per Container 6

Amount Per Serving	Per Serving	Per Waffle
Calories	180	90
Calories From Fat	50	25

	% Daily Value*	
Total Fat 6 g	9%	5%
Saturated Fat 1 g	5%	2%
Polyunsaturated Fat 1.5 9		
Monounsaturated Fat 3 g		
Cholesterol 0 mg	0%	0%
Sodium 430 mg	18%	9%
Potassium 85 mg	2%	1%
Total Carbohydrate 28 g	9%	5%
Dietary Fiber 4 g	16%	8%
Sugars 2 g		
Other Carbohydrates 22 g		
Protein 6 g		

Vitamin A	20%	10%
Vitamin C	0%	0%
Calcium	4%	2%
Iron	20%	10%
Thiamin	20%	10%
Riboflavin	20%	10%
Niacin	20%	10%
Vitamin B6	20%	10%
Folate	20%	10%
Vitamin B12	20%	10%

*Percent Daily Values are based on a 2,000 calorie diet. Your daily values may be higher or lower depending on your calorie needs:

	Calories:	2,000	2,500
Total Fat	Less than	65g	80g
Sat Fat	Less than	20g	25g
Cholesterol	Less than	300mg	300mg
Sodium	Less than	2,400mg	2,400mg
Potassium	Less than	3,500mg	3,500mg
Total Carbohydrate		300g	375g
Dietary Fiber		25g	30g

Calories per gram:

Fat 9 • Carbohydrate 4 • Protein 4

Note carefully the serving size and number of servings in the package!

The % Daily Value tells you how a serving contributes overall to a 2,000-calorie diet. Use these figures to get an idea of whether the food contains a little or a lot of a certain nutrient. A food is "high" in a nutrient if it contains 20% or more of the Daily Value.

This footnote helps consumers learn basic recommendations for a healthful diet—upper limits for fat, saturated fat, cholesterol, and sodium, and minimum targets for carbohydrate and fiber.

How Much to Buy?

Food	Purchase Weight or Measure	Approximate Yield
Fruits		
Apples	1 lb.	3 cups sliced
Apricots, dried	1 lb.	3 cups
Bananas	1 lb.	3–4 medium, or 2 cups mashed
Oranges	1 lb.	3–4 medium, or 2 cups pieces
Raisins	1 lb.	2-3/4 cups
Vegetables		
Alfalfa sprouts	1 lb.	6 cups
Broccoli, fresh	1 lb.	2-1/3 cups cooked
Cabbage	1 lb.	4 cups shredded raw, 2 cups cooked
Carrots, fresh	1 lb.	3 cups shredded raw
Lettuce, romaine	1 lb.	7-3/4 cups chopped
Onion	1 medium	1-1/4 cups chopped
Pepper, green	1 large	1 cup chopped
Potatoes, fresh	1 lb.	2-1/2 cups cooked, 2 cups mashed
Tomatoes, fresh	1 lb.	3–4 medium, 2-1/2 cups chopped
Grains		
Cornmeal, coarse	1 lb.	3 cups dry, 12 cups cooked
Oatmeal	1 lb.	5-1/3 cups dry, 16 cups cooked
Rice	1 lb.	2-1/2 cups dry, 8 cups cooked
Spaghetti, macaroni	1 lb.	8 cups cooked
Wheat flour	1 lb.	4 cups
Whole-wheat flour	1 lb.	3-3/4–4 cups
Dairy Foods		
Butter	1 lb.	2 cups, 4 sticks
Cheese, hard	1 lb.	4 cups shredded
Meat, Poultry		
Beef, 10% fat, ground	1 lb.	10-1/8 oz. cooked meat
Canadian bacon	1 lb.	11 oz. cooked meat
Chicken breast halves	1 lb.	8-7/8 oz. cooked chicken meat
Chicken drumsticks	1 lb.	6-1/2 oz. cooked chicken meat
Tuna, water packed	12-1/2-oz. can	11 oz. drained, 1-3/8 cups
Turkey, ground	1 lb.	10-2/3 oz. cooked meat
Other		
Beans, dried	1 lb.	2-1/4 cups dried, 6 cups cooked
Peanut butter	1 lb.	1-3/4 cups

Equivalents and Substitutions

Food	Amount	Equivalent
Baking powder	1 t.	1/4 t. baking soda + 1/2 t. cream of tartar *or* 1/4 t. baking soda + 1/2 cup buttermilk or yogurt and reduce liquid by 1/2 cup
Bread crumbs	1 cup	4 slices dried bread, crushed and run through a food processor *or* 3/4 cup cracker or cereal crumbs
Buttermilk	1 cup	1 cup plain yogurt *or* 1 T. lemon juice or vinegar + enough milk to make 1 cup; let stand 5 minutes
Catsup	1 cup	1 cup tomato sauce + 1/4 cup sugar + 2 T. vinegar + 1/4 t. ground cloves
Eggs, in baking	1 egg	1 t. cornstarch + 3 T. more liquid in recipe *or* 2 T. liquid + 2 T. flour + 1/2 T. oil + 1/2 t. baking powder
Flour, for thickening	1 T.	1 T. quick-cooking tapioca *or* 1-1/2 t. cornstarch *or* 2 T. granule cereal (e.g., farina or cornmeal)
Garlic, fresh	1 clove	1/8 t. garlic powder *or* 1/2 t. garlic salt and omit 1/2 t. salt from recipe
Herbs, fresh	1 T.	1 t. dried herb *or* 1/4 t. ground herb
Lemon juice	1 t.	1 t. vinegar
Milk	1 cup	1 cup soy, rice, or nut milk *or* 1 cup fruit juice for baking (add 1/2 t. baking soda if the juice is acidic)*
Sour cream	1 cup	1 cup plain yogurt *or* 1 cup low-fat cottage cheese + 1 T. lemon juice + 1 T. nonfat milk, pureed in blender or food processor to desired consistency
Sugar, brown	1 cup	1 cup white sugar + 1/4 cup molasses
Sugar, white	1 cup	1 cup brown sugar, packed *or* 3/4 cup honey or maple syrup and reduce 2 T. of other liquid in recipe *or* 1 cup date sugar *or* 1-1/2 cup fruit juice concentrate and reduce liquid in recipe by 2 T.
Tomatoes, fresh	1 lb.	1 cup tomato sauce
Tomato juice	1 cup	1 cup tomato sauce + 1 cup water
Tomato sauce	2 cups	3/4 cup tomato paste + 1 cup water
Tomato soup	10-3/4-oz. can	1 cup tomato sauce + 1/4 cup water

*Remember, these are not nutritional equivalents.

Basic Guide to Measurements

Reminder: Help with measuring is a great way to enable children to participate in the cooking process. In fact, checking the accuracy of your measuring equipment can make an interesting math and science activity.

Standard U.S. Liquid Measurements

3 teaspoons	= 1 tablespoon
4 tablespoons	= 1/4 cup or 2 ounces
5-1/3 tablespoons	= 1/3 cup or 2-2/3 ounces
12 tablespoons	= 3/4 cup or 6 ounces
16 tablespoons	= 1 cup or 8 ounces
2 cups	= 1 pint
2 pints	= 1 liquid quart
4 quarts	= 1 liquid gallon

Canned Goods Weights and Measures

8 ounces	= 1 cup
10-1/2–12 ounces	= 1-1/4 cups
14–16 ounces	= 1-1/2 cups
16–17 ounces	= 2 cups
1 lb. 4 ounces	= 2-1/2 cups
1 lb. 13 ounces	= 3-1/2 cups
No. 10 can	= 12–13-2/3 cups

Keeping Food Safe to Eat Is Up to You

We live in a time when many people are suspicious, almost afraid, of their food. Some fears about the safety of our food supply are reasonable, and some are not. It's important to realize that most of the dangers associated with food are due to the way *we* handle it in our own kitchens. In the United States, about 9,000 people die from food poisoning every year. Millions and millions of others have an uncomfortable few days with what they think is "stomach flu." Most of these illnesses could have been prevented through careful handling of food by the cook.

Food-borne illnesses are usually caused by bacteria. Some are caused by viruses or poisonous chemicals. We'll refer to bacteria and viruses together as **germs.**

Germs are found everywhere—in soil, in air, on animals' bodies (including ours), on fruits and vegetables, in milk—but before you swear you'll never eat or breathe again, realize that most aren't harmful to us (some are even helpful, like the bacteria that make yogurt). Other germs are a problem only if there are a *lot* of them around, or if they've had the chance to manufacture toxins that will hurt us even when the germs are dead. To survive, germs need:

- Food and water
- *Time* to reproduce or make toxins
- The right *temperature*
- A way to get around (they can't wiggle into our custard by themselves, but they *can* hitchhike on our fingers)

When we talk about preventing food poisoning, most of what we're dealing with involves giving the germs as little time as possible at the temperatures they like, so they can't do their dirty work. We also want to introduce as few bacteria as we can into our stew, or salad, in the first place. Food becomes unsafe to eat through six main mistakes:

- Poor personal hygiene on the part of people working with food
- Preparing food that may already have been spoiled or contaminated by poisons
- Storing food without proper care

- Handling food carelessly
- Using unclean equipment or working in a dirty kitchen
- Allowing insects or rodents to infest food supplies

Food safety is *very* serious business. What follows might seem like an impossibly long list of guidelines for keeping food safe to eat. But every point in the list is crucial, so it's worth reviewing over and over until all of these practices are second nature to you. Items that specifically apply to group settings are marked with a ★.

Start with Personal Hygiene

- Always wash your hands before you handle food.
- Wash your hands again after you:

> Use the toilet.
> Change a child's diaper or assist a child in the bathroom.
> Touch your face, hair, or any infected part of your body.
> Blow your nose, sneeze, or cough.
> Touch dirty rags, clothing, or work surfaces.
> Clear away dirty dishes and utensils.
> Touch raw food, especially meat, fish, or poultry.
> Handle money or smoke a cigarette.

Use the STOP DISEASE Method of Handwashing*

Use liquid soap from a dispenser and running water.
Rub your hands vigorously as you wash them.
Wash all surfaces, including:

> Backs of hands
> Wrists
> Between fingers
> Under fingernails

Rinse your hands well with running water.
Dry your hands with a paper towel.
Turn off the water using a paper towel instead of bare hands.
Discard towel in covered trash can controlled by a foot pedal.

Source: Childhood Emergencies—What to Do, A Quick Reference Guide, by Marin Child Care Council (formerly Project Care for Children), Bull Publishing Company, 1987.

- Keep your fingernails clean and short.

- Avoid wearing rings (except a simple band), bracelets, and anything that would dangle into the food.

- Keep your hair clean and long hair tied back.

- Wear clean clothing.

- Don't work with food when you're sick.

- Don't smoke in the kitchen.

Be Picky About the Foods You Serve

- Buy only from reputable stores or dealers.

- Don't buy or accept for delivery foods that look spoiled or infested with insects.

- Use only pasteurized milk and apple juice.

- ★ Don't serve home-canned foods to children you take care of.

- Don't serve raw eggs in any form (like eggnog), and don't allow children to taste items like raw cookie dough containing eggs. Liquid pasteurized egg products are fine.

- Don't serve spoiled or moldy foods, food from a bulging or leaky can, or anything else that looks or smells suspicious. If you have doubts, toss it, and don't take a little taste to test it! Some very dangerous foods taste okay.

- Pay attention to "use by" or "sell by" dates on food packages.

Store Foods Carefully

- Store foods at the right temperatures:

    Refrigerator: 32–40°F
    Freezer: 0°F or below
    Pantry: 65°F or below is best

- Immediately put perishable foods into the refrigerator or freezer after shopping or receiving a delivery.

- Stored foods should be dated, labeled if necessary, and kept off the floor.

- Place newer foods behind older ones in the storage area— "first in, first out."

- Don't store opened food in cans in the refrigerator. Transfer the food to glass or plastic containers.

- Cover all stored foods.

- Leave space for air circulation in the refrigerator. Don't line the shelves with foil. Keep it clean and check every day for food that should be tossed out. Check the thermometers in the refrigerator and freezer.

- Store cooked foods *above* raw foods in the refrigerator.

- Store packages of thawing meat or poultry in bowls or shallow pans so their juices can't drip on foods below.

- ★ Leftovers should be kept in the refrigerator for no more than 24 hours.

- Store foods separately from chemicals, cleaners, and so on.

- ★ Lunches and other perishable foods that children bring from home should be refrigerated until serving time.

If the Power Goes Out . . .

A fully stocked freezer will keep foods at safe temperatures for up to 2 days, a half-full freezer for 1 day. Keep the door closed!

A refrigerator will keep foods safe for only 4–6 hours. Perishable foods should be discarded, but generally fresh fruits and vegetables, hard and processed cheese, butter, margarine, and most condiments will be okay for longer periods. Discard anything that looks suspicious.

Handle Food with Respect

- Keep perishable foods at safe temperatures. If they're to be eaten cold, keep them at 40°F or below. If they're supposed to be hot, they must be 140°F or above. If you aren't going to serve hot foods soon, refrigerate them in uncovered shallow pans (less than 3 inches deep). The center of the food must reach 40°F or less within 4 hours. Cover when cool. Don't leave perishable foods out on the counter while you're working on a recipe with many steps.

- Wash fruits and vegetables thoroughly before using them.

- Wipe the tops of cans before you open them.

- Thaw frozen foods in the refrigerator or in the microwave. Bacteria can be happily setting up colonies on the outside of the food even when the center is frozen.

- Use oven temperatures of at least 325°F, and when using a crock-pot, bring the food to a boil before setting the heat on "low."

- Cook fish, poultry, eggs, and meat thoroughly.

- Taste those delicacies you're concocting with two spoons, the professional way. Spoon One goes into the food and then transfers it to Spoon Two (the spoons can't touch). Spoon Two goes into your mouth.

⭐ Avoid touching foods with your hands. Use scoops, tongs, other utensils, or disposable gloves when handling food that will be served uncooked to another person (for example, it's all right to cut carrots for soup with your bare hands, but not carrots that will be served raw).

▪ *Never* serve food that's left on anyone's plate to another person.

⭐ Discard any food that remains in serving bowls after family-style meal service in a child care setting.

▪ Don't mix leftover food and fresh-cooked food unless it's in good condition and the mixture will be used up immediately.

Final Cooking Temperatures

Egg-based dishes	160°F	Fish	145°F
Ground poultry	165°F	Ground beef, pork, lamb	160°F
Poultry pieces	170°F	Other cuts of meat	160°F
Whole poultry	180°F	Leftovers	165°F

Scrambled eggs are done when no visible liquid remains, poached and fried eggs when the whites are completely set and the yolk is starting to thicken.

How to take a chicken's temperature: A quick-read or digital thermometer is recommended. Insert the thermometer into the inner thigh area near the breast of the bird but not touching the bone. If stuffed, the stuffing must reach 165°F.

To test other foods for doneness, insert the thermometer into the thickest part of the food, away from fat, bone, and the pan itself. For thin items like meat patties, the thermometer can be inserted sideways, though a special thermometer called a thermocouple is even better. If your food wasn't done on first testing, clean your thermometer with hot soapy water and an alcohol prep pad before inserting it into the food again, to avoid introducing contamination into the food.

Keep the Kitchen and Your Equipment Clean

- Don't allow animals or cat litter boxes in the kitchen.

- Regularly clean your equipment, kitchen, and eating area (see *The Squeaky-Clean Kitchen Scrubbing Schedule*, p. 164).

- Don't let anyone sit on counters or work surfaces.

- Keep rugs out of food preparation areas.

- Wash the can opener in between uses. It's one of the most overlooked sources of germs in the kitchen!

- Air-dry rather than towel-dry dishes and utensils.

- Hold plates by the rims, drinking glasses by the bottoms, cups and silverware by the handles.

- Clean and sanitize any cutting board or utensil that has touched raw meat, poultry, or eggs before any other cooked or raw food comes in contact with it. It's a very good idea to have separate cutting boards for raw meat, fish, poultry, and for other foods.

- The debate over cutting board material continues, but plastic cutting boards are probably preferable to wooden boards because they can be cleaned more easily. Discard any board that has deep grooves in it.

- Don't use cracked tableware or containers; bacteria can find food and a nice place to live in the cracks.

- Don't serve or store foods in antique or imported pottery (especially from Mexico, China, Hong Kong, or India) unless it has been verified to be lead-free. Lead from the glazes can leach into food and has caused many cases of lead poisoning in the United States.

- Use freshly laundered towels and rags.

- Sanitize sponges occasionally with a bleach solution or run them through the dishwasher.

⭐ Tableware and serving pieces used in group settings must be sanitized. A dishwasher works; so does a bleach dip.

> ### To Sanitize with a Bleach Solution . . .
>
> Wash the table- or serviceware with hot water and detergent, rinse, then dip for 1 minute in a solution of 1/3 cup chlorine bleach to 5 gallons of water. Air-dry.

⭐ Disposable tableware is meant to be disposed of after a single use. *Do not* try to save money or the environment by washing and reusing it. The risk of spreading germs among children is too great.

Don't Put Out the Welcome Mat for Insects and Rodents

- Keep your kitchen immaculate.

- Store opened packages of food within tightly sealed containers.

- Remove garbage promptly and keep the outdoor garbage area clean.

- Don't store food under the sink.

- Keep doors and windows tightly screened. When screens get holes, fix them.

- Caulk openings and cracks around sinks, drain pipes, and water pipes. Repair cracks in walls.

- Inspect containers and cardboard boxes that you bring into your building. Cockroaches, especially, like to hitchhike in them.

- If you notice some pests around, take care of the problem before it gets bigger. Should you find that you'll have to use an insecticide, follow the directions carefully.

CAUTION!! These foods are among the most common sources of food poisoning:

Undercooked or improperly handled meat, poultry, eggs, fish, and dairy products

Raw milk

Cooked plant foods (fruits, vegetables, beans, or grains) or tofu left at room temperature for more than 2 hours

Homemade ice cream (with unpasteurized eggs)

Improperly canned low-acid foods, such as green beans, corn, spinach, mushrooms, olives, beets, asparagus, pork, beef, and seafood

The Squeaky-Clean Kitchen Scrubbing Schedule

We know that cleanup isn't usually the most attractive aspect of any job. A well-used kitchen can rapidly turn into a public health hazard, though, without conscientious cleaning. Then it's *really* no fun. The grime in a kitchen will never get out of hand if you set up a cleaning schedule and follow it. So here it is—preventive medicine for your kitchen:

Constantly

☐ Wipe up spills and splashes from:

Work surfaces	Range
Floors	Microwave
Walls	Refrigerator

☐ Wash equipment after each use:

Can opener	Blender
Mixer	Food processor

Daily

☐ Make sure all dishes, utensils, and so on, are washed.

☐ Wipe down work tables and counters and sanitize with a solution of 1 tablespoon chlorine bleach in 1 quart water.

☐ Wipe down range, microwave, refrigerator, and dishwasher.

☐ Sweep and damp mop kitchen floor.

☐ Take out the trash.

☐ Check refrigerator and freezer temperatures.

Weekly

☐ Scrub kitchen floor.

☐ Remove burners from range and clean underneath them.

☐ Clean the inside of the refrigerator. Throw out old food. A mixture of baking soda and water may be used to wipe the shelves and walls.

☐ Clean out the food trap in the dishwasher.

☐ Clean the filter from the smoke hood.

Saving Time in the Kitchen

If you're taking care of children by yourself, you know it's important to be supervising *them*, not a gourmet dish that's bubbling out of control on the stove. And even if you are in the position of cooking primarily for children, it's still nice to save time here and there so you can do other important things—like cleaning, maintaining equipment, doing bookwork, developing new recipes, and training staff. Here are some time-saving tips, learned the hard way during years of collective experience:

- Plan menus ahead of time, check for ingredients on hand, make a detailed shopping list, and shop only once a week.

- Remember that the children probably won't appreciate three elaborate menu items in a meal. *Keep it simple.* Skip the fancy sauces.

- It's okay to serve some cold foods, or even a full meal of them.

- Plan for leftovers that can show up later in another form. (Example: turkey loaf, served later as a cold sandwich filling or as cubes on a snack tray).

- Do as much in one pot or pan as possible. Avoid recipes that lead to a tower of dirty dishes in the sink. See if you can revise your old favorites to save steps.

- Make larger portions than you need and freeze some for later. Casseroles, soups, sauces, and quick breads lend themselves readily to this.

- Do as much of the food preparation as possible when the children aren't around or are napping, unless you want them to pitch in. You may find it works to set up an activity for them in the kitchen while you're doing certain phases of the food preparation.

- Use time-saving appliances like food processors, when they really will save time. Consider setup and cleanup time.

Safety for Adults in the Kitchen

Burns, cuts, and falls can put a damper on your fun in the kitchen. Don't let them happen to you! Follow these guidelines:

- Allow yourself enough time for the job. Most accidents happen when you're in a hurry or aren't paying attention to what you're doing.

- Wipe up grease or wet spots and pick up loose items from the floor immediately.

- Don't run or allow running in the kitchen.

- Use a ladder if you're reaching for items stored on high shelves.

- If you can, store heavier items on lower shelves.

- Keep your knives sharp; you are more likely to be cut by a dull knife, since you need to use more pressure.

- Store knives separately, not loose in a drawer with other utensils.

- Don't soak knives in a dishbasin; you could cut yourself reaching into the water.

- Make sure that your hands (and feet) are dry before plugging in or unplugging electrical appliances.

- Don't reach into a toaster with a metal utensil unless the toaster is unplugged.

- To unplug an appliance safely, turn it off, then hold the plug close to the electrical outlet and pull gently.

- Keep equipment in good repair. Be on the lookout for frayed cords and straining motors.

- Keep items that burn easily (pot holders, towels, curtains, billowy sleeves, and the like) away from burners and other sources of heat.

- Keep the oven and broiler clean. Grease buildup could lead to a fire.

- When cooking with a covered pan, take the lid off facing away from you to avoid being scalded.

Making a Kitchen Safe for Young Children

- Keep all poisonous products in locked cupboards.

- Keep all poisonous products in their original containers; don't transfer them into soda bottles or coffee cans.

- Use safety latches on cabinets.

- Keep potentially dangerous items like knives, matches, boxes with serrated edges, toothpicks, and plastic bags in one place, out of reach.

- Make sure that your drawers have safety catches so they don't crash to the floor when they're pulled out too far.

- When you're using the stovetop, keep pot handles turned toward the center of the stove.

- Watch out for appliance cords dangling over the counter. If you leave toasters, coffeemakers, and other appliances on the counter, unplug them when not in use, place them against the wall, and tuck the cords behind them.

- If you can, get a garbage disposal that operates only with a lid in place.

- Don't store alcoholic beverages, vitamins, and medicines in the refrigerator or any place accessible to a young child.

- Keep vanilla, almond, and other alcohol-containing extracts out of children's reach, too.

- Many children are burned by hot water from the tap. Supervise them closely at the sink.

- Teach children the proper way to use a knife (some don't realize which side of the blade is the cutting edge) and supervise always.

- Keep a first aid kit handy.

- Set aside child-safe kitchen equipment in a lower cabinet so the children can "play cooking" while you're working in the kitchen.

Using Your Microwave Safely

Because there is a wide array of models on the market, and because, with the speed of technology, new and different versions will be out each year, we recommend that you read the instructions that come with the microwave oven you are using and keep them handy for reference and service information.

Microwave ovens, when used and maintained properly, are considered to be extremely safe. There are some basic safety rules, however, that everyone who uses a microwave oven should know.

Important Safety Rules

- Follow the manufacturer's instructions for use.

- Keep the oven clean, especially around the door seal.

- Never tamper with any part of the oven.

- If you suspect any damage to the oven, be sure to call a qualified service person to check it out.

- Heat-proof glassware and glass-ceramic (Corning Ware type) cookware seem to be the best choices for use in the microwave, with round containers resulting in more even heating than square or rectangular ones. Here's how to test glass for microwave-cooking safety: Fill a glass measuring cup with 1 cup of water and put it in the microwave oven next to the container you are testing. (The cup of water is included because the oven should never be operated without food or liquid in it to absorb the energy.) Run the microwave oven on HIGH for one minute. *If the container stayed cool, it's okay to cook in it. If it was only lukewarm, it's okay to reheat in it. Don't use it in the microwave if it got warm.*

- Always choose containers that are colorless and plain; color and decoration can interfere with the transmission of microwaves.

- Other types of containers such as plastic yogurt or margarine tubs, and *even plastic containers that are marked "microwave-safe,"* may have chemical components that can "migrate" into the food at high temperatures.

- For the same reason, if you cover food with plastic wrap while cooking or heating, do not let the covering come in contact with the heating food. Also, be sure to use only the kind of plastic wrap that is recommended for use in the microwave, since other types can melt into the food.

- Avoid heat-susceptor packaging. At this time, its safety has not been thoroughly established.

- Recycled paper products should not be used in the microwave. They may contain small metal fragments that can set the paper on fire during cooking.

Preventing Microwave Burns

- Beware of microwave burns. The container or some portions of the food may be cool enough to touch, while other portions may be hot enough to cause external or internal (mouth and esophagus) burns. Fats and sugars can get especially hot in the microwave and must be handled with extreme caution.

- Puncture foods that have unbroken skins, such as potatoes, tomatoes, and sausage, to allow steam to escape and prevent bursting. Do not cook eggs in the shell for the same reason.

- To prevent being burned by escaping steam, puncture plastic wrap if you are using it to cover the cooking food.

- Stay with the oven if you're popping popcorn. Heat buildup can cause a fire.

- Do not heat baby bottles in the microwave. Uneven heating may result in hot spots in the bottle that are not readily apparent and can be quite dangerous.

- Heating baby food in jars can cause the food to erupt out of the jar and can also result in uneven heating. If you heat baby food in the microwave, place it in a shallow container, stir it well after heating to equalize the heat, and *always test it first* to be sure the food is not too hot for the baby.

Preventing Food Poisoning

- Check to be sure food is thoroughly and evenly heated or cooked. Cold spots can harbor harmful bacteria that can cause food poisoning.

- Discard foods forgotten in the microwave if they were there for more than 2 hours after thawing. Ordinary cooking won't destroy toxins that bacteria may have formed.

- Always cook meat, poultry, and fish thoroughly. Use a microwave temperature probe or check with a meat thermometer to be sure meat is cooked to a safe temperature—at least 160°F for pork, 180°F for poultry. Check temperature in several places. After cooking, it should be left to stand for 10–15 minutes under a foil tent to let temperatures equalize. Stuffing should be cooked separately to minimize the chance of bacterial growth.

- For questions about microwave cooking safety or packaging, call the nearest U.S. Food and Drug Administration office listed in your phone book.

Miscellaneous Microwave Facts, Tips, and Techniques

- Food cut into uniform sizes and shapes will cook more evenly.

- Unevenly shaped food should be placed with the thickest part toward the outside of the baking dish.

- Because the amount of liquid in a food affects the cooking time, foods with more moisture will get hotter than foods that are drier (for example, when heating a sandwich the filling may get hotter than the bread). Remember to test different parts.

- When cooking a number of items, such as potatoes, place them in an evenly spaced circle. This will allow air circulation and more even cooking.

- Stir, rearrange, and rotate foods to achieve even cooking. This is especially important when making sauces.

- Many foods cooked in a microwave oven continue to cook for 5–20 minutes after the oven is off. Some recipes for microwave cooking include this time in the directions. This is an important part of the cooking process, especially for dense foods such as roasts.

- Do not sprinkle meat or vegetables with salt until after they're cooked. Salt will draw liquid out of the food and interfere with the cooking process.

- One great advantage of a microwave oven is that it's able to defrost food quickly. Use the defrost or low power so that the food will not begin to cook on the outside before thawing on the inside. Alternate equal times of standing time and microwaving time while defrosting to allow the heat to become evenly distributed without starting to cook the food. For example, defrost 5 minutes, let stand 5 minutes, and so on.

- Some additional tips for defrosting:

    Cover the dish with waxed paper to help diffuse the microwaves.

    Separate the pieces as soon as they thaw enough and rearrange them more evenly.

    As soon as possible, stir, chop up, or rotate food.

    If some pieces thaw first, remove them while the others continue to thaw.

- To decrystallize honey or jam, remove the metal lid from the glass jar and microwave on HIGH for 1–2 minutes or until crystals have melted.

- Packages of tortillas can be softened and warmed by wrapping the number you need in paper towels and microwaving on HIGH for 6–7 seconds per piece.

- For easier cutting of the tough outer skin of a hard winter squash, microwave it uncovered on HIGH for 1–2 minutes and then let stand for 1–2 minutes more before cutting.

- To reheat casserole-type leftovers, place covered, microwave-safe container in oven on HIGH for 2 minutes per cup of refrigerated food. Stop and stir after 1 minute.

Children's Use of Microwave Ovens

It is a fact of modern life that children are frequent users of microwave ovens. (A 1988 study by Campbell Microwave Institute found 70% of children ages 6 to 12 using microwave ovens at home.) Thus, the potential is great for serious accidents. Here are some things to consider when assessing a child's ability to use a microwave oven safely.

- Does the child have the ability to understand cause and effect, for example, "If I do this, then that will happen"?

- Can the child competently read, understand, and follow directions?

- Is the child tall enough to remove food easily from the oven with both hands? Many of the serious burns reported have resulted from hot food spilling on the child who attempts to remove it from the oven.

- Is the child capable of understanding and upholding all of the safety rules on pages 168–170, *Using Your Microwave Safely*?

There is no age at which using any stove or oven is completely risk-free. However, the risk to children, because of their smaller size and limited experience, is likely to be greater than to adults. We strongly urge adults who permit children to use microwave ovens (or any stove or oven) to do so with extreme caution, thorough explanation of safety rules, and considerable practice in the presence of an adult. Here are a few additional safety tips if children will be using the microwave oven:

- Be sure that the oven is on a sturdy surface and can't be tipped.

- Have a table or counter nearby so that the cookware can be set down nearby immediately after removing it from the oven.

- Be sure that the child always uses oven mitts to minimize the risk of burns. Portions of the dish may be hot or hot food may spill over the edge.

- Make sure the child always lifts a lid or plastic wrap slowly, starting at the side away from the face.

Checklist for a Kid-Ready Kitchen

Feeding Necessities

☐ Child-appropriate tableware, serving utensils (serving spoons, tongs, pitchers, etc.)

☐ Infant or adaptive feeding equipment, if applicable

☐ High chairs and child-size tables and chairs

☐ Menu guidelines and recipes for kid-pleasing foods

☐ Forms for recording individual children's feeding needs and, if applicable, reports to parents

☐ Emergency food supplies

☐ Recycling setup, preferably one that the children can use

Food Safety

☐ Thermometers for refrigerator and freezer (Be sure to check these appliances to make sure they are at the appropriate temperatures.)

☐ Refrigerator, freezer, and pantry storage containers with tight-fitting lids or good seals

☐ Separate cutting boards—one for raw meats, poultry, and fish and another for raw produce and foods that have already been cooked

☐ Setup for air-drying dishes and food preparation equipment after washing

☐ Disinfectants (such as bleach) and appropriate storage/application containers. (Be sure you know the correct mixing proportions and safety precautions.)

☐ Meat or "quick-read" thermometer to test food temperatures and alcohol prep pads to disinfect the thermometer

☐ Disposable gloves approved for food service

☐ Hair restraints

Child Safety

- ☐ Safety devices for appliances and cupboards

- ☐ First aid kit

- ☐ Easily accessible instructions for performing the Heimlich maneuver

Food Safety and Sanitation Mini-Inspection

If you are serving children in a group setting, it's a good idea to do periodic checkups on the cleanliness and food handling practices in the kitchen. Although the following list is not a complete food safety inspection, it will direct you to problem areas that are commonly responsible for outbreaks of food-borne illness.

Personal Hygiene

- [ ] Food preparers must wash hands before handling food, between tasks, and before putting on gloves.

- [ ] Food preparers must wear clean clothes, restrain hair, have short, clean fingernails, and wear only simple jewelry.

- [ ] No one smokes in the kitchen.

Food Purchasing and Storage

- [ ] Purchase foods from reliable stores or vendors.

- [ ] Use only pasteurized milk and apple juice.

- [ ] Purchase food before the "sell by" date and use it within maximum storage times.

- [ ] Store food off the floor.

- [ ] Store newer foods behind or under older foods.

- [ ] Store food in a way that protects it from contamination (for example, covered containers).

- [ ] Stored foods must be free of mold, insect infestation, or other forms of spoilage.

- [ ] Check thermometers in the refrigerator and freezer daily to be sure they are at the appropriate temperature.

- [ ] Store chemicals and cleaners separately from food.

Food Handling

- ☐ Thaw food in the refrigerator, in the microwave, or under cold running water.
- ☐ Do not allow food to be in the "danger zone" for more than 2 hours.
- ☐ Taste food using two spoons—one for the food and one for the mouth.
- ☐ Food handlers must use gloves or utensils when touching food that will be served without further cooking.

Kitchen Cleanliness

- ☐ Work surfaces, equipment, utensils, and food storage areas must be clean to sight and touch.
- ☐ Air-dry washed items.
- ☐ Use separate cutting boards—one for raw meat, poultry, or fish, and another for other foods.
- ☐ Dishes and containers must be free of cracks.
- ☐ Use freshly laundered towels and rags; sanitize sponges regularly.
- ☐ Sanitize tableware after each use.
- ☐ Store garbage in appropriate containers; keep kitchen garbage cans clean.
- ☐ Keep window and door screens in good repair.
- ☐ Be sure there are no signs of insect or rodent infestations.

Chapter *Seven*
Environmental Concerns

At first glance, running a child care center or day care home, with the many regulations for sanitation, severe time constraints, and a tight budget, may seem incompatible with caring for the environment. Please don't give up yet! Among the many decisions you make about which cleaning products to use, how to dispose of garbage, and even such details as whether to run a half-full dishwasher, it's likely that you can find a few hassle-free ways to lessen the environmental impact of your business. You'll teach the children by your good example at the same time, and you may find them to be enthusiastic allies in your efforts.

Hints for an Earth-Friendly Kitchen

Each of us makes many choices every day that have an impact on the environment and affect the kind of world we're building for our children. With just a little thought and effort we can develop and maintain habits that contribute to a healthier planet. Try posting a reminder list in the kitchen of three or four earth-friendly improvements you are pretty sure you can make. When those become second nature, post a new list. What you do *does* make a difference.

To Save Water

- Wash dishes in a dishpan instead of under running water.

- Rinse the dishes with the faucet on halfway and only on while in use (50% of wasted water in homes is due to letting the tap run unnecessarily).

- If you use a dishwasher, run it only when it is full.

- When peeling fruits or vegetables that will need to be washed, set them aside in a colander until they're all peeled, then wash them all at once.

- Fix leaky faucets right away. Even tiny leaks waste lots of water. Meanwhile, catch the drips in a container for watering plants.

- Use a low-flow aerator (available at most hardware stores) on your faucet.

- If you have a water meter, check it to find hidden leaks. (If there is a leak, it will register use even when all the water in the house is turned off.)

To Save Energy

- Use cold water instead of hot whenever possible.

- Keep a container of cold drinking water in the refrigerator to avoid having to let the faucet run until the water gets cold.

- Keep the refrigerator and freezer only as cold as you need to—refrigerator 32–40°, freezer 0°.

- Make sure the refrigerator door seal is tight.

- Periodically use a brush or vacuum to clean the condenser coils on the back of the refrigerator. (Unplug it while doing this.) Dirt and dust make it more difficult for the coils to stay cool.

- If you have a manual-defrost freezer, defrost it regularly. Frost buildup causes the motor to run longer.

- Defrost frozen foods in the refrigerator—it will help keep the refrigerator cold, using less energy.

- Don't leave the refrigerator door open unnecessarily.

- For cooking small portions, pressure cookers, toaster ovens, and microwave ovens are more energy-efficient than conventional ovens. For large items such as turkeys, microwaving is the least efficient.

- Preheat the oven only when it is really necessary, and then, for the shortest possible time. (Ten minutes is usually adequate.)

- Don't open the oven door while baking; you'll let a lot of heat escape. Use a timer and look through the oven window.

- Match the pot size to the burner, using the smallest of both for the job, and use lids on pots to speed up cooking.

- Use glass or ceramic baking dishes for baking—they retain heat well and you can lower the oven temperature 25°.

- Use compact fluorescent lights, which are three to four times more energy-efficient than incandescent bulbs.

- Insulate your hot water heater and accessible hot water pipes.

Planning a Kitchen for Energy Efficiency

If you are designing a new kitchen, or remodeling an existing one, you have a great opportunity to build energy efficiency right into your plans.

- Purchase energy-efficient appliances—check their federally mandated Energy Guide Labels to compare and rate them.

- Choose a refrigerator with a top freezer compartment rather than a side-by-side model, which uses up to 35% more energy.

- Choose a chest-type freezer over an upright if you have the space. They are 10–15% more energy-efficient. Also, an automatic-defrost model consumes 40% more electricity than an equivalent-size-and-style manual-defrost model.

- Select a dishwasher with a built-in water heater. With an insulating water heating jacket for your hot water heater, you will be able to keep your household water temperature lower (110–120°). The dishwasher will only heat the amount of water necessary to wash the dishes at the required 140°F.

- Plan to install the dishwasher away from the refrigerator or freezer. If that's not possible, put insulation between them. Heat and moisture from the dishwasher makes the refrigerator or freezer use more energy.

- Purchase a gas range with electric ignition instead of a pilot light. You will be cutting gas consumption by about 40% a year.

- Choose a convection oven over a conventional one. You will be able to lower temperatures and shorten cooking times.

- Install a solar hot water system.

- Include a built-in recycling system that is designed to coordinate with local recycling requirements.

- Refer to David Goldbeck's book, *The Smart Kitchen: How to Design a Comfortable, Safe, Energy-Efficient and Environmentally Friendly Workspace*, Woodstock, NY: Ceres Press, 1989, and also to the other resources listed in Appendix E to help you with your planning.

Think of Mother Earth When You're Shopping

Most of us grew up during the "disposables" or "throw-away" generations. Now that we are faced with the dire consequences, we find ourselves struggling to change some very ingrained environmentally harmful habits. With less than 5% of the world's population, our nation generates 25% of its pollutants and more than 30% of its garbage. Every day, each American throws out an average of 4 pounds of garbage. That totals a *daily* garbage heap of 438,000 tons—enough to fill 63,000 garbage trucks! By becoming "green" consumers, we can directly reduce the amount of waste.

Here's how to shop with ecology in mind:

- First and foremost—if you don't really need it, don't buy it!

- Choose reusable items over disposable items whenever possible.

- Be picky about packaging:

    Look for products that have minimal packaging.

    Choose products packaged in recycled (look for the ♻ symbol) or recyclable materials, or in reusable containers.

    Choose products packaged in materials that are most easily recyclable in your community.

    Buy eggs in cardboard cartons rather than foam plastic.

    Avoid purchasing anything in foam plastic.

    Let the store manager know why you are making these choices.

    Write or call the manufacturers and let them know why you've chosen to buy or not to buy their products. (You can usually find their address and phone number on the container. Many companies list an 800 phone number for consumers.)

- Bring your own canvas or string bags with you when you shop.

- When you must use bags from the store, choose paper bags, which can be recycled, over plastic bags (most of which are neither biodegradable nor recyclable). Reuse bags by bringing them the next time you shop.

- Read labels—try not to purchase products with harmful ingredients.

- Buy the large size or buy in bulk.

- When you do make purchases in recyclable containers, be sure to actually recycle them.

- Talk to your children about why you are making these choices; this will help them develop their own "ecology awareness."

- Complete the loop by buying consumer goods made from recycled materials. This is critical to keeping the demand for recycled materials high and our recycling systems viable.

Making Everyone a Part of Your Recycling Plan

Whether it's in the home or in the child care setting, establishing a recycling program works best if everyone is involved. Adults can take responsibility for gathering or purchasing necessary supplies and transporting wastes to the recycling center; older children can help with research, planning, setup, and maintenance of the program; and younger children can help by decorating boxes to use as storage containers and helping to decide where to keep them and by sorting recyclables.

Here are some ideas to help you establish a successful recycling program:

- Find out what local recycling programs are available in your community and find out what items can be recycled.

- If you do not have a curbside pick-up program in your community, decide on a practical schedule for going to the recycling center.

- Decide on the most convenient place(s) to store the recyclables —kitchen, garage, back porch, closet, and so on. If you don't have lots of space in a nearby, convenient spot (e.g., the kitchen), use small containers there and, when full, empty them into larger bins in another storage area (e.g., the basement). The more convenient your system, the quicker you will adapt to using it.

- Select containers, preferably with handles or on wheels, that won't be too heavy or bulky to carry when they fill up. Some possible choices: sturdy cardboard cartons, paper grocery bags, empty milk crates, plastic laundry baskets, rattan baskets, or recycling storage units specially designed for the purpose. (See "Appendix E—Resources" for places to order these.)

- As they accumulate, sort your recyclable items into the containers to be set out for curbside pick-up or delivered to the recycling center.

- If you have a yard, establish a compost for recycling food waste (other than meat products) and other organic materials.*

- Be creative about recycling items that can't be taken to the recycling center. Clothes and household goods that are in usable condition can be donated to nonprofit organizations. Many items are usable for arts, crafts, and science projects with children. A current fashion trend is jewelry, art pieces, and clothing made of recycled material—a sign of the times!

- If there is no recycling program in your community, join with other concerned residents and get one started. *The Recycler's Handbook: Simple Things You Can Do,* by The Earthworks Group, will tell you how to begin.

EPA Nationwide Recycling Hotline:

1–800–CLEANUP

*To learn more about composting, turn to page 192.

Homemade and Nontoxic Cleaning Products

What's a safe and economical way to keep your home and center squeaky clean? You can make your own nontoxic cleaning products.

Many of the commercial household cleaning products that we have become accustomed to using contain harsh, toxic chemicals that add to environmental pollution and may also be harmful to our skin and lungs. (The average American home uses approximately 25 gallons of hazardous chemicals per year!) When you purchase cleaning products, read labels and avoid buying products that include harmful ingredients (these are required by law to have some type of warning label or hazard symbol).

Examples of some of the more common and familiar hazardous substances included in cleaning products are *ammonia,* which is harmful to the skin, eyes, and lungs; *chlorine bleach,* which can be highly irritating to the eyes, nose, throat, and lungs, and *can result in deadly fumes if mixed with ammonia;* and *cresol,* an ingredient in many disinfectants, which can cause poisoning by ingestion and inhalation.

More and more companies are responding to consumer demands for environmentally safe products. With a bit of kitchen chemistry, you can make your own safe and effective alternative cleaners, too.

Here are some cleaning products for you to try. The ingredients can be found in your grocery or hardware store or pharmacy.

General All-Purpose Cleaners

- Mix equal parts of white vinegar and water for general cleaning.

- Mix 3 tablespoons washing soda with 4 cups warm water. Rinse with clean water.

- Mix vinegar and salt together for a good surface cleaner.

- Dissolve 4 tablespoons baking soda in 1 quart warm water or use baking soda on a damp sponge to clean and deodorize surfaces. Baking soda can also be made into a paste and used with an old toothbrush to clean tile grout.

Disinfectants

(*Note:* It is possible that these alternatives will not pass muster with child care licensing authorities.)

- Mix 1/2 cup borax with 1 gallon hot water. Use on a sponge or cloth to disinfect kitchen and/or bathroom surfaces.

- Hydrogen peroxide will disinfect surfaces.

- Isopropyl alcohol wiped on surfaces and allowed to dry is another effective disinfectant.

Dishwashing Soaps

- Use any phosphate-free dishwashing liquid.

- Use pure bar soap rubbed on a cloth or sponge.

Scouring Powders

- Sprinkle baking soda, borax, table salt, or washing soda on any surface where you would normally use a scouring powder. Scrub with a damp cloth or plastic mesh scrubber and rinse.

Oven Cleaners

- Sprinkle water and then lots of baking soda in the oven. Scrub with steel-wool pads and more water as needed.

- To maintain an already reasonably clean oven, mix 2 tablespoons nonphosphate dishwashing liquid soap with 1 tablespoon borax in a spray bottle and fill with warm water. Spray the solution in the oven and leave for 20 minutes or more before wiping clean. Spread newspapers on the floor to catch drips.

Silver Polish

- Apply a paste of baking soda mixed with water. Then rub, rinse, and dry the silver.

- Line the bottom of the kitchen sink with a sheet of aluminum foil. Fill with hot water and add 1/4 cup of baking soda, rock salt, or table salt. Put the silver into the water for 2–3 minutes, then wash in soapy water and dry.

Use toothpaste on an old toothbrush to remove tarnish from crevices. Rinse with warm water and polish with a soft cloth or chamois.

Brass and Copper Polish

Use lemon juice or a slice of lemon sprinkled with baking soda. Rub with a soft cloth, rinse, and dry.

Glass Cleaner

Mix equal parts white vinegar and water in a spray bottle. Spray on window or mirror and dry with crumpled newspaper.

Drain Cleaners

Prevent clogging by keeping a drain strainer over the sink drain and never pour grease down the drain. Pour a pot of boiling water down the drain once or twice a week.

For clogged drains, first try a plunger or a mechanical snake. If it's still clogged, pour 1/2 cup salt and 1/2 cup baking soda down the drain, followed by 6 cups of boiling water. Let it sit for several hours before flushing with more water.

Another formula for clearing clogged drains is to pour 1/2 cup of white vinegar and a handful of baking soda down the drain and cover it tightly for 1 minute. Then rinse with hot water.

Air Freshener

Simmer vinegar or herb mixtures or spices (e.g., cinnamon sticks or cloves) in water.

Furniture Polishes

Use plain mayonnaise, straight from the jar. Rub on the wood with a soft cloth.

Mix 2 parts olive oil with 1 part lemon juice.

Mix 3 parts olive oil with 1 part white vinegar.

Source: Debra Lynn Dadd, *Nontoxic & Natural: How to Avoid Dangerous Everyday Products and Buy or Make Safe Ones,* Jeremy P. Tarcher, Inc., Los Angeles, 1984; and Debra Lynn Dadd, *The Nontoxic Home,* Jeremy P. Tarcher, Inc., Los Angeles, 1986.

Setting Goals and Making Changes, or "Every Little Bit Helps"

If you're like we are, you would like to make lots of changes for the better —improve eating habits and environmental habits, add new activities to do with the children, read more, take a few classes, and on and on. Maybe you've even decided that "Starting on Monday, I'll never use sugar again," or "Next month we'll begin to recycle." Realistically, change is usually a long, slow process, and taking an approach that acknowledges this fact is likely to result in more success. Also, adults who have realistic expectations of themselves and can be proud of their own achievements, even the small ones, will be able to have the same patient, supportive attitude toward the children they care for.

Some guidelines:

- Set only small, achievable goals, and if you discover they weren't small enough, adjust them so that you will succeed. Remind yourself that any positive change is a plus. If you recycle a little, it's better than not at all. If you cut down a bit on fat and sugar, you're heading in the right direction.

- Incorporate health and environmental changes into your life through activities that you do anyway, such as buying ecologically sound alternatives to products you usually use, or adding one new healthy recipe to your menu plan each week.

- When you are doing things that are good for your health and for the environment, talk about them matter-of-factly with the children. Each time we describe our actions to children, we are helping to instill or strengthen awareness. They will be learning "why's" without a lecture.

■ Acknowledge efforts that children make to be environmentally sensitive. Let them know that you notice and appreciate what they do. Perhaps the next generation will consider environmental abuses socially unacceptable.

■ We adults know how hard it can be to change our old ways. Make the most of children's natural flexibility and adaptability. Let's help the next generation learn healthy, responsible habits from the beginning.

Build changes into your life gradually and patiently, and before you know it new habits will become second nature.

Building a Compost Heap

Composting is a great way to help children learn the benefits of recycling organic garbage. The size of your compost will depend on how much space you have. Just follow these steps:

- Choose an out-of-the-way spot in your yard, preferably a level, well-drained, sunny spot, but a shady one will work, too. A 3′ × 3′ plot is a good size to retain heat and compost faster, but use whatever size space you have. *If you don't have a large enough dirt area, you can use a planter box.*

- A simple compost bin can be enclosed with chicken wire fencing formed into a cylinder or into a square by attaching it to four metal or wood posts.

- Line the bottom with moist peat moss, shredded paper, leaves, or grass clippings. Sprinkle lightly with water as you add the layers.

- Buy some earthworms at a local nursery or bait shop and put them into the compost mixture. Their continual tunneling helps to build rich and fertile soil and ensure a successful compost.

- As you accumulate them, keep adding any food scraps (other than meat or dairy products) and other organic substances such as wood chips or garden clippings. High-nitrogen substances such as blood meal, bone meal, and manure can also be added to speed up the decaying process.

- Turn the mixture with a pitchfork or shovel every few days. To avoid flies, keep food scraps covered with grass clippings, dirt, or leaves.

- Talk with the children about the changes taking place as you tend the compost together. Observe the worms at work. They're fun to watch and can help children learn respect for the value of all living things and the jobs they do.

- When the compost is broken down and ready to use, usually in 2 to 8 weeks, dig in with the children and add your new "home-made" soil to the vegetable garden, around bushes and trees, and to potted plants. If you sift it, you can use it as a planting mixture for sprouting garden seeds.

Appendix A

A Basic Scheme for Nutrition Education

A child starts to learn about food the day she is born. As she receives her first feeding by breast or bottle, she learns that it is pleasurable to eat; her hunger is satisfied and she enjoys the contact with her caregiver. When she takes her first spoonful of mashed bananas, she learns that her hunger can be quieted by something new—something sweet and slightly lumpy that slides from a spoon into her mouth. Each new food is a profound experience! As she grows and sits at the family table, reads books, watches television, and helps prepare foods, she learns more about the place food has in her social structure and what adults consider to be appropriate foods for nourishment. Learning about food happens constantly and automatically.

But are the messages this child gets regarding food likely to teach her what she needs to know about eating healthfully, enjoying eating, and becoming a savvy and socially responsible consumer? If this child is typical, she will have picked up a mish-mash of ideas about food, some of which are fine and some of which aren't helpful at all. This should be no great surprise, because the typical adult is in the same situation!

Recognizing that children need a good knowledge base about food and nutrition, many child care centers, homes, and schools have implemented nutrition education programs. The best is comprehensive in its approach, meaning that the site's menus, the example set by teachers and other adults, books, videos, and toys used, formal nutrition education activities and field trips, and participation by parents reinforce consistent messages about eating well and happily. For example, children are unlikely to learn about the pleasures of trying new foods if the center's menus rotate among hamburgers, hot dogs, and spaghetti with meat sauce. They will continue to think that sweet foods always accompany celebrations if every holiday or birthday is celebrated with cupcakes or candies. They will not learn to recycle waste if containers are not provided for recyclable material in the lunchroom.

Teaching children what they need to know about food starts with adults learning about good nutrition and applying its principles in their own lives every day. The children who eat brown rice and broccoli enthusiastically are generally those who have seen their parents and teachers or caregivers doing it; they think that's how people are *supposed* to eat. Too often nutrition education for child care staff and parents focuses on children's nutrition issues. It's important for people who work with children to know about these things, but at least as much effort should go into helping them improve their own nutrition.

Teaching Kids About Food, Step by Step

Build the Foundation

▪ *Learn and practice the basics of good nutrition yourself.* A class at your local college or adult education center may be available; if not, some suggested books are listed in Appendix E. Keep abreast of nutrition news by reading reliable magazines or journals.

▪ *Serve meals that are consistent with current nutritional guidelines.* If children are bringing their own food to the site, how do their bag lunches or snacks look? Some child care centers and schools encourage parents to refrain from sending foods high in sugar or salt to school and have guidelines regarding appropriate foods for celebrations.

▪ *Fill the children's environment with nutrition-positive decorations, toys, books, and videos.* Take a look at your classroom, child care site, or home. Are there posters of healthful foods or families from around the world sharing meals? When you decorate the children's paperwork with stickers, do you use "lollipops" or "apples"? Does the math textbook teach that 4 candy bars + 5 candy bars = 9 candy bars?

Construct a Framework of "Natural" Learning Experiences

▪ *Equip your classroom for food preparation activities.* This need not be costly; many inexpensive kitchen tools are available that are easy for children to manage. Projects should be fairly simple and geared to the children's level of development. Even assembling a salad can be exciting for a young child. There are many good children's cookbooks; stick with those having recipes for more than cookies and candy. And remember that constant adult supervision is a must.

■ *Set up some food-growing experiences for the children.* A children's garden is wonderful, but if space or time isn't available, many foods can be grown in pots outside or in a windowsill. Sprouts are another fun project.

■ *Take children shopping for food.* Regular grocery stores offer plenty of opportunities for "food education," but be sure to check out other shopping resources; for example, farmer's markets and ethnic groceries.

■ *Arrange field trips to places where food is grown or manufactured.* Your local cooperative extension agent can usually provide you with listings of farms that conduct tours or allow you to "pick your own." And there is probably a bakery, restaurant, or food-processing plant in your area that arranges tours.

■ *Establish a system of environmentally conscious waste disposal.* Have the children sort their own trash for recycling and use a minimum of nonrecyclable materials in food service. Maintaining a compost heap with certain food wastes is a wonderful adjunct to your garden as well.

■ *Use mealtimes as occasions to talk about food origins, cultural food habits, and various nutrition concepts.* For example, preschoolers might be asked which of the foods served come from animals, whereas older children might be asked to identify those high in fat or vitamin C. Children can be encouraged to share information about how (or whether) their own families use certain foods.

Supplement with Other Nutrition Education Activities

■ *Games, riddles, puzzles, art projects, flannelboard stories, songs, puppets, dramatic play, and science experiments can all be used to enrich the program* of "food education" you've established. Numerous curricula and idea books are available. *Teaching Children About Food,* the companion volume to this book, has lots of ideas, and we've listed other books in Appendix E. You may want to organize your nutrition education around certain concepts, say, on a monthly basis. Cooking projects, stories, games, and menus can help teach a particular theme. Assess what the children already know about food and nutrition before you choose the themes you will develop; knowledge and skills will vary widely within the same age group. Be sure the children are well grounded in the simpler concepts before moving on to more sophisticated ones.

Appendix B
Nutrition Basics

■ **Nutrition** is the science concerned with food and how it is used by the body. It is also the combination of processes by which a person eats, digests, absorbs, utilizes, and excretes food substances.

■ Nutrition is a young science—the first vitamin was discovered about 70 years ago, and we assume that more nutrients will be discovered in years to come. There are over 40 known nutrients, and no one food contains them all.

■ **Nutrients** are the substances found in food that work together to provide energy, promote growth, and regulate body processes. The six major classes of nutrients are:

Carbohydrates	Vitamins
Proteins	Minerals
Fats	Water

Proteins, fats, and carbohydrates provide **calories,** which are small units of energy your body can use to do its work or stay warm.

The tables on pages 201–203 describe briefly the functions and good food sources of the major nutrients.

■ Everyone has different nutritional needs, which depend on age, sex, body size, heredity, activity levels, state of health, and even climate! Although more information is becoming available, we still don't know for certain what all of those needs are.

■ Some nutrients are needed in large quantities and some in small ones. In the United States, nutrient requirements have been, up to now, expressed as **Recommended Dietary Allowances,** or **RDAs.** As this book goes to press, a new and expanded system of guidance called the **Dietary Reference Intakes (DRIs)** is being developed. Some nutrients will continue to have RDAs, others will have Adequate Intakes (AIs), and acceptable upper limits for nutrient intakes will be given as Tolerable Upper Intake Levels (ULs). These DRIs are based on the best available scientific research, and they will have a far-reaching impact on consumer education, fortification of food products, and planning dietary standards for nutrition programs.

It is important to remember that DRIs have their limitations when we use them to measure the quality of an individual's diet. For one thing, although they are expressed as daily requirements, they are actually daily intakes averaged over a week or more. Thus, falling short of a nutritional requirement one day is unlikely to cause any harm; it's what's eaten over a longer term that's important. In addition, the DRIs are meant to be used as goals but not applied rigidly, because individual nutritional needs vary. For example, suppose that someone habitually ingested just 50% of his RDA for vitamin C. We couldn't necessarily assume he is suffering from a vitamin deficiency! Maybe his body needs only 25% of the RDA. But then again, he might need 95% of the RDA (unfortunately, human beings aren't born with owner's manuals, so we don't really know how much of each nutrient will make each person's body work best). It would be fair to say that if this fellow habitually got about 50% of the RDA for vitamin C, he would have a greater *risk* of a deficiency than someone who took in 100% of the RDA. For this reason, it's a good idea to aim for food patterns that supply nutrients in quantities close to the DRIs.

■ Although it is true that some people in the United States don't get enough of certain nutrients, it is far more common for us to get too *much* of others, namely, fat, sugars, and sodium. Excessive intakes of these substances, along with a lack of fiber, are related to the "diseases of affluence" that kill millions and millions of Americans: heart disease, high blood pressure, diabetes, and cancer.

■ Getting the recommended number of servings from the Food Guide Pyramid helps ensure dietary intakes consistent with guidelines for disease prevention and optimum growth and development (see page 70).

■ In the field of nutrition right now, exciting research is being conducted on substances in plant foods called **phytochemicals.** These substances, produced by plants to protect themselves from invading viruses, bacteria, and fungi, aren't considered nutrients, but they may help prevent some cancers, heart disease, and other chronic health problems. Carotenoids, flavinoids, indoles, isoflavones, capsaicin, and protease inhibitors are among the phytochemicals being studied. Avoid running to the store to buy supplements containing one or several of these substances, and follow Mom's advice to eat lots of fruits and vegetables instead (a bit of tea and chocolate now and then probably won't hurt either!). And stay tuned. . . .

A User-Friendly Guide to Some Major Nutrients

Nutrients	Primary Functions	Rich Food Sources
Energy Nutrients (supply calories)		
• *Proteins*	• Supply amino acids to be used for growth and maintenance of the body	• Meat, poultry, fish, eggs, milk, cheese, dried beans, tofu, peanut butter
• *Carbohydrates*	• Primary source of energy for the body's activities	• *Complex carbohydrates:* Breads, cereals, rice, pasta, tortillas, potatoes • *Sugars:* Sugar, honey, jelly, molasses, candy, milk, fruits

Fiber is also a carbohydrate, but it can't be digested by humans, so it provides bulk or "roughage" and no calories. Good sources are whole grains, fresh fruits and vegetables, dried fruits, and dried beans.

• *Fats*	• Provide energy, cushion vital organs, and supply essential fatty acids that maintain skin and membranes	• Oils, butter, margarine, meat, lard, cream, olives, coconut, avocados, nuts

Fat Facts

Fats are made up of different combinations of fatty acids. These fatty acids may be saturated (solid at room temperature) or mono- or polyunsaturated (liquid at room temperature). Saturated fats are the ones that raise blood cholesterol. They are *usually* found in animal foods, like meat or milk (palm oil and coconut oil are two vegetable oils that are highly saturated, however).

Cholesterol is found only in foods of animal origin. It is possible for a food to have no cholesterol in it but still be very high in fat (and calories!). Corn oil, for example, is cholesterol free but 100% fat.

continued . . .

Major Nutrients, continued...

Nutrients	Primary Functions	Rich Food Sources
Water-Soluble Vitamins		
• Thiamin (B$_1$)	• Helps the body use carbohydrates for energy; important for health of nervous system	• Pork, organ meats, yeast, eggs, green leafy vegetables, whole or enriched grains, dried beans
• Riboflavin (B$_2$)	• Helps the body get energy from carbohydrates, fats, and proteins; important for healthy mucous membranes	• Milk, organ meats, yeast, cheese, eggs, green leafy vegetables, whole or enriched grains
• Niacin	• Helps the body release energy from foods; promotes healthy skin, digestive tract, and nervous system	• Liver, yeast, whole or enriched grains, beef, pork, peanuts
• Vitamin B$_6$	• Helps the body use proteins and fats; keeps nervous system healthy	• Yeast, whole grains, fish, poultry, meats, bananas, green leafy vegetables
• Folic acid (folate/folacin)	• Helps make new body cells through its role in making RNA and DNA; helps make red blood cells	• Leafy vegetables, some fruits, dried beans, liver, wheat germ, fortified cereals, most enriched grain products
• Vitamin B$_{12}$	• Helps the body make its genetic material; vital for health of nerve tissue	• Meat, poultry, fish, eggs, milk products, a few specially fortified plant foods
• Vitamin C	• Helps form collagen; keeps bones, teeth, and blood vessels healthy; antioxidant	• Citrus fruits, tomatoes, peppers, potatoes, cantaloupe, strawberries, cabbage

Nutrients	Primary Functions	Rich Food Sources
Fat-Soluble Vitamins		
• *Vitamin A*	• Helps in growth and maintenance of skin and membranes; needed for healthy eyes and night vision	• Liver, cream, egg yolk, butter, fortified dairy products; green, orange, and yellow vegetables and fruits
• *Vitamin D*	• Helps form and maintain bones and teeth; aids in calcium absorption	• Fatty fish, liver, eggs, butter, fortified dairy foods
• *Vitamin E*	• Helps form red blood cells and other tissues; protects fatty acids and vitamin A	• Vegetable oils, wheat germ, whole grains, liver, green leafy vegetables
• *Vitamin K*	• Needed for normal blood clotting	• Cabbage, cauliflower, liver, vegetable oils, green leafy vegetables
Minerals		
• *Calcium*	• Builds and maintains bones and teeth; needed for blood clotting and muscle contraction	• Milk products, fish eaten with bones, dried beans, broccoli, bok choy, collards, kale, blackstrap molasses
• *Iron*	• Forms components of blood that carry oxygen to cells	• Liver, meat, dried beans, dried fruits, fortified cereal
• *Fluoride*	• Keeps bones and teeth strong	• Fluoridated water, tea, sardines
• *Iodine*	• Part of thyroid hormones	• Seafood, iodized salt, seaweed
• *Water (the most important nutrient)*	• An essential component of the body's structure; a solvent, transports nutrients and wastes, regulates body temperature	• Beverages and most solid foods

How Can You Tell Whether a Child Is Getting Proper Nutrition?

A physician or registered dietitian is in the best position to judge whether a child is truly well nourished, but in general, you can feel reasonably assured that a child is getting the nutrition she needs if she is growing well, is vigorous, and seems to have good resistance to illness (of course, most children will have occasional colds or bouts with flu). There are other indicators of good nutrition as well. A child who is well nourished will have:

- Erect posture and straight arms and legs (excepting infants)
- Good muscle tone
- Smooth skin, slightly moist, and with good color
- Good attention span, normal reflexes, psychologically stable
- Good appetite, normal elimination
- Normal heart rate and rhythm, normal blood pressure
- Normal sleeping habits
- Shiny hair, firmly rooted, and healthy scalp
- Smooth, moist lips
- Smooth, red tongue, not swollen
- Gums with a good pink color, no swelling or bleeding
- Teeth that are clean and free of cavities, well-shaped jaw
- Bright, clear eyes with healthy pink membranes
- Firm nails with pink nailbeds

We do not recommend that you take it upon yourself to get into the medical diagnosis business, but you can alert families to signs that professional evaluation and treatment might be in order. Obviously, not all of these criteria are appropriate to use in the case of some children with physically handicapping conditions.

Appendix C
Special Topics

Allergies to Foods

Depending upon whom you believe, 0.3% to 38% of all children have food allergies. The truth is that no scientifically accurate count of the number of children with food allergies exists; pediatric allergists generally estimate the figure at around 1% to 2% of all children.

Food allergies are hard to diagnose, and even the most respected allergy specialists disagree about the best method to use. They also disagree on the range of health conditions that can be caused by allergies. Colic, migraine headaches, and hyperactivity have been linked to food allergies by some researchers, but not all.

We do know that symptoms of food allergies usually appear in the first year of a child's life and often disappear within nine months or less. And we also know that children are much more likely to have food allergies if their parents do (though not always to the same foods!).

In a true food allergy, the body's immune system reacts to contact with the offending substance (**allergen**) by making **antibodies.** In some cases, food allergies are only minor inconveniences. They can, however, also produce chronic health complaints, and in extreme cases, life-threatening reactions. Through a series of mechanisms in the tissues of the body, symptoms are produced that may include:

- Hives
- Nausea and vomiting
- Eczema
- Diarrhea
- Anaphylactic shock
- Sleep disturbances
- Coughing
- Swelling of the throat
- Nasal congestion
- Sneezing
- Conjunctivitis
- Asthma

A reaction can take from a few minutes to several days to occur. The severity of the reaction can depend upon:

- How much of the allergen was eaten
- How often the food was eaten
- Physical or emotional stress

The foods most likely to cause allergies in children are: cow's milk, soy, wheat, and eggs. Corn, oranges, chocolate, peanuts, legumes, rice, fish, beef, pork, and chicken are other potential allergens.

Children can also have **sensitivities** or **intolerances** to foods, which are often confused with allergies; for example, lactose intolerance, which is the inability to digest the sugars in milk, and sensitivities to food colorings and MSG.

A child should have a professional evaluation when food allergies or intolerances are suspected. It's a shame when a child suffers unnecessarily from allergy-related symptoms. It's also a shame when a child is forced to avoid enjoyable foods that may not even be a problem for her. And there have been cases of growth failure in children when their parents "diagnosed" food allergies and restricted their diets without guidance.

Be aware that allergies are not to be taken lightly and can result in some troublesome feeding situations:

- Children can develop aversions to eating when they've been scared by severe allergic reactions or when restrictions make mealtimes unpleasant.

- Highly restrictive diets can be boring; they can also lead to serious nutrient deficiencies if they aren't well planned.

- Children may use eating "forbidden" foods, or not eating at all, to manipulate their parents or caregivers.

Guidelines for Managing Food Allergies in Child Care

- Establish a written policy on parent/caregiver responsibilities in allergic conditions.

- Have a physician's statement on file that describes the allergy and recommended substitutions.

- Make sure a list of children's names with their allergies and "forbidden" foods is readily available for any adult who might be involved in preparing food or serving it to the children.

- If a child is subject to life-threatening reactions from foods, obtain authorization to administer the appropriate medications and the necessary training to do so safely.

**Anaphylactic shock can be fatal!
Its warning signs are:**

Itching and flushing of the skin

Severe nausea or diarrhea

Swelling of the respiratory passages

- Children with multiple food allergies, or allergies to foods that are primary sources of nutrients (as milk is in the United States), should be monitored by a physician or dietitian. Parents and caregivers may wish to receive counseling together regarding appropriate food choices.

- Be matter-of-fact about a child's food restrictions. Let the child take increasing responsibility for his food selections, as his awareness of what must be avoided grows. Tell other children in the group why the restrictions are necessary; hopefully they'll be supportive of their peer.

- Remember that children generally hate being singled out. Become adept at planning menus that everyone can eat, and when you find that you must make substitutions for a child, be sure that what she gets is as nice as what everyone else is getting. Don't make it too spectacular, though, or you'll have everyone else clamoring for that special treatment! (We recall one preschool classroom that was disrupted every lunch hour for weeks when a child's mother brought him fast-food chicken nuggets as his "allergy-free" lunch. Needless to say, none of the other children were interested in the standard menu.)

- Become thoroughly familiar with foods that potentially contain the allergens you're avoiding. Read labels like crazy. Beware of "hidden" allergens in foods.

- Make every effort to replace the nutrients that will be missing when a child must avoid major foods and food groups. For example, apple juice is not a substitute for milk. Sure, they're both beverages, but apple juice has virtually none of milk's protein, calcium, riboflavin, vitamin A, or vitamin D.

Check Appendix E in the back of this book for allergy cookbooks and suppliers of specialty foods.

Milk Allergies

Some foods or ingredients to avoid

Milk	Casein
Cheese	Caseinate
Cottage cheese	Whey
Yogurt	Lactalbumin
Butter	Sodium caseinate
Margarine with milk solids	Lactose
Milk chocolate	Cream
Creamed foods	Calcium caseinate
Custards and puddings	Nonfat milk solids
Lactate solids	

Substitutes for dairy foods

Fortified soy milk Nut milks

Soy formulas Juices, in baked goods

Tofu Broth, in sauces or soups

Fortified rice milk Oat milk

Alternative food sources of important nutrients

Protein: Meats, poultry, fish, eggs, dried beans, peanut butter, tofu

Calcium: Spinach, collards, kale, turnip greens, broccoli, bok choy, soybeans, tofu (made with calcium sulfate), mustard greens, canned salmon with bones (they're soft!), sardines, corn tortillas (made with lime), blackstrap molasses, calcium-fortified orange juice, fortified soy or rice milk

Riboflavin: Mushrooms, beet greens, spinach, broccoli, romaine lettuce, bok choy, asparagus, dried peaches, bean sprouts, fortified cereals

Egg Allergies

Some foods or ingredients to avoid

Eggs Meringues

Egg whites Many baked goods

Egg yolks Many breaded/batter-fried

Some egg substitutes items

Mayonnaise Albumin

Some salad dressings Globulin

Egg noodles Livetin

Most fresh pasta Ovomucin

Custards, tapioca Ovomucoid

pudding Vitellin

Substitutes for eggs in recipes

Ener-G Egg Replacer®

Extra 1/2 teaspoon
   baking powder for
   each egg missing

Arrowroot powder as a binder

Tofu for pudding-like texture;
   can be "scrambled," too

Most dried pasta

Alternative food sources of important nutrients

Protein: Meats, poultry, fish, dairy products, dried beans,
            nut butters

Vitamin A: Fortified milk and margarine, yellow/orange
            and green leafy fruits and vegetables

Citrus Allergies

Alternative sources of vitamin C

Cantaloupe	Papaya	Strawberries
Green peppers	Broccoli	Cabbage
Chiles	Tomatoes	Potatoes

Wheat Allergies

Some foods or ingredients to avoid

Wheat	Postum, malted milk
Wheat germ	Most baked goods
Wheat bran	Most crackers
Modified food starch	Macaroni, spaghetti
Graham flour	Noodles
Farina	Gravies, cream sauces
Semolina	Fried food coating
Gluten	Most baking mixes
Vegetable starch	Soy sauce (read label)
Vegetable gum	Some hot dogs, sausages
Enriched flour	Some salad dressings
Hydrolyzed vegetable protein	MSG
Some yeast (Fleishman's is	

wheat-free)

Substitutes for wheat in recipes

Cornstarch, tapioca, rice
    flour as thickeners
Wheat-free breads, crackers
Rice cakes
Corn tortillas
Oatmeal
Polenta
Cream of rice

Wheat-free pasta
Popcorn
Rice flour
Barley flour
Potato flour
Oat bran
Rice bran
Wheat-free cereal crumbs

Baking mix: 1 cup cornstarch, 2 cups rice flour, 2 cups soy
    flour, 3 cups potato flour (bake at lower temper-
    ature for a longer time, and you may want to cut
    down on the added fat in the recipe)

Alternative food sources of important nutrients

Complex carbohydrates,
    B-vitamins, fiber:

Other whole grains (corn,
barley, millet, rice, oats),
potatoes, dried beans

Soy Allergies

Some foods or ingredients to avoid

Soybeans
Soy flour
Soybean oil
Soy protein isolate
Texturized vegetable
    protein (TVP)
Vegetable starch
Vegetable gum
Tofu
Hydrolyzed vegetable
    protein

Soy sauce
Teriyaki sauce
Worcestershire sauce
Soy milk
Soy infant formulas
Some margarines
Soy nuts
Tempeh
Miso
Vegetable protein
    concentrate

Corn Allergies

Some foods or ingredients to avoid

Cornmeal

Cornstarch

Masa harina

Corn oil

Corn syrup

Corn sweetener

Vegetable starch

Vegetable gum

Modified food starch

Some baked goods

Some baking powder

Corn tortillas

Corn chips

Some cold cereals

Pancake syrups

Many candies

Corn solids

Substitutes for corn in recipes

Other flours

Potato starch, rice flour, arrowroot, tapioca as thickeners

Beet or cane sugar

Pure maple syrup

Baking soda and cream of tartar for leavening

Honey

Wheat flour tortillas

Anemia and Iron Deficiency

Normally oxygen is carried to the body's tissues as part of a molecule called **hemoglobin** in the red blood cells. When there's not enough hemoglobin around, a condition called anemia is the result. Most anemia is caused by **iron deficiency.** Iron-deficiency anemia is a common nutritional problem in the United States, affecting primarily children 12 to 36 months old, teenage boys, and women of childbearing age. Iron-deficiency anemia is found among children of all income levels, although it is more common in children from poorer families.

Unfortunately, at a critical time in infancy, iron-deficiency anemia may cause irreversible abnormalities in brain growth and development. Iron deficiency may also make a child more susceptible to lead poisoning, which can cause growth stunting and neurological problems. Even before outright anemia appears, iron deficits can have serious effects on the body's functioning. Infants with iron deficiency appear fearful, tense, unresponsive to examiners, and generally "unhappy." Older children with mild iron deficiency have exhibited:

- A shortened attention span

- Irritability

- Fatigue

- Inability to concentrate on tasks

- Poor performance on vocabulary, reading, math, problem-solving, and psychological tests

- Lowered resistance to infection

How heartbreaking that children may do poorly in school or be labeled "lazy" or "unmanageable," when in fact they are suffering from a preventable nutritional problem!

Iron deficiency can have several causes: a diet that's lacking in good sources of iron; poor absorption of iron in the intestines; increased requirements for iron, particularly during periods of rapid growth; heavy or persistent losses of blood; and some infections. When young children become iron-deficient, it's often because they didn't get enough iron during their first year of life or because they've been consuming too much milk and not enough iron-rich foods.

What you can do to prevent iron deficiency

- Give infants *iron-fortified formula* or *breast milk* up to the age of 1 year. Breastfeeding mothers may want to discuss iron supplementation with their pediatricians.

- When feeding cereal to infants who are between 4 to 6 months and 1 year old, use *iron-fortified infant cereals.*

- Don't feed children whole cow's milk during their first year; it can cause some gastrointestinal bleeding.

- Serve children *iron-rich foods* frequently for snacks as well as for meals. Organ meats, shellfish, and muscle meats are the richest sources of highly absorbable iron; don't feed liver more than once a week, though, or vitamin A toxicity can result. Nuts, green vegetables, whole grains, enriched breads and fortified cereals, and dried fruits are also good sources of iron.

- The iron in nonmeat foods is absorbed better when meats or *vitamin C–rich foods* are served at the same meal. Dairy products, eggs, and tea hinder the absorption of nonmeat iron.

- Don't allow children to fill up on milk and ignore other foods. A pint of milk a day is plenty for children between the ages of 1 and 3 years; 2-1/2 cups a day is sufficient between ages 3 and 8 years.

Choking on Food

Every five days, a child in the United States dies from choking on food. Young children lack the chewing skills to deal with foods that are hard or tough. And foods that are round or sticky can block their airways, which are smaller than those of adults.

Although children have been known to choke on apple pieces, peanut butter sandwiches, cookies, carrots, popcorn, beans, and even bread, four foods that have caused the most deaths are:

- Hot dogs
- Nuts
- Hard candies
- Grapes

Every adult who takes care of children should be aware of the simple precautions that can drastically reduce the risk of choking.

Choking Prevention

- *Always* supervise children while they are eating.
- Insist that children eat calmly and while they're sitting down.
- Encourage children to chew their food well.
- Infants should be fed solid foods only while they're sitting up.
- Make sure that the foods you serve the children are appropriate for their chewing and swallowing abilities. Do not give the following foods to children younger than 4 years of age, unless they are modified (see p. 67):

Hot dogs	Popcorn
Nuts	Peanut butter
Grapes	Marshmallows
Hard candies	Chips
Hard pieces of fruits or vegetables	Pretzels
	Fish with bones
Raisins	Large chunks of meat

- Never use styrofoam cups and plates for young children; pieces can easily break off.

- Don't allow children to eat in the car or bus; if a child started choking, it might be hard to get the vehicle to the side of the road safely in order to help her.

CHOKING (When Conscious)

Have someone call EMS # 911 immediately!

Fig. I

Infant (Birth to I Year)

1. Supporting infant's head and neck, straddle over forearm, with head lower than trunk, and administer 4 back blows, high, between the shoulder blades. *(Fig. I)*

2. Supporting infant's head and neck, turn on back and give four chest thrusts with 2–3 fingers 1/2″ deep, at one finger-width below the nipples (midsternal region). *(Fig. 2)*

Fig. 2

3. Repeat steps I and 2 until obstruction clears.

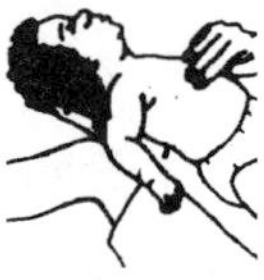

Child (Older Than I Year) and Adults

Ask "Are you choking?" If victim cannot speak, cough, or breathe, take the following action (Heimlich maneuver):

1. Kneel behind the child (stand behind a taller child or adult). *(Fig. 3)*

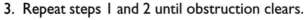

Fig. 3

2. Wrap your arms around the child's waist.

3. Make a fist with one hand. Place your fist (thumbside) against the child's stomach in the midline just above the navel and well below the rib cage.

4. Grasp your fist with your other hand.

5. Press inward and upward into stomach with a quick thrust. *(Fig. 4)*

Fig. 4

6. Repeat thrust until obstruction is cleared.

Abdominal thrusts (Heimlich maneuver)
should not be done on an infant.

Source: *Childhood Emergencies—What to Do: A Quick Reference Guide,* by Marin Child Care Council (formerly Project Care for Children). Palo Alto: Bull Publishing Company, 1989.

CHOKING (When Unconscious)

CALL EMS # 911. **If necessary, you can leave the phone off the hook and shout information into the phone while attending to the child.**

Infant (Birth to 1 Year)

An infant who has become unconscious should be placed in a supine (lying on back) position.

1. Perform jaw tongue lift *(Fig. 5)* and sweep the mouth only for visible objects. *Do not use "blind" finger sweeps of the mouth as the object can be pushed back, causing further obstruction.*

2. Attempt to ventilate *(Fig. 6)*. If airway remains blocked, proceed to step 3.

3. Perform 1 set of 4 back blows, then 4 chest thrusts *(see Figs. 1 and 2).*

Repeat steps 1, 2, and 3 until airway is clear or medical help arrives.

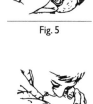
Fig. 5

Fig. 6

IMPORTANT: If child is coughing, do not interfere! If child cannot cough, speak, or cry, and/or is turning blue, use these techniques immediately!

Child (Older Than 1 Year) and Adults

A child who has become unconscious should be placed in a supine (lying on back) position.

1. Perform jaw tongue lift *(Fig. 7)* and sweep the mouth only for visible objects. *Do not use "blind" finger sweeps of the mouth as the object can be pushed back, causing further obstruction.*

2. Attempt to ventilate. If airway remains blocked, proceed to step 3.

3. Deliver compressions by kneeling at the child's feet or straddling the child's legs, pressing the heel of one hand on the midline of the abdomen, slightly above the navel, pressing the free hand over the positioned hand and locking your elbows, and giving 6–10 rapid upward abdominal thrusts. *(Fig. 8)*

Repeat steps 1, 2, and 3 until airway is clear.

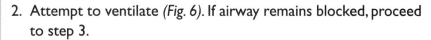
Fig. 7

Fig. 8

Calcium and Osteoporosis

Calcium is the most abundant mineral in our bodies. Ninety-nine percent of it is stored in our bones; the rest is found in fluids inside and outside of the body cells, where it performs crucial roles in the movement of nerve impulses, contraction of muscles, movement of materials across cell membranes, and clotting of blood. The calcium concentrations in these fluids are so important that the body will dissolve bone if necessary to make the mineral available to them. In this way, the bones act as a form of "calcium bank account." As people age, they start to lose more calcium from their bones (osteoporosis) and may suffer fractures on very little impact. Women have this problem more than men, and heredity, exercise, and many other factors play a role. Prevention of osteoporosis involves building up as hefty a bank account of calcium as possible during the years when bone-building can occur and minimizing the loss of bone in later years.

Scientists are working very hard to determine when the critical times of life for building bone mass happen, how much calcium we need to ingest during these times, and what other dietary factors may be involved. It does appear that childhood is a window of opportunity for preventing osteoporosis and that getting enough calcium even at a very young age could help. The extent to which eating too many animal-protein foods, drinking a lot of phosphoric-acid-containing soda drinks (primarily colas), and eating too much salt affect our bones is still under investigation. Recently the Institute of Medicine made these recommendations for calcium intake for children:

- Children ages 1 through 3 years: 500 mg per day
- Children ages 4 through 8 years: 800 mg per day
- Children ages 9 through 18 years: 1,300 mg per day

What do these recommendations mean in practical terms? For infants who are breastfed or receiving infant formula, you needn't worry; they'll get the calcium they need. For older children, you can usually figure that they'll get about 200 mg of calcium in their usual consumption of various foods. The other 600 to 1,100 mg is usually supplied by milk and dairy products such as yogurt or cheese. One cup of low-fat milk contains about 300 mg of calcium. So, a child up through age 8 can get the calcium she needs from 2 cups of milk, an older child from 3-1/2 to 4 cups of milk. A study of child care sites found that children don't drink as much milk when juice is also on the table, so if you're wondering how to get the children to drink more milk, this is something you might want to consider. Most children under the age of 9 years are getting enough calcium in their diets, but if a child can't or won't drink milk, some care is needed in planning for adequate calcium intake, although the fortification of some common foods is making this easier. The following table demonstrates some alternative sources of calcium.

Some Foods That Have as Much Calcium as a Cup of Milk

Mozzarella or cheddar cheese	1-1/2 oz.
Yogurt	3/4 cup
Calcium-fortified orange juice	1 cup
Calcium-fortified soy milk	1 cup
Cooked kale	3 cups
Cooked broccoli	1-3/4 cups
Tofu (with calcium sulfate)	10 oz.
Salmon (canned, with bones)	4 oz.
Dried figs	9 pieces
Corn tortillas (with lime)	5
Cooked pinto beans	3 cups

Constipation and Fiber

Some people think that constipation means not having a bowel movement every day. Actually, the number of days between bowel movements isn't really the issue. Constipation is defined as having bowel movements that are hard and passed with pain or difficulty. An occasional hard stool need not cause special concern, but if a child has persistent constipation and her abdomen is swollen, her physician should examine her to make sure there isn't an underlying disease.

True constipation is rare in infants. There is a wide variation in the normal number of bowel movements a baby may have in a day, or even in a week; it isn't necessary to have one daily. It's also normal for infants to strain and turn red in the face while having a normal bowel movement, alarming as this may be to an adult bystander. Parents often change formulas hoping to solve this "problem," but generally it isn't necessary.

Toddlers sometimes develop constipation after they've had painful bowel movements. They hold them in, trying to avoid the discomfort. But what happens is that when they hold their bowel movements in, the intestines draw the water out of them, which makes them harder and of course more painful. You can see the potential for a vicious cycle here. In these situations, physicians will often temporarily prescribe a stool softener. Hopefully, the child will get the idea that it doesn't always hurt to go to the bathroom, and he'll be more willing to "answer nature's call."

When older children are constipated, it is often because they can't use the bathroom when they need to, like when they're running on tight schedules or have to wait for recess at school. Also, some kids don't want to use school bathrooms, if they aren't given the privacy they want.

Maybe you're wondering at this point if we're ever going to talk about the role of nutrition in constipation. We're getting to that; but you should know that constipation can have other causes, too. So if you look at what a child's been eating, and there doesn't seem to be a problem with it, consider the factors already mentioned.

Okay, now for the nutrition part. You know that dietary fiber contributes to regular bowel function. **Fiber** is the part of our food (usually plant matter) that we can't digest. It attracts water into the intestines, which makes the stool softer and bulkier. Most children—and most adults, for that matter—don't get enough fiber in their diets. That's too bad, because in addition to helping maintain normal bowel function, fiber may help reduce the risk of cardiovascular disease, some cancers, and adult-onset diabetes.

The American Health Foundation offers a guideline for fiber intake for children 3 years and older that's easy to remember: *age plus 5* (grams of fiber). For example, a 6-year-old should get 11 grams of fiber daily. A diet with sufficient calories and plenty of unprocessed foods and fresh produce will pretty much ensure adequate fiber intake. But you need to practice moderation. Children can be deprived of needed nutrients when they're restricted to high-fiber, low-calorie foods. We generally don't recommend fiber supplements (like bran concentrates), either.

Constipation Prevention Plan

Offer children fiber-rich foods often. Whole grains, fresh fruits and vegetables, dried fruits, dried beans, nuts, and popcorn are good sources of fiber.

Make sure children drink water when they're thirsty. It helps fiber do its job.

Encourage children to use the bathroom when they feel the urge to go, and allow them enough time to take care of their business. Make sure the bathroom is a pleasant enough place to be!

Encourage plenty of physical activity. Exercise is thought to be beneficial in maintaining bowel regularity.

Dental Health

Nutrition affects the health of teeth in two ways. First, adequate amounts of certain nutrients are necessary for the formation of teeth. Second, the foods that go into the mouth can cause tooth decay.

All of the primary ("baby") teeth and some permanent teeth are already forming in a baby's jaw before he is born. The teeth depend on nutrients for development until the last permanent tooth erupts. Sufficient amounts of protein, calcium, phosphorus, magnesium, and the vitamins A, C, and D must be present if healthy teeth are to develop. The minerals fluoride, iron, and zinc help make the teeth resistant to decay.

Most people don't realize that tooth decay is actually the result of **infection** passed on to children by parents or caregivers (babies aren't born with the bacteria that cause tooth decay). We don't tell you this to keep you from kissing your children! But the fact is that children tend to have fewer cavities when their parents practice good oral hygiene. So pay close attention . . . this is important for everyone.

The bacteria that cause tooth decay use the carbohydrates in foods we eat, both for energy and for making **plaque** that helps them stick to the teeth. The bacteria also produce acids that dissolve tooth enamel and form **cavities.**

You're familiar with the sugars that feed these bacteria—table sugar, brown sugar, honey, maple syrup, molasses, and corn syrup are the principal ones. In addition, bacteria can produce sugar by breaking down the starches in foods such as potatoes and bread, if these foods stay in the mouth long enough. That means a dry, unsweetened cracker stuck to the teeth might be more harmful than a can of soda!

So, if a tooth is to end up with a cavity, three things are necessary:

- Bacteria . . . to produce the acids that dissolve the tooth's enamel

- Carbohydrates . . . to feed the bacteria and glue them to the tooth

- Time . . . for the bacteria to do their work

When we talk about preventing cavities, we're generally trying to make sure at least one of these factors is missing. For example, brushing teeth removes food particles, as well as some of the bacteria in the plaque.

To Keep Tooth Decay Away

Serve a well-balanced diet, being careful to include good sources of calcium and phosphorus.

Cut down on foods that are high in sugar, such as soda pop, candy, cookies, pastries, jams, syrups, and presweetened breakfast cereals.

Avoid foods that stick to the teeth. Raisins, other dried fruits, fruit rolls, and gummy-style fruit candies fall into this category.

Serve raw vegetables often. They scrub the teeth and stimulate the flow of saliva, which can help protect the teeth.

If you are going to serve a sweet food, do it at mealtime, not as an ongoing snack. This will cut down on the amount of time the teeth are exposed to the sugar.

Encourage children to brush their teeth after meals. If that's not possible, they should at least floss and brush their teeth once a day. Be sure children brush their teeth after eating sticky foods.

Children should be drinking fluoridated water. Find out whether your water supply has fluoride. Bottled waters have differing levels, too.

Never send a child to bed with a bottle, unless it has plain water in it.

20 Non-Candy Items That Children Love . . .

They will feel perfectly at home in trick-or-treat bags, Christmas stockings, piñatas, Easter baskets, or as holiday gifts and favors.

Stickers	Playing cards
Pencils and pens	Coins
Erasers	Stamps for collecting
Tiny farm animals	Colorful socks
Pocket-size cars	Movie passes
Small books	Crayons
Music tapes	Note pads
Small bouncing balls	Dime-store jewelry
Jacks	Hair ornaments
Tangerines or other small fruits	Individual packets of sunflower seeds or nuts

Diarrhea

Diarrhea has been defined as the passage of frequent, watery stools. There are some children who have bowel movements that are normal for them but look like diarrhea, just as some children have bowel movements so infrequently that their parents think they're constipated. Parents and caregivers have to determine what is normal for a particular child. In addition to being a bother, to say the least, diarrhea can affect a child's nutritional status. And what a child is eating can sometimes be a cause of diarrhea.

Acute Diarrhea

Usually caused by a viral or bacterial infection called enteritis, acute diarrhea may be accompanied by fever and vomiting. It can be a serious problem for infants or very young children because they can become dehydrated. Consequently, many parents use glucose-electrolyte maintenance beverages such as Pedialyte® to replace fluids lost from vomiting, diarrhea, and fever. These beverages are readily available in supermarkets and drug stores, but *they should be used only as advised by a physician. They are not meant to be substitutes for feeding.* Parents and caregivers often make the mistake of waiting too long to resume feeding a child who has had a bout with enteritis. While eating *may* cause more stool volume, the child actually does gain some value from the food.

Here's what the American Academy of Pediatrics recommends:

- Don't feed the child if he is vomiting a lot, has significant dehydration, or his abdomen is swollen (call the doctor!).

- When there is no vomiting or dehydration, resume feeding the child.

  Infants can usually tolerate breast milk well.

  Some infants need to drink lactose-free formula for a few days, but most will do fine with their regular formula.

  The child should be offered a normal diet, though fatty foods and foods high in sugar are best avoided.

  Keep the child's fluid intake high.

Chronic Nonspecific Diarrhea

Also called "toddler diarrhea," this condition can occur any time between 6 months and 5 years of age. The child will have 4 or 5 stools a day, 4 or 5 days out of a month, yet have no specific diseases and exhibit normal growth and development. Chronic nonspecific diarrhea isn't particularly dangerous, but it is messy, and in some cases dietary changes can help solve the problem. After the child's physician has ruled out parasites or infections that need treatment, it may be worth experimenting with diet rather than waiting for the child to outgrow the condition.

- Susceptible children can get diarrhea when fat is restricted too severely in their diets. Fat slows down the digestive process, so adding some fat to the diets of these children may alleviate the diarrhea.

- Children may also develop diarrhea when they're allowed to drink excessive amounts of juice or sweetened liquids. Some children seem to have a sensitivity to the sugars in juices and will get diarrhea when they drink even modest amounts. Apple, pear, and grape juice have all been found to cause sugar malabsorption in some children.

- It's a good idea to avoid serving foods with artificial sweeteners to children because these may contribute to diarrhea.

It is usually not necessary to restrict dairy products, eggs, or wheat in the diets of children with chronic diarrhea; in fact, children risk nutrient deficiencies when such restrictions are applied without careful planning.

Diabetes and Other Chronic Diseases

The purpose of this section is not to give you specific instructions about caring for children with diabetes or other diseases. Rather, we're going to bring up some nutritional issues related to diabetes and suggest ways to handle them.

Parents and caregivers are usually very concerned about doing the right thing for a child with a chronic health condition, as they should be. Things go better, however, when they are neither intimidated nor overprotective. It's important to follow a medical treatment plan while allowing the child to take increasing responsibility for himself and enjoy being as much like other children as possible.

While chronic health conditions vary, common nutritional issues are bound to come up when caring for children who have them:

- It can be difficult to follow a prescribed dietary plan without interfering with a child's decisions about the kinds and amounts of foods to eat.

- Children generally detest being treated differently from other children, and they will probably resent having to eat special foods.

- Children with chronic diseases need to learn self-care skills; this includes making appropriate food choices in unsupervised situations.

- These children may eat forbidden foods—or not eat at all—in an attempt to manipulate their parents' and caregivers' behavior.

Diabetes

About one in every 600 children develops diabetes, usually the "insulin-dependent" form of the disease. Most people produce the hormone insulin, which moves glucose (sugar) from the blood into the cells of the body, where it can be used for energy. People with diabetes either don't produce insulin, or the insulin they do produce isn't effective. So the glucose stays in the bloodstream, while the cells are starved for fuel. High blood sugars can have serious short- and long-term consequences.

Treatment of insulin-dependent diabetes generally involves (1) injections of insulin to make up for what's lacking in the body, (2) a food plan formulated to avoid very high or very low blood sugars and to provide the nutrients for normal growth and development, and (3) a program of exercise, which helps stabilize blood sugars and maintain normal weight.

In order to care for a child with diabetes, you will need to know:

- The symptoms of **hypoglycemia** (low blood sugar) and **ketoacidosis** (the result of high blood sugars), and what to do about them

- How to plan meals and snacks—the types of food offered, the amounts, and the timing. The diabetic diet is basically the same healthy diet we recommend for everyone!

- When necessary, how to help the child test blood sugars and inject insulin

- How to help the child manage her exercise regime

Cystic Fibrosis

Cystic fibrosis is an inherited glandular disease. It affects digestion and absorption, causes the loss of vital minerals in perspiration, and can lead to chronic lung infections. Treatment may include pancreatic enzyme replacement for better digestion and antibiotics to fight infections.

Children with cystic fibrosis don't always get the nourishment from food they need to grow well. They may require extra calories, specially formulated fats that they can absorb, extra salt when they've been sweating a lot, and vitamin and mineral supplements.

Inborn Errors of Metabolism

Some children are born without the enzymes needed to handle particular food elements such as sugars and amino acids. Toxic levels of these elements can build up in the blood, causing damage to the nervous system and hindering growth. Phenylketonuria (PKU), galactosemia, and fructose intolerance are examples of inborn errors of metabolism that call for strict dietary modifications. Often special formulas and food products are necessary.

Acquired Immune Deficiency Syndrome (AIDS)

Children with AIDS may have a number of medical problems that make it difficult for them to eat enough and for their bodies to make use of what they do eat. They need high-calorie, high-protein foods. Often, their foods must be modified to reduce irritation; for example, nonacidic foods are necessary when a child has sores in her mouth. Food safety is always important in child care, but it takes on a new dimension when caring for someone who is so highly susceptible to food poisoning. We recommend that you call on a registered dietitian who specializes in AIDS if you will be caring for a child with the condition.

Children with Chronic Diseases . . . Nutrition Guidelines

When it is possible to arrange it, parents and child care providers can benefit from receiving training *together* in the care of children with chronic health conditions. That way there can be a better understanding and coordination of efforts.

Avoid making a big deal out of serving special foods. Try to plan meals and snacks that *everyone* can eat. When you must enforce restrictions, be matter-of-fact about it and serve an enjoyable substitute.

Allow the child as much control in the feeding situation as you can. Even when their range of options is limited, children still like to make decisions about what they're going to eat. Teach the child to recognize foods that contain "forbidden" ingredients. Allow the child to participate in planning menus.

Enlist the other children as "buddies" who can alert you to signs of low blood sugar in their friend or who can help the child stick to her regimen.

Eating Disorders

Lots of parents consider their children to be problem eaters. It's normal for children to go through periods of lagging appetites, pickiness, and preferring candy bars to vegetables. But occasionally a child's eating problem is serious enough to be called an *eating disorder.* It may manifest itself as failure to thrive, obesity, excessive pickiness, or monumental struggles between the child and the parent or caregiver about eating. (What we usually think of as eating disorders—anorexia nervosa and bulimia—don't show up until adolescence or later.)

Child feeding expert Ellyn Satter stresses that an eating disorder consists of a severe disturbance in eating or feeding accompanied by an emotional problem. There are lots of circumstances in which eating disorders can develop, from too much pressure to eat more or less food, to problems in the parents' marital relationship. When adults begin to exercise an inappropriate amount of control over a child's eating, when the situation is highly charged emotionally, and when no one is willing to change, it's time to see a therapist. The underlying emotional issues need to be resolved before eating can return to normal.

Helping to Prevent Eating Disorders

It's important for a family to be functioning well and for the individual family members to be emotionally healthy.

Adults should be role models for healthy attitudes toward eating and body image.

The child should be supported in following his own internal sense of food regulation. Parents and caregivers should neither withhold food from a child nor force a child to eat.

Teach the child to feel good about herself, no matter what body size and shape she has acquired.

Food-Drug Interactions

Rare is the child who at some time doesn't receive medication for an illness. She may need antibiotics for a short time for an infection, or she may require long-term drug therapy for asthma or seizures. Many people are unaware that foods and medications can interact to produce unwanted effects. This is especially important for children, because they may suffer longer from their illnesses or experience poor growth and nutrient deficiencies if the food-drug interactions aren't taken into account.

Foods can alter the effectiveness of a drug by:

- Reducing or increasing the amount of the drug absorbed
- Changing the way the drug is used in the body
- Causing more or less of the drug to be excreted in the urine

Drugs can affect a child's nutritional state by:

- Changing the way foods taste and smell
- Increasing or reducing appetite
- Causing nausea, vomiting, or diarrhea
- Changing the amounts of nutrients that are absorbed
- Altering the way nutrients are used in the body
- Causing more or less of a nutrient to be excreted in the urine

**When You Must Administer
Medications to a Child, Ask:**

Whether the drug should be taken with food
or on an empty stomach

If any foods should be *avoided*

If any nutrients should be *emphasized*

*Call a pharmacist if you have any questions
about food-drug interactions.*

Junk Food

We try not to label foods as "good" or "bad." Instead, we look for "good eating habits" and "bad eating habits." Good eating habits provide the necessary nutrients in appropriate amounts to maintain well-being. Bad eating habits do not.

It's hard to think of any foods that would actually be harmful for most children to eat *once in a while.* But it's easy to name dozens of foods that have little nutritional value and could lead to health problems if consumed *frequently.* These are what concerned adults call "junk foods," and they are characteristically high in sugar, salt, or fat. Candy, cookies, sodas, and snack chips are examples.

Parents and caregivers have valid concerns regarding the following:

- Frequent consumption of sugary foods can cause tooth decay.

- Eating a lot of junk foods can give a child less appetite for the truly nutritious foods he needs for growth.

- It's easy to take in too many calories when eating foods high in fat and sugar (however, research has *not* shown that overweight children eat any more high-calorie foods than do thinner children).

The problem is, children don't look at the situation this way. They don't worry about developing nutrient deficiencies; they just know they like to eat foods that taste good.

The sweetness or saltiness of junk foods makes them particularly appealing. Babies are born with a preference for sweet flavors, and children can acquire a taste for salt, even cravings for it, when they've habitually eaten salty foods. Children also want to eat what the other kids are eating.

Adults and children can get into some major battles over junk foods. Parents and caregivers who are sincerely trying to provide good nutrition for kids may prohibit them from eating these foods. What usually happens next isn't too surprising: the forbidden foods become *very* attractive. Have you noticed how children whose parents never allow them to eat foods with sugar go absolutely wild over sweets at parties and at their grandparents' houses?

Yes, it's true that we don't *need* junk foods. Most of us are better off without them, especially as we grow older and more sedentary and as our caloric needs go down. But because it is unlikely that sweet, fatty, and salty foods are going to disappear anytime soon, and because many people find them enjoyable, the reasonable thing to do is teach children how to work them into an otherwise healthful way of eating.

As we said earlier, eating a piece of candy every now and then is not likely to do harm; it's when candy is providing a significant portion of a child's calories that nutritional problems will occur. You can maintain your commitment to good nutrition *and* allow children to experience an occasional cupcake or handful of snack chips.

- The best way to teach children how to manage junk foods is to serve them occasionally without any more fuss than you would for carrot sticks or cheese slices. If the children ask why they can't have these foods more often, just let them know that they aren't as good for them as other foods, but they're okay once in a while.

- Minimize the damage by making your own nutritious versions of junk foods. You can make cookies with less sugar, muffins instead of frosted cupcakes, or baked potato sticks rather than french fries. Think about the attributes of junk foods when you're concocting substitutes for them; most junk foods are at least one of the following: sweet, salty, crunchy, bubbly, eaten with the fingers, or served in individual portions in some kind of cute packaging. Fight back! Use your imagination!

- Emphasize the other celebratory aspects of holidays and birthdays besides eating. Plan lots of games, songs, storytelling, and similar activities. Give prizes and party favors that aren't candy (see page 223).

- *Never* use food as a reward for good behavior or as consolation for upsets and injuries.

- Be careful about the amount of time children spend watching television. It's hard for kids *not* to be interested in nutritionally questionable foods when confronted with dazzling advertising.

Lactose Intolerance

Lactose is a form of sugar found in almost all animal milks, including human milk. If a person doesn't have the enzymes in the small intestine to digest lactose (which is the case for *most* adults in the world), it goes into the large intestine, where bacteria cause it to ferment. This fermentation process results in acids and gases that can cause abdominal cramps, flatulence, and diarrhea.

Children can generally handle the lactose in dairy products until they're about 5 or 6 years old. After that, their tolerance to lactose will depend upon heredity. (Scientists tell us that northern Europeans, Hungarians, members of the Fulani and Tussi tribes in Africa, the Punjabi from India, and perhaps Mongolians are able to digest lactose as adults. The rest of the world's peoples cannot, unless they can count some of these "lactose digesters" among their ancestors.)

A physician can test for lactose tolerance. If a child is lactose intolerant, you will need to change what you're feeding him:

- Many people with lactose intolerance can digest fermented dairy products: yogurt, hard cheese, cottage cheese, and acidophilus milk.

- Enzyme preparations such as Lactaid® can be added to milk; they "predigest" the lactose.

- Some children can tolerate regular milk if they simply drink smaller portions more frequently.

- If a child is unable to tolerate *any* dairy products, be sure to offer him foods rich in the nutrients he'll be missing, such as calcium.

Low-Fat Diets and Children

Several health organizations have made dietary recommendations aimed at reducing our risks of heart disease, cancer, and stroke. Common to all of them is the advice to limit fat intake to no more than 30% of calories, to cut the saturated fat in our diets to 10% of calories or less, and to eat an average of no more than 300 mg cholesterol daily. Many adults are taking these recommendations seriously—eating less red meat, taking the skin off their chicken, and switching from whole milk to low-fat or nonfat milk. And they're wondering if it's okay to do the same for their children.

There's been a lot of research into the relationship between lifestyle factors (including diet) and heart disease. Some of the findings have led experts to recommend low-fat diets for children:

- In countries where adults have high rates of heart disease, both children and adults have higher blood cholesterol levels than in countries where the incidence of heart disease is low.

- People from countries where heart disease rates and blood cholesterol levels are lower tend to eat less saturated fat and cholesterol than people from countries with higher heart disease rates.

- Children develop fatty streaks in their blood vessels, which *may* develop into the lesions of atherosclerosis, at an early age. Autopsies show that children with lesions have higher levels of LDL (low density lipoprotein—"bad") cholesterol and VLDL (very low density lipoprotein—also "bad") cholesterol in their blood.

- Children with high fat intakes are more likely to have serum cholesterol levels in the middle or high range.

Health experts disagree, sometimes heatedly, on the implications of these findings. Questions that need to be settled are: Does what children eat (or does having high blood cholesterol) affect their chance of getting chronic diseases like atherosclerosis when they're adults? Will making the recommended changes in diet actually lower blood cholesterol levels enough to affect the risk of disease? And will restricting fat in their diet lead to poor growth or nutrient deficiencies?

In some cases, fears about children on low-fat diets have been justified. There have been reports of children who suffered growth failure because their parents limited the fats in their diets too severely. With professional nutritional guidance, children on low-fat diets can thrive. But without guidance, children usually replace the lost fat calories with sugar calories. Even when they get enough calories for growth, they may lack the vitamins and minerals that are essential for health and development.

No doubt the controversy will continue; meanwhile, the best argument for providing low-fat foods to children is that eating patterns and preferences are formed in childhood. It isn't necessary to count every gram of fat a child takes in; what's important is that he learns while he's young to enjoy eating poultry, seafood, low-fat dairy products, whole grains, fruits, and vegetables. It will be much harder to change his eating habits when he's an adult.

This book contains many suggestions for reducing fat and saturated fat in the foods you serve. You'll find that many changes are easy to make. Keep in mind that there are other risk factors for heart disease that are important to work on during childhood—and adolescence, too—such as obesity, lack of physical fitness, and cigarette smoking.

- *Never* restrict fat in the diet of a child younger than 2 years old.

- Don't restrict fat in the diet of a child who is underweight and a fussy eater.

- Avoid getting too involved in what children are eating. Offer healthful choices, but don't hover over them, monitoring every pat of butter or slice of cheese.

- Children may need to eat more often, because foods low in fat aren't satisfying for long, and because they may not be able to eat enough at regular mealtimes to get the calories they require.

- Be a good role model for a healthy lifestyle, conscientious without being fanatic. You've heard the old saying: Too much worrying about your health can be bad for your health.

Overweight Children

Our society is obsessed with thinness. And in the midst of this obsession, more and more children are becoming overweight, or to be more precise, obese. (*Obesity* is excessive body fat, versus *overweight*, in which excessive weight could be coming from heavy bones, large muscles, *or* too much fat. We will use the terms somewhat interchangeably, because heavy children have certain problems regardless of where their weight comes from.)

Heavy children are likely to be viewed as unlikeable or lacking in self-control. They may suffer from a poor self-image and a sense of failure, and they usually feel pressure to lose weight by dieting. Whether they will be obese as adults generally depends on how long they've been obese, how obese they are, and whether or not they are obese as adolescents. In truth, *we have no way of knowing* whether a particular child will be obese when she reaches adulthood.

Adult health problems associated with obesity include high blood pressure, respiratory diseases, gallstones, orthopedic conditions, and diabetes. (It's worth noting, however, that some obese adults are quite healthy.) During childhood, it's generally believed that obesity causes more social and psychological problems than physical ones.

Why are some people obese? Basically, they have taken in more calories than their bodies can use, so the leftovers are stored as fat. But contrary to popular belief, obese people don't necessarily eat more than thinner ones. There are no simple explanations for why some people gain excess fat and others don't, but here are some of the possible reasons:

- Heredity

- Lack of physical activity

- The composition of the diet (calories from fat appear to be stored as fat more easily than calories from other sources)

- Slower metabolism, which is largely inborn but may be influenced by such factors as repeated attempts at weight loss or the number of daily meals

- Overeating, which may be the result of:

  > Eating too fast
  >
  > Being out of touch with true feelings of hunger
  > and satisfaction
  >
  > Eating in response to stress or traumatic events

Unfortunately, concerned adults sometimes use tactics with overweight children that cause more serious problems than the overweight itself. Putting pressure on children about their weight can lead to:

- Obsession with food, dieting, and body image

- Lowered self-esteem and an overwhelming sense of failure

- Damage to the adult-child relationship due to protracted struggles over food choices, food quantities, and exercise

The most common mistake that parents and some physicians make is to put children on restricted diets. For one thing, as mentioned earlier, not all overweight children are big eaters. Limiting their calories may interfere with normal growth and development. Furthermore, children who aren't allowed to eat until they feel satisfied, or to eat the foods that they enjoy, may feel deprived and singled out; such children tend to become obsessed with eating. And when adults exert too much control over what children eat, the children never learn to manage eating for themselves.

Overweight children are victims of other ill-advised tactics. One mother told us of the humiliation her daughter felt when her upper-arm fatfold measurements were read aloud to her sixth-grade class. And this very conscientious young student received a failing grade in her gym class because she couldn't quite run a mile. Can you imagine how this girl might feel about her body and exercise when she grows up, thanks to these early experiences? Forcing the exercise issue can be just as counterproductive as restricting food intake.

We aren't advocating letting children—overweight or not—eat whatever they want, whenever they want. And we don't think children should be encouraged to spend all of their free time in front of the television set, either. Adults are *supposed* to be in charge of the kinds of foods that are offered to children and the timing of meals and snacks. And adults *should* set limits on sedentary activities like watching television—for everyone, including themselves.

Helping an overweight child, or preventing a child from becoming overweight, involves setting up the best situation you can for nurturing, feeding, and active play, then trusting the child to make her own decisions within that structure. Recognize that you don't *know* how a child's body will turn out when she's older, nor do you need to subscribe to society's rather limited view of what constitutes the "ideal body."

What You Can Do to Help an Overweight Child

- *Foster a positive self-image.* Let him know he's loveable and has something valuable to contribute, no matter how his body turns out.

- *Encourage lots of physical activity.* Provide plenty of opportunities for active play. Set limits on sedentary activities like watching television—for everyone, not just the overweight child.

- *Promote healthful eating habits.* Serve healthful foods at regular times and let the child make his own decisions regarding eating.

- *Attend to emotional health.* If the child has unmet emotional needs or is dealing with trauma, make sure he gets the help he requires.

- *Be a good role model.* Eat healthfully without falling into the "dieting trap." Stay active and value yourself.

Pesticides and Other Chemicals in Our Food

Consumers are told that the American food supply is the safest in the world, yet many of us are uncomfortable with the idea of "all those chemicals" in our food. Some of these fears seem to be justified; others are not. After all, even "natural" foods are made up of chemicals; for that matter, so are our bodies.

Not all "natural" chemicals are good for us, just as not all synthetic chemicals are bad. Most of us can accept that. What we resent are the invisible substances, which could cause cancer, birth defects, or other problems, and may be lurking in our foods without having good reason to be there!

Much of the furor over contaminants in foods surrounds pesticide residues. The Alar "scare" in 1989 brought the issue of pesticides in foods to public attention in a big way. Parents, especially, are concerned about the dangers their children might face while eating the very fruits and vegetables that are supposed to be so *good* for them. Meanwhile, respected scientists continue to debate the hazards and virtues of pesticides. To stimulate your thinking (and inquiring), we summarize the points of controversy for you.

Experts who feel that pesticide residues in our foods are of grave danger to our health assert that:

- Many of the ingredients in pesticides have not been tested thoroughly for their toxic effects or their effects in combination with other chemicals.

- The Food and Drug Administration has established tolerated amounts or "action levels" for only a fraction of the chemicals in our food.

- Action levels are set with the assumption that a consumer eats a certain amount of a food *per year*, which may be quite unrealistic.

- Many pesticides aren't detected by the tests now in use.

- Imported foods may contain residues of pesticides that are banned in the United States, despite testing of samples on entry to the country.

- Children face greater risks from pesticides because:

    Relative to their body weight, they eat and drink more of the foods likely to have high levels of contaminants (fruit and apple juice, for example).

    They're more susceptible to the effects of toxins and cancer-causing substances, because their body cells are dividing rapidly, and their immune systems are immature.

    They will be living longer than people who are adults now, so cancer will have a longer time to show up in their bodies.

The Food Quality Protection Act of 1996 requires the collection of sufficient information on infants' and children's food consumption to accurately determine the risk of pesticide residues to their health. Government agencies and scientists are trying to resolve some other issues, as well, such as how much to rely on tests with animals when determining chemical safety.

There are scientists who feel that the risks from pesticides are exaggerated. They argue that:

- We eat a lot more natural pesticides, those that are made by plants in self-defense, than synthetic ones, and at least half of these natural compounds may be able to cause cancer.

- We have general bodily defenses against *all* toxins, no matter what their source.

- Tolerance levels for pesticides are set with huge margins of safety.

- Many fruits and vegetables contain substances that probably prevent cancer, and the benefits from these foods outweigh the risks.

- Consumers may not be able to afford enough fruits and vegetables if the more "natural" methods increase their cost.

Although health experts disagree on the extent of the hazards posed by pesticide residues, they do agree that it's better to go ahead and eat fruits and vegetables than to avoid them out of fear. There are steps you can take to minimize your exposure to pesticides. We'll outline them for you at the end of this section.

Food (and water) may contain other contaminants as well. Fungal poisons, heavy metals like lead and mercury, industrial chemicals, animal hormones and antibiotic residues, chemicals that migrate into food from packaging, and food colorings, flavorings, and many other food additives have the potential to cause health problems. Some of this contamination occurs naturally; some is the outcome of poorly handled industrial waste, agricultural practices, and consumer demand for foods that taste and look a certain way. Changes will be needed in industrial practices and governmental enforcement to solve some of these problems.

You don't have to feel like a victim, however; you can do a lot to make sure the foods you serve are as safe as possible. For one thing, realize that one of the greatest dangers we face is food poisoning from bacteria or viruses—often a product of our *own* mishandling of food. Serve a wide variety of foods and "spread out" the potential contaminants. Seek out foods that are organically grown or free of artificial colorings and flavorings. Remember, you "vote" with your shopping dollars! Know where your food comes from; avoid, for example, buying fish caught in polluted waters. You can keep yourself informed about these issues by subscribing to such publications as the *Nutrition Action Healthletter* or writing to:

Americans for Safe Food
1501 16th St., NW
Washington, DC 20036

How to Minimize Your Exposure to Pesticides

Buy produce that is grown organically or with Integrated Pest Management.

Buy produce grown in the United States, especially broccoli, bell peppers, melons, cauliflower, green beans, tomatoes, and cucumbers. The produce manager at your market should be able to tell you where such items were grown.

Wash fruits and vegetables in water to which you've added a few drops of dishwashing detergent; use a scrub brush and rinse well.

Peel produce that has been waxed; it's obvious when cucumbers have been waxed, but apples, bell peppers, citrus fruits, eggplants, tomatoes, sweet potatoes, and squash may be waxed as well. Stores *should* have a sign letting consumers know when produce has been waxed.

Trim the fat from meat, poultry, and fish. These foods, as well as butter, lard, cheese, and whole milk, may contain *more* pesticide residues than produce! That's because pesticides tend to accumulate in fat.

Peas and dried beans usually have the lowest levels of pesticide residues. Serve them often! Besides, they're very nutritious and inexpensive.

Plant a garden and grow your own. Better yet, let the children do it.

Sodium

Sodium is an essential mineral for the functioning of our bodies. However, the amount we need is actually very small compared to the amount many of us consume. The sodium in our food is primarily in the form of **sodium chloride,** or table salt; a teaspoon of salt contains about 2,300 milligrams of sodium. Some sodium is also contributed by additives like sodium bicarbonate (baking soda) and monosodium glutamate (MSG). Only about 10% of the sodium in our foods is naturally present; the rest is added during cooking and at the table (15% of our total intake) and during food manufacturing (75% of intake). Cereals and baked goods, processed meats, and dairy products are the major sources of sodium in the American diet.

Many consumers have been trying to cut down on salt consumption because of evidence that connects sodium with high blood pressure. In truth, most people don't develop high blood pressure from eating a lot of salt. But it's impossible to predict who will and who won't, so health authorities recommend moderation in sodium intake for everyone.

It has not been proven that children get high blood pressure from eating a lot of salt, but it is clear that a preference for salty foods can be cultivated by eating them frequently. This could lead to problems later on, if these children grow up to be some of the adults who *do* develop hypertension as the result of salt sensitivity. It makes sense, then, to exercise moderation in the use of salt and foods high in sodium when feeding children. They should learn to enjoy the natural taste of foods.

We've provided suggestions for reducing salt during your food preparation earlier in this book (p. 77). And many tasty reduced-sodium versions of favorite foods have appeared on supermarket shelves in response to consumer demand!

Although specific guidelines for children's sodium intake aren't yet available, most health experts advise that we all keep our daily sodium intake below about 2,400 milligrams.

Sodium Content of Foods Children Commonly Eat

Food	Serving	Sodium (mg)
Corn flake cereal	1 oz.	351
Shredded wheat biscuits	1 oz.	3
Tomato soup	10 oz.	1,050
Tomato juice	8 oz.	744
Milk	8 oz.	130
Orange juice	8 oz.	2
Low-fat cottage cheese	1/2 cup	435
Processed American cheese	1 oz.	238
Cheddar cheese	1 oz.	190
Plain low-fat yogurt	1 cup	159
Beef hot dog	1	425
Bologna	2 slices	450
Tuna, water-packed	2 oz.	312
Chicken breast, roasted	2 oz.	42
Peanut butter	2 T.	167
Canned baked beans	1 cup	810
Canned spaghetti and meatballs	7.5 oz.	1,000
Pizza	1 slice	500–1,000
Fast-food deluxe hamburger	1	1,510
Cheese goldfish crackers	10	117
Pretzel	1	54
Butter-flavored crackers	3	97
Tortilla chips	1 oz.	99
Dill pickle	2 oz.	700
Mustard	1 T.	212
Ketchup	1 T.	154
Mayonnaise	1 T.	80

Sources: Sodium Scoreboard, Center for Science in the Public Interest, 1501 16th St., NW, Washington, DC 20036; "Wrap-Up: Sodium," University of California, Berkeley, *Wellness Letter* 2:4, 1986.

Special Needs and Feeding

Children with developmental or physical disabilities are prone to the same nutritional problems that affect their peers: obesity, iron-deficiency anemia, underweight, and tooth decay. Their risks of nutrient deficiencies and excesses are greater, however, because they may have trouble eating or have altered nutrient requirements. And it can be more difficult for a child with disabilities to develop the self-esteem that comes, among other things, from successfully managing eating.

Nutrition-related concerns that may arise when a child has developmental delays or physical handicaps include:

- An increased requirement for calories, due to medications, diseases, or central nervous system damage

- A decreased requirement for calories, due to inactivity, slow metabolism, or medications; this can lead to obesity

- Drug-nutrient interactions, which may change vitamin needs

- Lack of sensation of hunger or satiety in some children with central nervous system damage

- Feeding difficulties, which include

    Limited sucking ability (infants)
    Inability to sit up and balance the head
    Lack of strength or control in the arms and wrists
    Difficulty coordinating biting, chewing, and swallowing
        without choking or drooling
    Difficulty grasping utensils or removing food from them
    Excessive gagging and vomiting
    Extreme sensitivity to food temperatures

- Constipation, resulting from slowed bowel action, inactivity, lack of fiber in the diet, or inadequate fluids

It can be quite a challenge to manage your feeding relationship with a child who has a disability. She will go through the same developmental sequence of eating skills and behaviors that you would expect of any child, but she will probably do it more slowly. It may be very tempting to feed her only the foods that she can eat very easily, or not to let her feed herself because she makes such a mess. It might also be tempting to try to make her eat more or eat less when you are concerned about how she's growing.

Children with handicaps are entitled to, and need, the benefits of good nutrition as much as any other children. They are also entitled to progress as far as possible in their development, to have as much control over their lives as they can, and to be treated respectfully, with consideration for their feelings and comfort. It is outside of the scope of this book to teach you the specifics of feeding children with special needs, but we will give you some general guidelines:

- Allow the child to eat foods of progressively more challenging textures as he appears able.

  Avoid prolonged use of bottle feeding.
  Be alert for cues (they may be subtle) that the child is ready for solid foods and coarser textures.

- Help the child to develop self-feeding skills.

  Don't feed a child if he is at all capable of feeding himself.
  Make sure the child is comfortable; supports for his head, arms, trunk, or feet may be necessary so that he can sit upright.
  He may need adaptive feeding equipment.
  Take it step by step, allowing the child to experience success before moving on to more difficult skills.

- Respect the child's preferences regarding types and amounts of food eaten (from what *you* offer, of course), pace of eating, and even whether he will eat.

- Avoid overindulgence with sweet foods and unlimited snacking. Children with handicaps need limits, too.

- Find out if any of the child's medications interact with nutrients.

- When you would like training or you're having problems feeding a child with special needs, seek out professionals in your community who can help: occupational therapists, physical therapists, speech therapists, dietitians, and behavior modification specialists. See Appendix E for more information.

Sugar, Food Additives, and Children's Behavior

Parents exchange knowing looks when a mother describes how her darling child turned into a monster during the days following Halloween. And teachers fear that birthday-party cupcakes will send an entire class into a hyperkinetic frenzy. Don't blame it on the sugar . . . all kids get "wild" sometimes!

Between 1% and 5% of children have **attention deficit disorder (ADD)** and may have hyperactivity. This disorder is characterized by restlessness, distractibility, impulsive behavior, and a low tolerance for frustration. No one really knows what causes it. But desperate, exhausted parents sometimes wonder if there might be something to all this talk about sugar and food additives, especially food colorings.

Despite the popularity of the Feingold diet in the 1970s, it has been very hard for scientists to prove a link between dietary components and hyperactivity. When a child's diet is changed, his behavior may improve because his parents expect it to. Or there might be changes in family dynamics. Maybe the child feels better because he's eating a more nourishing diet than he was before.

The majority of research trials in which neither the parents, the child, nor the observers knew whether the child received sugar (or an additive) or a placebo have failed to find a connection between dietary components and behavior. Some studies have even indicated that sugar has a calming effect on children! In fairness, we must say that a few research studies have found that a *very* small number of children do respond to sugar or additives with behavior changes. The results of one study, albeit a small one, suggest that children's hormones may respond differently from adults' to large doses of sugar on an empty stomach.

Most health experts believe that there are other reasons why children get "hyper" after they've eaten sugar, such as the general excitement or fatigue that accompanies celebrations. Maybe they become super-excited about being able to indulge in otherwise "forbidden" treats.

It's a good idea to consult a physician before imposing an unnecessarily restrictive diet on a child. Diets completely free of sugar and food additives can be a lot of work for the adults and traumatic for the child. At the same time, there are good reasons for limiting the amounts of sugar and additives in the foods you serve. Frequent sugar intake causes tooth decay. Eating lots of sugary foods can displace other more nutritious foods in the diet, leading to borderline nutrition. And while some food additives seem to be safe, there are questions about the safety of others, including some coloring agents, nitrates, nitrites, and saccharin. Many additives, especially colorings, can be easily avoided.

There are other aspects of children's food patterns that *can* have effects on their behavior. They are:

- **Nutrient deficiencies.** Deficiencies of most nutrients will affect behavior. The most common deficiency in the United States is iron deficiency. The brain is very sensitive to a lack of iron, and this can have profound effects: fatigue, distractibility, irritability, reduced tolerance for challenging tasks, and headaches.

- **Skipping meals.** Children need to eat at least every 4 to 6 hours to supply their brains with needed glucose. Children who skip breakfast or other meals tend to be irritable and unable to concentrate on the tasks at hand. That's why midmorning snacks are a good idea, and why kids should eat their breakfast!

- **Caffeine.** Caffeine is often overlooked as a source of "wild" behavior in children. But for a child's size, a 12-ounce can of cola can contain the caffeine equivalent to 3 or 4 cups of coffee for an adult.

- **Food allergies.** Although most allergists don't believe that food allergies themselves can cause behavior problems, a child who feels miserable because of allergy symptoms is likely to be difficult to manage.

This sounds like the same old-fashioned advice we heard when we were children, but there really is no substitute for regular, well-balanced meals and snacks, regular sleep, and regular exercise. It's a good idea to monitor television viewing, too; many of the shows children enjoy are violent and overstimulating. Sometimes the simplest interventions are the last ones we consider. Consider them first!

A Common-Sense Approach to Dealing with Children and Sugar

Never use sweet foods as a reward for eating other parts of a meal or for "good" behavior.

When serving sugary foods, make them part of a meal or snack containing protein (milk with a cookie, for example).

Sweet foods should also have some nutritional value, that is, contain some protein, fiber, vitamins, and/or minerals.

Serve snacks other than sweets regularly.

Reduce sugar intake when possible.

Have children brush their teeth after eating sweet foods.

Television

The average child in the United States spends more time watching television than in any other activity except sleeping. It is estimated that 2- to 5-year-olds watch 25 hours of television per week, children aged 6 to 11 watch 22 hours per week, and adolescents watch 23 hours per week. How all of this television viewing affects a child will depend upon what she sees and for how long she sees it. Television can have a *huge* impact on children's nutrition, as you will see.

Here's what nutritionists don't like about television:

- It's a sedentary activity.

- Children see about 25,000 commercials a year, of which about half promote foods of low nutritional value. Younger children are particularly inclined to believe claims that the products being advertised are *good* for them.

- It encourages children to manipulate their parents' purchasing decisions at the grocery store.

- It is conducive to mindless snacking.

- It can hinder social interaction at mealtimes.

- It has been associated with obesity, high blood cholesterol levels, low levels of physical fitness, and lowered metabolic rate. (Note: "Association" doesn't necessarily mean "proof of cause.")

Television does have its good features, however:

- It can be a source of useful information presented in a way that is very attractive to children.

- It can be a trigger for talking about nutrition and health behaviors.

Watching television may not be an option in your home or child care center. If it is, there are ways you can emphasize its positive aspects and downplay the negative ones.

Television and Good Nutrition *Can* Be Friends

Be selective about what children are watching. Some stations make more of an effort to present nutrition-friendly messages than do others.

Watch television *with* the children. Talk about the eating and health behaviors portrayed on the programs. Discuss the ways consumers can be misled by advertising.

Limit viewing time. Balance passive activities like television watching with physical activity.

Don't allow children to eat while they watch television.

Underweight Children

Some children are destined to be small. Others have the potential to grow larger or grow more quickly, but for some reason they don't. Sometimes in our weight-conscious society we get very concerned about a child who is overweight, yet fail to notice when a child isn't growing as well as she could. Faltering growth can be a serious problem, with many causes:

- Some children require more calories for their size than others, due to heredity or activity, and caregivers may underestimate their food needs.

- Children may eat poorly because they are exceedingly finicky, can't handle sitting at the table for long, are resistant to what they perceive as pressure to eat, or suffer from anxiety or depression.

- Children can exhibit poor growth when their parents severely restrict fat or calories in their diets.

- Children may have limited self-feeding skills or difficulty chewing and swallowing the food that is offered.

- Certain disease processes can interfere with growth.

A child who is lagging in her growth should be evaluated by a physician, of course, and treatments vary. You as a parent or caregiver can do much to help the underweight child:

- Make sure that you provide a supportive and attractive environment for eating.

- Provide regular meals and snacks, including foods the child enjoys, *with no pressure* on the child to eat.

- Check to make sure there's enough fat in the child's diet.

- Observe whether the child has any problems with chewing or swallowing the foods you offer; you may be offering foods too advanced for the child, or she may need professional help.

- Be alert to signs that the child is anxious, withdrawn, or depressed; therapy may be in order.

- Accept the child's body, no matter how she turns out.

Vegetarianism

People may choose not to eat meat, or any foods of animal origin, for religious, health, ethical, or political reasons. Much of the world's population is vegetarian for economic reasons. Some vegetarians eat no meat, poultry, or fish but do eat eggs and dairy products (**lacto-ovo-vegetarians**); some avoid eggs as well (**lacto-vegetarians**); and some eat no animal products whatsoever (**vegans**).

A vegetarian diet can't guarantee good health, just as eating meat doesn't guarantee poor health. But vegetarians do seem to enjoy some health benefits, including lower blood cholesterol levels, lower blood pressure, and less risk of osteoporosis, gallstones, and diabetes. In the past, many child-health experts expressed concern as to whether vegetarian diets were beneficial for children, but now most agree that a well-planned lacto-ovo- or lacto-vegetarian diet is compatible with normal growth and development.

Vegan diets are viewed with more concern. Researchers have found that vegan children tend to be shorter and lighter than other vegetarians or children who eat meat, though they fall within the normal range of growth. By the age of 10 years, vegan children tend to catch up in height, but remain lighter than children on mixed diets. There have been a few horror stories of rickets, vitamin B_{12} deficiencies, and outright malnutrition among vegan children, but usually their parents were using misguided feeding practices or the breastfeeding mothers had dietary deficiencies.

Vegan diets are typically high in fiber and low in calories; it can be difficult for a small child to eat enough to satisfy her calorie requirements. Fiber can hinder the absorption of iron, calcium, and zinc. The transition from breast milk or formula to solid foods is an especially vulnerable time for vegan children. Inadequate protein, calcium, essential fatty acids, riboflavin, iron, zinc, vitamin D, or vitamin B_{12} are potentially matters of concern in a vegan diet, especially if the child is a picky eater and rejects good sources of these nutrients.

It's quite simple to work out an adequate diet for a child who eats dairy products and eggs. Planning to meet the needs of the vegan child requires considerably more effort.

Meal Planning for Vegan Children

Use soy or rice milk or formula fortified with vitamins D and B_{12}.

Use cooked dried beans, nuts and nut butters, and seeds as meat alternates (high in protein).

Tofu can be a good source of calcium, but only if it is made with calcium sulfate—check the label. Corn tortillas (made with lime) and greens such as kale, bok choy, and collards are also high in calcium. Calcium-fortified orange juice or soy or rice milk is another option.

Serve foods rich in vitamin C at meals to enhance iron absorption.

Children may require more frequent meals and snacks because vegan meals tend to be filling but low in calories.

Consider serving eggs and dairy products to very young children or children who are picky eaters and not growing well (with parental approval, of course).

For excellent discussions of vegetarian meal planning and delicious recipes, we highly recommend *The New Laurel's Kitchen,* by Laurel Robertson, Carol Flinders, and Brian Ruppenthal, published by Ten Speed Press, Berkeley, California.

Vitamin and Mineral Supplements

More than half of preschool- and school-age children receive multivitamin/ mineral supplements. Often these children aren't the ones who could really benefit from them.

Parents usually give vitamin and mineral supplements to their children because they feel the need for insurance against the ups and downs of their children's appetites. Some use supplements as alternatives to conventional medical therapy for a variety of health problems. For some children supplements may be helpful, for others they are harmless but a waste of money, and for others they can cause significant problems. It's important to know this about vitamin and mineral supplements:

- It isn't necessarily true that if a little of a nutrient is good, more is better; some nutrients are toxic at high doses, and they may interfere with the body's ability to use other nutrients. Children who are on megavitamin or megamineral therapy need close monitoring by their health care providers.

- Vitamin and mineral supplements can give parents a false sense of security about their children's diets. Supplements contain only a fraction of the many nutrients needed for health.

- Children can get the message that pills, not nutritious foods, are necessary for growing into healthy adulthood.

- Children have mistaken vitamin or mineral tablets for candy and have suffered fatal overdoses.

The American Academy of Pediatrics has determined that most children don't need vitamin or mineral supplements. Those who probably do are:

- Children whose diet is significantly limited because of severe allergies, developmental delays, feeding problems, or poor appetite

- Children living in neglectful or abusive situations

- Children who follow a vegan diet

- Pregnant teenagers

Having said all this, we know that despite our best efforts, many children still don't eat enough fruits and vegetables, and a basic multivitamin/mineral tablet may take some pressure off the feeding situation. Parents who decide to give their children vitamin or mineral supplements should treat them as medications and keep them out of the reach of young children. Keep offering fruits and vegetables. And unless instructed otherwise by a physician, it's best to avoid giving a supplement that contains more than 100% of the RDA for any nutrient.

Appendix D
References

Chapter One
What You Should Know About Feeding Children

Birch, L. L., Johnson, S. L., and Fisher, J. A. Children's eating: The development of food acceptance patterns. *Young Children* Jan: 71, 1995.

The Relationship Between Nutrition and Learning: A School Employee's Guide to Information and Action. Washington, DC: National Education Association of the United States, 1989.

Satter, E. *How to Get Your Kid to Eat . . . But Not Too Much.* Palo Alto: Bull Publishing Company, 1987.

Sombke, L. How our meals have changed. *USA Weekend,* November 11–13, 1988.

Story, M., and Brown, J. E. Do children instinctively know what to eat? The studies of Clara Davis revisited. *New England Journal of Medicine* 316: 103, 1987.

U.S. Department of Health and Human Services, Public Health Service, *The Surgeon General's Report on Nutrition and Health.* Washington, DC: U.S. Government Printing Office, 1988.

Chapter Two
Feeding and Growth

Beal, V. The preschool years (one to six). In *Nutrition in the Life Span.* New York: John Wiley & Sons, 1980.

Committee on Nutrition, American Academy of Pediatrics. Follow-up or weaning formulas. *Pediatrics* 83: 1067, 1989.

Committee on Nutrition, American Academy of Pediatrics. The use of whole cow's milk in infancy. *Pediatrics* 72: 253, 1983.

Committee on Nutrition, American Academy of Pediatrics. The use of whole cow's milk in infancy. *Pediatrics* 89: 1105, 1992.

DeBruyne, L. K., and Rolfes, S. R. Focal point 3: Dental health. *Life Cycle Nutrition: Conception Through Adolescence.* St. Paul: West Publishing Company, 1989.

DeBruyne, L. K., and Rolfes, S. R. Infants: A nurtured beginning. *Life Cycle Nutrition: Conception Through Adolescence.* St. Paul: West Publishing Company, 1989.

Exchange Lists for Meal Planning. The American Diabetes Association, Inc., and The American Dietetic Association, 1986.

Fomon, S. J. Reflections on infant feeding in the 1970s and 1980s. *American Journal of Clinical Nutrition* 46: 171, 1987.

Food and Nutrition Service. *Feeding Infants: A Guide for Use in the Child Care Food Program.* Washington, DC: U.S. Department of Agriculture, 1988.

Gortmaker, S. L., Dietz, W. H., and Cheung, L. W. Y. Inactivity, diet, and the fattening of America. *Journal of the American Dietetic Association* 90: 1247, 1990.

Hagan, J. Out of the jar or homemade: What's best for baby and when? *Environmental Nutrition* 13: 1, 6–7, 1990.

Keating, J. P., Schears, G. J., and Dodge, P. R. Oral water intoxication in infants: An American epidemic. *American Journal of Diseases of Children* 145: 985, 1991.

Leach, P. *Your Baby and Child from Birth to Age Five,* 2nd ed. Alfred Knopf, 1995.

Morgan, K. J., and Zabik, M. E. Amount and food sources of total sugar intake by children ages 5 to 12 years. *American Journal of Clinical Nutrition* 34: 404, 1981.

Nelms, B. C., and Mullins, R. G. *Growth and Development: A Primary Health Care Approach.* Englewood Cliffs, NJ: Prentice Hall, 1982.

Pediatric Nutrition Handbook. Elk Grove Village, IL: American Academy of Pediatrics, 1993.

Pipes, P. L. Infant feeding and nutrition. *Nutrition in Infancy and Childhood,* 5th ed. St. Louis: Times Mirror/Mosby College Publishing, 1993.

Pipes, P. L., and Trahms, C. M. Nutrition: Growth and development. *Nutrition in Infancy and Childhood,* 5th ed. St. Louis: Times Mirror/Mosby College Publishing, 1993.

———. The preschool-age child. *Nutrition in Infancy and Childhood,* 5th ed. St. Louis: Times Mirror/Mosby College Publishing, 1993.

Radbill, S. X. Infant feeding through the ages. *Clinical Pediatrics* 20: 613, 1981.

Redel, C. A., and Shulman, R. J. Controversies in the composition of infant formulas. *Pediatric Clinics of North America* 41(5): 909, 1994.

Satter, E. *Child of Mine: Feeding with Love and Good Sense.* Palo Alto: Bull Publishing Company, 1991.

———. *How to Get Your Kid to Eat . . . But Not Too Much.* Palo Alto: Bull Publishing Company, 1987.

Chapter Three
Planning How and What to Feed Children

American Public Health Association and American Academy of Pediatrics. *Caring for Our Children: National Health and Safety Performance Standards—Guidelines for Out-of-Home Child Care Programs.* Washington, DC: APHA and Elk Grove, IL: AAP, 1992. See especially pp. 115–139.

Bedinghaus, J. B., and Doughten, S. Childhood nutrition: From breastmilk to burgers. *Primary Care* 21: 655, 1994.

Child Care Food Program. *Simplified Buying Guide: 1992 Edition.* Sacramento: California State Department of Education, 1992.

Deutsch, R. M., and Morrill, J. S. *Realities of Nutrition.* Palo Alto: Bull Publishing Company, 1993.

Nutrition Division, Calgary Health Services. *Day Care Nutrition and Food Service Manual.* Calgary, Alberta: Calgary Health Services, 1988.

Pipes, P. L. Infant feeding and nutrition. *Nutrition in Infancy and Childhood,* 5th ed. St. Louis: Times Mirror/Mosby College Publishing, 1993.

Resnicow, K. The relationship between breakfast habits and plasma cholesterol levels in schoolchildren. *Journal of School Health* 61: 81, 1991.

Satter, E. The feeding relationship. *Child of Mine: Feeding with Love and Good Sense.* Palo Alto: Bull Publishing Company, 1991.

U.S. Department of Agriculture and U.S. Department of Health and Human Services. *Nutrition and Your Health: Dietary Guidelines for Americans,* 4th ed. Washington, DC: U.S. Government Printing Office, 1995.

Chapter Six
Running a Ship-Shape Kitchen

Bailey, J. *Keeping Food Fresh.* New York: Harper & Row, 1989.

Blume, E. Germ wars: Cleaning up our food. *Nutrition Action Healthletter* 13(6): 1, 1986.

Blumenthal, D. An unwanted souvenir . . . lead in ceramic ware. *FDA Consumer,* December 1989–January 1990.

Duyff, Roberta Larson. *The American Dietetic Association's Complete Food and Nutrition Guide.* Minneapolis: Chronimed, 1996.

Farley, D. Keeping up with the microwave revolution. *FDA Consumer,* March 1990.

Hillman, H. *Kitchen Science,* revised ed. Boston: Houghton Mifflin Company, 1989.

How safe is the microwave for kids? *American Health,* September 1990.

Kurtzwell, P. Labeling rules for young children's food. *FDA Consumer,* March 1995.

Large microwave ovens. *Consumer Reports,* November 1990.

Lefferts, L. Y., and Schmidt, S. Microwaves: The heat is on. *Nutrition Action Healthletter* 17:1, 1990.

Microwave heating of infant formula and breast milk. *Child Health Alert,* July 1990.

Miller, R. Mother Nature's regulations on food safety. *FDA Consumer,* April 1988.

Satter, E. Diarrhea. *Child of Mine: Feeding with Love and Good Sense.* Palo Alto: Bull Publishing Company, 1991.

Shugart, Grace, and Molt, Mary. *Food for Fifty,* 9th ed. New York: Macmillan Publishing Company, 1993.

Sunset Microwave Cookbook. Menlo Park, CA: Lane Publishing, 1981.

U.S. Department of Agriculture, Human Nutrition Information Service. *Shopping for Food and Making Meals in Minutes Using the Dietary Guidelines.* Washington, DC: U.S. Government Printing Office, 1989.

Willis, J. L. (ed.). *FDA Consumer Special Report: Focus on Food Labeling.* Rockville, MD: Food and Drug Administration, 1993.

Chapter Seven
Environmental Concerns

Dadd, D. L. *Nontoxic and Natural: How to Avoid Dangerous Everyday Products and Buy or Make Safe Ones.* Los Angeles: Jeremy Tarcher, Inc., 1984.

———. *The Nontoxic Home.* Los Angeles: Jeremy Tarcher, Inc., 1986.

Earthworks Group. *50 Simple Things Kids Can Do to Save the Earth.* Kansas City: Andrews and McMeel, 1990.

———. *The Recycler's Handbook: Simple Things You Can Do.* Berkeley: Earthworks Press, 1990.

Earthworks Group and PG&E. *30 Simple Energy Things You Can Do to Save the Earth.* Berkeley: Earthworks Press, 1990.

Elkington, J., Hailes, J., Hill, D., and Makower, J. *Going Green: A Kid's Handbook to Saving the Planet.* New York: The Penguin Group, 1990.

Hadingham, E., and Hadingham, J. *Garbage! Where It Comes From, Where It Goes.* New York: Simon and Schuster, Inc., 1990.

Heloise. *Heloise: Hints for a Healthy Planet.* New York: The Putnam Publishing Group, 1990.

Kimbrell, A. C. Environmental house cleaning. *The Green Lifestyle Handbook: 1001 Ways You Can Heal the Earth.* New York: Henry Holt & Co., 1990.

Lamb, M. *2 Minutes a Day for a Greener Planet: Quick and Simple Things Americans Can Do to Save the Earth.* New York: Harper & Row Publishers, Inc., 1990.

MacEachern, D. *Save Our Planet: 750 Everyday Ways You Can Help Clean Up the Earth.* New York: Dell Publishing, 1990.

Morris, D. A materials policy from the ground up. *The Green Lifestyle Handbook: 1001 Ways You Can Heal the Earth.* New York: Henry Holt & Co., 1990.

Smith, K. Home economics. *The Green Lifestyle Handbook: 1001 Ways You Can Heal the Earth.* New York: Henry Holt & Co., 1990.

Appendix A
A Basic Scheme for Nutrition Education

Christakis, G. (ed.). *Nutritional Assessment in Health Programs.* Washington, DC: American Public Health Association, Inc., 1973.

Duyff, R. L. *The American Dietetic Association's Complete Food and Nutrition Guide.* Minneapolis: Chronimed, 1996.

Standing Committee on the Scientific Evaluation of Dietary Reference Intakes, Food and Nutrition Board, Institute of Medicine. *Dietary Reference Intakes: Calcium, Phosphorus, Magnesium, Vitamin D, and Fluoride.* Washington, DC: National Academy Press, 1997 (Prepublication Copy).

Appendix C
Special Topics

Allergies to Foods

Bock, S. A. Prospective appraisal of complaints of adverse reactions to foods in children during the first 3 years of life. *Pediatrics* 79: 683, 1987.

Bock, S. A., and Sampson, H. A. Food allergy in infancy. *Pediatric Clinics of North America* 41: 1047, 1994.

Cant, A. J. Food allergy in childhood. *Human Nutrition: Applied Nutrition* 39A: 277, 1985.

Levine, E. Food allergies: Cause for concern or over-diagnosed malady? *Environmental Nutrition* 12(11): 1, 1989.

Pipes, P. Special concerns of dietary intake during infancy and childhood. *Nutrition in Infancy and Childhood,* 4th ed. St. Louis: Times Mirror/Mosby College Publishing, 1989.

Roesler, T. A., Barry, P. C., and Bock, S. A. Factitious food allergy and failure to thrive. *Archives of Pediatric and Adolescent Medicine* 148: 1159, 1994.

Roesler, T. A., Bock, S. A., and Leung, D. Y. M. Management of the child presenting with allergy to multiple foods. *Clinical Pediatrics* Nov: 608, 1995.

Anemia and Iron Deficiency

Florentino, R. F., and Guirriec, R. M. Prevalence of nutritional anemia in infancy and childhood with emphasis on developing countries. *Iron Nutrition in Infancy and Childhood.* New York: Nestle, Vevey/Raven Press, 1984.

Fomon, S. J. Reflections on infant feeding in the 1970s and 1980s. *American Journal of Clinical Nutrition* 46: 171, 1987.

Kline, N. A practical approach to the child with anemia. *Journal of Pediatric Health Care* 10: 99, 1996.

Oski, F. A. Iron deficiency—facts and fallacies. *Pediatric Clinics of North America* 32: 493, 1985.

———. Iron deficiency in infancy and childhood. *New England Journal of Medicine* 329: 190, 1993.

The Relationship Between Nutrition and Learning: A School Employee's Guide to Information and Action. Washington, DC: National Education Association, 1989.

Satter, E. Feeding the toddler. *Child of Mine: Feeding with Love and Good Sense.* Palo Alto: Bull Publishing Company, 1991.

Calcium and Osteoporosis

Abrams, B., and Berman, C. Women, nutrition, and health. *Current Problems in Obstetrics, Gynecology, and Fertility* 16: 1, 1993.

Fassler, A. L. C., and Bonjour, J. P. Osteoporosis as a pediatric problem. *Pediatric Clinics of North America* 42: 811, 1995.

Meyer, M., and Larson, E. Osteoporosis and the vegetarian diet. *Vegetarian Journal* Nov/Dec: 8, 1995.

Norris, J. M., Beaty, B., Klingensmith, G., Yu, L., Chase, H. P., Erlich, H. A., Hamman, R. F., Eisenbarth, G. S., and Rewers, M. Lack of association between early exposure to cow's milk protein and b-cell autoimmunity. Diabetes Autoimmunity Study for the Young (DAISY). *The Journal of the American Medical Association* 276: 609, 1996.

Standing Committee on the Scientific Evaluation of Dietary Reference Intakes, Food and Nutrition Board, Institute of Medicine. *Dietary Reference Intakes: Calcium, Phosphorus, Magnesium, Vitamin D, and Fluoride.* Washington, DC: National Academy Press, 1997 (Prepublication Copy).

Thomas, L. F., Keim, K. S., Long, E. M., and Zaske, J. M. Factors related to low milk intake of 3- to 5-year-old children in child care settings. *Journal of the American Dietetic Association* 96: 911, 1996.

Wyshak, G., and Frisch, R. E. Carbonated beverages, dietary calcium, the dietary calcium/phosphorus ratio, and bone fractures in girls and boys. *Journal of Adolescent Health* 15: 210, 1994.

Choking on Food

Food and Nutrition Service. *Feeding Infants: A Guide for Use in the Child Care Food Program.* Washington, DC: U.S. Department of Agriculture, 1988.

Harris, C. S., Baker, S. P., Smith, G. A., and Harris, R. M. Childhood asphyxiation by food: A national analysis and overview. *Journal of the American Medical Association* 251: 2231, 1984.

Marin Child Care Council (formerly Project Care for Children). *Childhood Emergencies— What to Do: A Quick Reference Guide.* Palo Alto: Bull Publishing Company, 1987.

Pipes, P. L., and Trahms, C. M. The preschool-age child. *Nutrition in Infancy and Childhood,* 5th ed. St. Louis: Times Mirror/Mosby College Publishing, 1993.

Constipation

Conference on Dietary Fiber in Childhood, New York, May 24, 1994. A summary of conference recommendations on dietary fiber in childhood. *Pediatrics* 96(5): 1023, 1995.

Dwyer, J. T. Dietary fiber for children: How much? *Pediatrics* 96(5): 1019, 1995.

Hillemeier, C. An overview of the effects of dietary fiber on gastrointestinal transit. *Pediatrics* 96(5): 997, 1995.

McClung, H. J., Boyne, L., and Heitlinger, L. Constipation and dietary fiber intake in children. *Pediatrics* 96(5): 999, 1995.

Rappaport, L. A., and Levine, M. D. The prevention of constipation and encopresis: A developmental model and approach. *Pediatric Clinics of North America* 33: 859, 1986.

Saldanha, L. Fiber in the diet of U.S. children: Results of national surveys. *Pediatrics* 96(5): 994, 1995.

Williams, C. L., and Bollella, M. Is a high-fiber diet safe for children? *Pediatrics* 96(5): 1014, 1995.

Williams, C. L., Bollella, M., and Wynder, E. L. A new recommendation for dietary fiber in childhood. *Pediatrics* 96(5): 985, 1995.

Dental Health

DeBruyne, L. K., and Rolfes, S. R. Focal point 3: Dental health. In *Life Cycle Nutrition: Conception Through Adolescence.* St. Paul: West Publishing Company, 1989.

Diabetes and Other Chronic Diseases

Diet for cystic fibrosis. *Manual of Clinical Dietetics.* Chicago: The American Dietetic Association, 1988.

Inborn errors of metabolism. *Manual of Clinical Dietetics.* Chicago: The American Dietetic Association, 1988.

Pipes, P., and Glass, R. Developmental disabilities and other health care needs. *Nutrition in Infancy and Childhood,* 5th ed. St. Louis: Times Mirror/Mosby College Publishing, 1993.

Satter, E. Feeding the child with special needs. *How to Get Your Kid to Eat . . . But Not Too Much.* Palo Alto: Bull Publishing Company, 1987.

Siminerio, L. M., and Betschart, J. *Children with Diabetes.* Alexandria, VA: The American Diabetes Association, Inc., 1986.

Diarrhea

Cohen, S. A., Hendricks, K. M., Eastham, E. J., Mathis, R. K., and Walker, W. A. Chronic non-specific diarrhea, a complication of dietary fat restriction. *American Journal of Diseases in Childhood* 133: 490, 1979.

Committee on Nutrition, American Academy of Pediatrics. Use of oral fluid therapy and posttreatment feeding following enteritis in children in a developed country. *Pediatrics* 75: 358, 1985.

Green, H. L., and Ghishan, F. K. Excessive fluid intake as a cause of chronic diarrhea in young children. *Journal of Pediatrics* 102: 836, 1983.

Hyams, J. S., Etienne, N. L., Leichtner, A. M., and Theuer, R. C. Carbohydrate malabsorption following fruit juice ingestion in young children. *Pediatrics* 82: 64, 1988.

Hyams, J. S., and Leichtner, A. M. Apple juice: An unappreciated cause of chronic diarrhea. *American Journal of Diseases in Childhood* 139: 503, 1985.

Kneepkens, C. M. F., and Hoekstra, J. H. Chronic nonspecific diarrhea of childhood: Pathophysiology and management. *Pediatric Clinics of North America* 43: 375, 1996.

Lloyd-Still, J. D. Chronic diarrhea of childhood and the misuse of elimination diets. *Journal of Pediatrics* 95: 10, 1979.

Nutritional management of diarrhea in childhood. *Manual of Clinical Dietetics.* Chicago: The American Dietetic Association, 1988.

Provisional Committee on Quality Improvement, Subcommittee on Acute Gastroenteritis, American Academy of Pediatrics. Practice parameter: The management of acute gastroenteritis in young children. *Pediatrics* 97: 424, 1996.

Satter, E. Diarrhea. *Child of Mine: Feeding with Love and Good Sense.* Palo Alto: Bull Publishing Company, 1991.

Eating Disorders

Satter, E. Eating disorders. *Child of Mine: Feeding with Love and Good Sense.* Palo Alto: Bull Publishing Company, 1991.

———. Eating disorders. *How to Get Your Kid to Eat . . . But Not Too Much.* Palo Alto: Bull Publishing Company, 1987.

Food-Drug Interactions

Powers, D. E., and Moore, A. O. *Food Medication Interactions.* Phoenix: F-M I Publishing, 1986.

Junk Food

Accounting for taste. *University of California at Berkeley Wellness Letter* 7: 7, 1990.

Satter, E. Nutritional tactics for preventing food fights. *How to Get Your Kid to Eat . . . But Not Too Much.* Palo Alto: Bull Publishing Company, 1987.

Shapiro, L. R., Crawford, P. B., Clark, M. J., Pearson, D. J., Ray, J., and Huenemann, R. L. Obesity prognosis: A longitudinal study of children from the age of 6 months to 9 years. *American Journal of Public Health* 74: 968, 1984.

Lactose Intolerance

Committee on Nutrition, American Academy of Pediatrics. Practical significance of lactose intolerance in children: Supplement. *Pediatrics* 86: 643, 1990.

Low-Fat Diets and Children

Committee on Diet and Health, Food and Nutrition Board, National Research Council. Recommendations. *Diet and Health Implications for Reducing Chronic Disease Risk.* Washington, DC: National Academy Press, 1989.

Committee on Nutrition, American Academy of Pediatrics. Prudent life-style for children: Dietary fat and cholesterol. *Pediatrics* 78: 521, 1986.

Committee on Nutrition, American Academy of Pediatrics. Statement on cholesterol. *Pediatrics* 90: 469, 1992.

Gaull, G. E., Giombetti, T., and Yeaton Woo, R. W. Pediatric dietary lipid guidelines: A policy analysis. *Journal of the American College of Nutrition* 14: 411, 1995.

Gidding, S. S., Deckelbaum, R. J., Strong, W., and Moller, J. H. Improving children's heart health: A report from the American Heart Association's Children's Heart Health Conference. *Journal of School Health* 65: 129, 1995.

Lifshitz, F., and Moses, N. Growth failure: A complication of dietary treatment of hypercholesterolemia. *American Journal of Diseases in Childhood* 143: 537, 1989.

National Cholesterol Education Program. Report of the expert panel on blood cholesterol levels in children and adolescents. *Pediatrics* 89 (suppl.): 525, 1992.

Newman, W., Freedman, D. S., and Voors, A. W. Relation of serum lipoprotein levels and systolic blood pressure to early atherosclerosis. *New England Journal of Medicine* 314: 138, 1986.

Nicklas, T. A., Webber, L. S., Johnson, C. C., Srinivasan, S. R., and Berenson, G. S. Foundations for health promotion with youth: A review of observations from the Bogalusa heart study. *Journal of Health Education* 26 (suppl.): S18, 1995.

Nicklas, T. A., Webber, L. S., Koshak, M., and Berenson, G. S. Nutrient adequacy of low fat intakes for children: The Bogalusa heart study. *Pediatrics* 89: 221, 1992.

Olson, R. E. The dietary recommendations of the American Academy of Pediatrics. *American Journal of Clinical Nutrition* 61: 271, 1995.

Pugliese, M. T., Weyman-Daum, M., Moses, N., and Lifshitz, F. Parental health beliefs as a cause of nonorganic failure to thrive. *Pediatrics* 80: 175, 1987.

Tershakovec, A. M., Shamiz, R., Van Horn, L., and Shannon, B. Dietary recommendations for children. *American Journal of Clinical Nutrition* 62: 443, 1995.

Overweight Children

Gortmaker, S. L., Dietz, W. H., and Cheung, L. W. Y. Inactivity, diet, and the fattening of America. *Journal of the American Dietetic Association* 90: 1247, 1990.

Hermann, M. *EN* speaks with obesity expert. *Environmental Nutrition* 13: 1, 1990.

Liebman, B. Calories don't count . . . equally. *Nutrition Action Healthletter* 16(1): 8, 1989.

Peck, E. B., and Ullrich, H. D. *Children and Weight: A Changing Perspective.* Berkeley: Nutrition Communications Associates, 1988.

Satter, E. Helping all you can to keep your child from being fat. *How to Get Your Kid to Eat . . . But Not Too Much.* Palo Alto: Bull Publishing Company, 1987.

Satter, E. Internal regulation and the evolution of normal growth as the basis for prevention of obesity in children. *Journal of the American Dietetic Association* 96: 860, 1996.

Pesticides and Other Chemicals in Our Food

American Dietetic Association. Position statement: Food and water safety. *Journal of the American Dietetic Association* 97: 184, 1997.

Ames, B. Dietary carcinogens and anticarcinogens. *Science* 221: 1256, 1983.

Lefferts, L. Pass the pesticides. *Nutrition Action Healthletter* 16: 1, 1989.

Marwick, C. Pesticides pose concern about children's diet. *Journal of the American Medical Association* 270: 802, 1993.

Montgomery, A. America's pesticide-permeated food. *Nutrition Action Healthletter* 14: 1, 1987.

Sodium

Food and Nutrition Board, National Research Council. *Recommended Dietary Allowances.* Washington, DC: National Academy of Sciences, 1989.

Sodium Scoreboard. Washington, DC: Center for Science in the Public Interest.

U.S. Department of Agriculture and U.S. Department of Health and Human Services. *Nutrition and Your Health: Dietary Guidelines for Americans,* 4th ed. Washington, DC: U.S. Government Printing Office, 1995.

Wrap-Up: Sodium. *University of California at Berkeley Wellness Letter* 2: 4, 1986.

Special Needs and Feeding

Pipes, P., and Glass, R. Developmental disabilities and other health care needs. *Nutrition in Infancy and Childhood,* 5th ed. St. Louis: Times Mirror/Mosby College Publishing, 1993.

Satter, E. Feeding the child with special needs. *How to Get Your Kid to Eat . . . But Not Too Much.* Palo Alto: Bull Publishing Company, 1987.

Sugar, Food Additives, and Children's Behavior

Bachorowski, J., Newman, J. P., Nichols, S. L., Gans, D. A., Harper, A. E., and Taylor, S. L. Sucrose and delinquency: Behavioral assessment. *Pediatrics* 86: 244, 1990.

Kaplan, B. J., McNichol, J., Conte, R. A., and Moghadam, H. K. Dietary replacement in preschool-aged hyperactive boys. *Pediatrics* 83: 7, 1989.

Rowe, K. S., and Rowe, K. J. Synthetic food coloring and behavior: A dose response effect in a double-blind, placebo-controlled, repeated-measures study. *Journal of Pediatrics* 125: 691, 1994.

Sugar may jolt adrenaline in kids. *Environmental Nutrition* 13(7): 3, 1990.

Whitney, E. N., Cataldo, C. B., and Rolfes, S. R. Nutrition and behavior. *Understanding Normal and Clinical Nutrition.* St. Paul: West Publishing Company, 1988.

Wolraich, M. L., Lindgren, S. D., Stumbo, P. J., Stegink, L. D., Appelbaum, M. I., and Kiritsy, M. C. Effects of diets high in sucrose or aspartame on the behavior and cognitive performance of children. *New England Journal of Medicine* 330: 301, 1994.

Wolraich, M. L., Wilson, D. B., and White, J. W. The effect of sugar on behavior or cognition in children: A meta-analysis. *Journal of the American Medical Association* 274: 1617, 1995.

Television

Committee on Communications, American Academy of Pediatrics. Children, adolescents, and television. *Pediatrics* 85: 1119, 1990.

Committee on Communications, American Academy of Pediatrics. The commercialization of children's television. *Pediatrics* 89: 343, 1992.

DuRant, R. H., Baranowski, T., Johnson, M., and Thompson, W. O. The relationship among television watching, physical activity, and body composition of young children. *Pediatrics* 94: 449, 1994.

Klesges, R. C., Shelton, M. L., and Klesges, L. M. Effects of television on metabolic rate: Potential implications for childhood obesity. *Pediatrics* 91: 281, 1993.

Promoting Nutritional Health During the Preschool Years: Canadian Guidelines. Network of the Federal/Provincial/Territorial Group on Nutrition and National Institute of Nutrition, 1989.

Schmidt, S. Hawking food to kids. *Nutrition Action Healthletter* 16: 1, 1989.

Sylvester, G. P., Achterberg, C., and Williams, J. Children's television and nutrition: Friends or foes? *Nutrition Today* 30: 6, 1995.

Taras, H. L., and Gage, M. Advertised foods on children's television. *Archives of Pediatric and Adolescent Medicine* 149: 649, 1993.

Trahms, C. Factors that shape food patterns in young children. *Nutrition in Infancy and Childhood*, 5th ed. St. Louis: Times Mirror/Mosby College Publishing, 1993.

TV, kids' cholesterol linked. *San Francisco Chronicle,* November 14, 1990.

Underweight Children

Satter, E. The child who grows poorly. *How to Get Your Kid to Eat . . . But Not Too Much.* Palo Alto: Bull Publishing Company, 1987.

Vegetarianism

O'Connell, J. M., Dibley, M. J., Sierra, J., Wallace, B., Marks, J. S., and Yip, R. Growth of vegetarian children: The farm study. *Pediatrics* 84: 475, 1989.

Saunders, T. A. B. Vegetarian diets and children. *Pediatric Clinics of North America* 42: 955, 1995.

Trahms, C. Vegetarian diets for children. *Nutrition in Infancy and Childhood,* 5th ed. St. Louis: Times Mirror/Mosby College Publishing, 1993.

Vitamin and Mineral Supplements

American Academy of Pediatrics, Committee on Nutrition. Vitamin and mineral supplement needs of normal children in the United States. *Pediatrics* 66: 1015, 1980.

Appendix E

Resources

Publications

General Nutrition

*The American Dietetic Association's
    Complete Food and Nutrition Guide*
    by Roberta Larson Duyff.
    Minneapolis: Chronimed, 1996.

Jane Brody's Nutrition Book by Jane Brody.
    Toronto: Bantam Books, 1987.

The New Laurel's Kitchen by L. Robertson,
    C. Flinders, and B. Ruppenthal.
    Berkeley: Ten Speed Press, 1986.

Nutrition Action Healthletter
    Center for Science in the Public Interest
    1875 Connecticut Avenue, NW
    Suite 300
    Washington, DC 20009-5728
    (202) 332-9110
    Current nutrition research and
    consumer issues; also great recipes.

Tufts University Diet and Nutrition Letter
    P. O. Box 57857
    Boulder, CO 80322-7857
    (800) 274-7581

Consumer Information Catalog Booklets,
    contact:
    Superintendent of Documents
    Consumer Information Center-T
    P. O. Box 100
    Pueblo, CO 81002
    (719) 948-4000
    http://www.pueblo.gsa.gov

*University of California at Berkeley
    Wellness Letter*
    Wellness Letter Subscription Department
    P. O. Box 420148
    Palm Coast, FL 32142
    (800) 829-9080
    Nutrition, fitness, and stress management
    newsletter.

The Vegan Handbook, edited by Debra
    Wasserman and Reed Mangels, Ph.D.
    The Vegetarian Resource Group
    P. O. Box 1463
    Baltimore, MD 21203
    (410) 366-8343

Child Nutrition

Caring for Our Children. National Health and Safety Performance Standards: Guidelines for Out-of-Home Child Care Programs. American Public Health Association and American Academy of Pediatrics. Washington, DC (APHA) and Elk Grove, IL (AAP), 1992.

Child of Mine: Feeding with Love and Good Sense by Ellyn Satter, RD, MS, MSSW. Palo Alto: Bull Publishing Company, 1991.

How to Get Your Kid to Eat . . . But Not Too Much by Ellyn Satter, RD, MS, MSSW. Palo Alto: Bull Publishing Company, 1987.

The Relationship Between Nutrition and Learning: A School Employees' Guide to Information and Action
National Education Association
Human and Civil Rights
1201 Sixteenth Street, NW
Washington, DC 20036
(800) 229-4200
Nutrition and optimum learning; how schools can make sure all children have access to good nutrition.

Tiny Tummies Nutrition News
P.O. Box 2171
Sausalito, CA 94966
(415) 389-6494
Written by a registered dietitian, this monthly newsletter offers nutrition information for parents and children.

Allergies

Allergy Products Directory
Prologue Publications
P. O. Box 640
Menlo Park, CA 94026
Listings for food products and their sources.

Caring and Cooking for the Allergic Child by Linda Thomas. New York: Sterling Publishing, 1980.

Coping with Food Allergy by Claude A. Frazier, M.D. Revised ed. New York: Times Books, 1985.
Good information on food allergies with extensive recipe section.

Dairy-Free Cookbook by Jane Zukin. Rocklin, CA: Prima Publishing, 1991.

Delicious Milk-Free Recipes
Loma Linda Foods
11503 Pierce Street
Riverside, CA 92515

Gluten-Free Diet
National Celiac-Sprue Society
5 Jeffrey Road
Wayland, MA 01778

Tasty Rice Recipes for Those with Allergies
Rice Council of America
P. O. Box 74021
Houston, TX 77274

Breastfeeding Support

Breastfed Babies Welcome Here! A Guide for Childcare Providers
U.S. Department of Agriculture
(703) 305-2554

"Guidelines for Breastfeeding Promotion and Support in Child Care"
Pamphlet available through the Colorado Child and Adult Care Food Program
(303) 692-2400

Diabetes

American Diabetes Association, Inc.
Diabetes Information Service Center
1660 Duke Street
Alexandria, VA 22314
(800)ADA-DISC
Local affiliates can also provide information.

Diabetes Mellitus—A Practical Handbook by Sue K. Milchovich, RN, BSN, CDE, and Barbara Dunn-Long, RD. Palo Alto: Bull Publishing Company, 1990.

Everyone Likes to Eat: How Children Can Eat Most of the Foods They Enjoy and Still Take Care of Their Diabetes, 2nd ed., by Hugo J. Hollerorth, Ed.D., and Debra Kaplan, RD, MS. Minneapolis: Chronimed Publishing, 1993.

Exchanges for All Occasions: Meeting the Challenge of Diabetes by Marion J. Franz, RD, MS. Minneapolis: Diabetes Center, Inc., 1987.
Diabetic exchange lists, recipes, and hints for managing events like illness, travel, and children's parties.

Kids, Food, and Diabetes by Gloria Loring. Chicago: Contemporary Books, Inc., 1986. The mother of a child with diabetes, the actress/author provides guidelines, recipes, and "coping hints" for dealing with diabetes.

Prana Publications
5623 Matilija Avenue
Van Nuys, CA 91401
(800) 735-7726
Source of many self-help books for people with diabetes, including a large collection of books for children with diabetes and for their parents or caregivers.

Special Needs

American Occupational Therapy Assoc., Inc.
1383 Piccard Drive
P. O. Box 1725
Rockville, MD 20850-4375

CARE: Special Nutrition for Kids
by the Alabama State Department of Education, 1993.
Distributed through The National Food Service Management Institute
P. O. Drawer 188
University, MS 38677-0188
(800) 321-3054

Feeding Young Children with Cleft Lip and Palate
Minnesota Dietetic Association
1821 U Avenue, Suite S-280
St. Paul, MN 55104

Managing the School-Age Child with a Chronic Health Condition, Georgianna Larson, RN, PNP, MPH (ed.). Wayzata, MN: DCI Publishing, 1988.

Mealtimes for Persons with Severe Handicaps by R. Perske, A. Clifton, B. M. McLean, and J. Ishler Stein. Baltimore: Paul H. Brookes, 1986.

United Cerebral Palsy Associations, Inc.
66 East 34th Street
New York, NY 10016
(212) 481-6344

Food Safety

Educational Foundation of the National Restaurant Association
(800) 765-2122
Offers a variety of handbooks and complete training packages about food safety.

Food Safety at Home, School, and When Eating Out
The Chef and the Child Foundation, Inc.
P. O. Box 3466
St. Augustine, FL 32085
(904) 824-4468
This activity and coloring book teaches children about food safety.

For Our Kids' Sake: How to Protect Your Child Against Pesticides in Food by Anne Witte Garland. San Francisco: Sierra Club Books, 1989.

Cookbooks

Cooking Light [magazine]
  P. O. Box 830549
  Birmingham, AL 35282-9810

Eating Well [magazine]
  P. O. Box 52919
  Boulder, CO 80322-2919
  (303) 604-1464

Healthwise Quantity Cookbook by S. Turner, MPH, RD, and V. Aronowitz, MPH, RD. Washington, DC: Center for Science in the Public Interest, 1990.

Jane Brody's Good Food Book by Jane Brody. Toronto: Bantam Books, 1987.
More than 350 healthful recipes and lots of good basic nutrition information.

Microwave Diet Cookery by M. Cone and T. Snyder. New York: Simon and Schuster, 1988. How to use the microwave oven to prepare low-calorie, healthy meals.

The New Laurel's Kitchen by L. Robertson, C. Flinders, and B. Ruppenthal. Berkeley: Ten Speed Press, 1986.

Kitchen Lore

Keeping Food Fresh: How to Choose and Store Everything You Eat by Janet Bailey. Revised ed. New York: Harper & Row Publishers, 1989. Fascinating information on selecting and storing foods as well as general tips on food safety.

Kitchen Science: A Guide to Knowing the How's and Why's for Fun and Success in the Kitchen. Revised ed. Boston: Houghton Mifflin Company, 1989. Answers such questions as: How do non-stick coatings work? Why does meat get tougher as it cooks? Why does red cabbage turn bluish purple when cooked?

Social and Environmental Concerns

Anti-Bias Curriculum: Tools for Empowering Young Children by Louise Derman-Sparks and the A.B.C. Task Force. Washington, DC: National Association for the Education of Young Children, 1989. Companion video also available.

Clean and Green: The Complete Guide to Nontoxic and Environmentally Safe Housekeeping by Annie Berthold-Bond. Woodstock, NY: Ceres Press, 1994.

The Consumer Guide to Home Energy Savings
  American Council for an Energy-Efficient Economy
  1001 Connecticut Avenue, NW, #535
  Washington, DC 20036
  (202) 429-8873

Discovering the World: Empowering Children to Value Themselves, Others, and the Earth. S. Hopkins and J. Winters, eds. Philadelphia, PA: New Society Publishers, 1990.

Food First Curriculum: An Integrated Curriculum for Grade 6 by Laurie Rubin. San Francisco, CA: Institute for Food and Development Policy, 1984.

Garbage: The Practical Journal for the Environment
  P. O. Box 51647
  Boulder, CO 80321-1647
  Excellent resource for home waste reduction.

Garbage! Where It Comes From, Where It Goes by Evan Hadingham and Janet Hadingham. New York: Simon and Schuster, Inc., 1990.

Going Green: A Kid's Handbook to Saving the Planet by J. Elkington, J. Hailes, D. Hill, and J. Makower. New York: Puffin Books, 1990.

An Introductory Guide to Bilingual Bicultural/Multicultural Education: Beyond Tacos, Eggrolls, and Grits by Gloria Gomez. Dubuque: Kendall/Hunt Publishing Company, 1982.

Shopping for a Better World: The Quick and Easy Guide to Socially Responsible Supermarket Shopping
Council on Economic Priorities
30 Irving Place
New York, NY 10003-9990
(800) 822-6435
Helps consumers select products made by companies whose policies and practices they support.

Skipping Stones
Aprovecho Institute
80574 Hazelton Road
Cottage Grove, OR 97424
(503) 942-9434
Quarterly multiethnic international children's magazine.

Teaching and Learning in a Diverse World: Multicultural Education for Young Children by Patricia G. Ramsey
Toys 'n Things Press
(800) 423-8309

What Are We Feeding Our Kids? by Michael Jacobson, Ph.D., and Bruce Maxwell. New York: Workman Publishing, 1994.

50 Simple Things Kids Can Do to Recycle by The EarthWorks Group. Berkeley: EarthWorks Press, 1994. This book is full of recycling projects for children, offers clear explanations of recycling concepts, and has an extensive listing of resources for books, pamphlets, videos, and recycling curricula.

50 Simple Things Kids Can Do to Save the Earth by The EarthWorks Group. Kansas City: Andrews and McMeel, 1990.

Children's Book Press
1461 Ninth Avenue
San·Francisco, CA 94122
(415) 664-8500
A nonprofit publisher specializing in multicultural children's literature.

Kids for Saving the Earth
P. O. Box 47247
Plymouth, MN 55447-0247
(612) 559-1234
International membership organization for kids who pledge to "be a defender of my planet." Members receive certificate, resources, guidebook, and more.

Natural Resources Defense Council
40 West 20th Street
New York, NY 10011
(212) 727-2700
Special project on environmental problems affecting children. *TLC* newsletter has pull-out section for children.

Gardening with Children

Gardening Wizardry for Kids by L. Patricia Kite. New York: Barron's, 1995. Lots of activities and interesting information about plant foods.

The Growing Classroom . . . Garden-Based Science by Roberta Jaffe and Gary Appel. Menlo Park, CA: Addison-Wesley Publishing Company, 1990. A comprehensive garden-based curriculum for schools.

Nutrition Activities with Kids

Creative Food Experiences for Children by Mary T. Goodwin and G. Pollen. Revised ed. Washington, DC: Center for Science in the Public Interest, 1980. Classic guide to teaching children ages 3 to 10 about good nutrition.

Eat, Think, and Be Healthy! by Paula K. Zeller and M. Jacobsen, Ph.D. Washington, DC: Center for Science in the Public Interest, 1987. Nutrition activities and handouts for grades 3–6 with recipes for foods kids can make. Basic nutrition, smart consumerism.

I Love Animals and Broccoli by Debra Wasserman and Charles Stahler. 1985. The Vegetarian Resource Group
P. O. Box 1463
Baltimore, MD 21203
Healthy eating, caring about animals, world hunger.

Cooking with Kids

Cook and Learn: Pictorial Single-Portion Recipes by Beverly Veitch and Thelma Harms. Menlo Park: Addison-Wesley Publishing Company, 1981.

Easy Menu Ethnic Cookbooks
Lerner Publications Company
Minneapolis, MN
Cooking the African Way
Cooking the Caribbean Way
Cooking the Chinese Way
Cooking the English Way
Cooking the French Way
Cooking the German Way
Cooking the Greek Way
Cooking the Hungarian Way
Cooking the Indian Way
Cooking the Israeli Way
Cooking the Italian Way
Cooking the Japanese Way
Cooking the Korean Way
Cooking the Lebanese Way
Cooking the Mexican Way
Cooking the Norwegian Way
Cooking the Polish Way
Cooking the Russian Way
Cooking the Spanish Way
Cooking the Thai Way
Cooking the Vietnamese Way

The Healthy Start Kids' Cookbook: Fun and Healthy Recipes That Kids Can Make Themselves by Sandra K. Nissenbuerg, MS, RD. Minneapolis: Chronimed Publishing, 1994.

KidsCooking: A Very Slightly Messy Manual by the editors of Klutz Press. Palo Alto: Klutz Press, 1987.

Learning Through Play: Cooking, A Practical Guide for Teaching Young Children by Lisa Feeney. New York: Scholastic Inc., 1992. (800) 724-6527
This book is a must-have for anyone cooking with groups of children. It covers kitchen setup and safety, activity plans for cooking with healthful ingredients, and a section on cooking with children who have special needs and developmental guidelines.

Math in the Kitchen by Laura Mackey. Monterey, CA: Evan-Moor Corp., 1994. There aren't many recipes in this book, but it's an excellent example of integrating food education into the overall curriculum. From the publishers of *Math in the Garden.*

Pretend Soup and Other Real Recipes: A Cookbook for Preschoolers and Up by Molly Katzen and Ann Henderson. Berkeley: Tricycle Press, 1994.

The Travel-the-World Cookbook by Pamela Marx. Glenview, IL: GoodYearBooks, 1996.

Miscellaneous Books

The American Dietetic Association
216 W. Jackson Boulevard
Chicago, IL 60606-6995
(800) 877-1600, ext. 5000
Offers a variety of educational materials for an adult audience.

The Book Lady, Inc.
8144 Brentwood Industrial Drive
St. Louis, MO 63144
(800) 766-READ
Large selection of food-themed books
for children.

NAEYC Early Childhood Resources Catalog
1834 Connecticut Avenue, NW
Washington, DC 20009-5786
(800) 424-2460
Outstanding books, pamphlets, posters,
and more for early childhood educators
from the National Association for the
Education of Young Children.

NCES (Nutrition Counseling Education
Services)
1904 East 123rd Street
Olathe, KS 66061-5886
(800) 445-5653
Books, videos, games, and other
teaching aids.

Scholastic, Inc.
P. O. Box 7502
Jefferson City, MO 65102
(800) 724-6527
Books, videos, and professional
resources.

Toys 'n Things Press: Resources for the Early
Childhood Professional
A division of Resources for Child Caring
450 North Syndicate, Suite 5
St. Paul, MN 55104
(800) 423-8309
Excellent books and other learning
materials for adults and children.

Supplies

Earth-Friendly Products

Co-op America Catalog
2100 M Street, Suite 403
Washington, DC 20063
(202) 223-1881
Ecological products, energy-saving
devices, and more.

Ecco Bella, The Environmental Store
6 Provost Square, Suite 602
Caldwell, NJ 07006
(800) 888-5320
Nonanimal tested, biodegradable
products.

EcoSource, Products for a Safer, Cleaner
World
9051 Mill Station Road
Sebastopol, CA 95472
(800) 688-8345

Gardener's Supply
128 Intervale Road
Burlington, VT 05401
(802) 863-1700
Chemical-free pest control supplies,
composting equipment, and more.

Seventh Generation, Products for a
Healthy Planet
360 Interlocken Blvd., Ste. 300
Broomfield, CO 80021
(800) 456-1177
Energy-saving devices, ecological household cleaners, recycling supplies. Catalog
includes lots of tips.

Specialty Foods

Ener-G Foods, Inc.
5960 1st Avenue S
P. O. Box 84487
Seattle, WA 98124-5787
(800) 331-5222
Gluten-, wheat-, milk-, soy-, and corn-
free food products. Recipes also available.

Fearn Natural Foods
4520 James Place
Melrose Park, IL 60160
Baking mixes for allergy diets; found
in most health food stores.

Loma Linda Foods
11503 Pierce Street
Riverside, CA 92515
A variety of food products for
allergy diets.

Learning Materials and Toys

Animal Town
P. O. Box 485
Healdsburg, CA 95448
(800) 445-8642
Beautiful catalog of nature games,
books, cooperative games, posters,
toys, and much more.

Fisher-Price®
East Aurora, NY 14052
(800) 432-5437
Super Mart Super Cart shopping cart
comes with play money and groceries;
Magic Scan Checkout Counter and other
Fun with Food™ toys.

FOODPLAY Productions
221 Pine Street
Northampton, MA 01060
(800) FOODPLAY
Nutrition videos and guidebooks.

Hand in Hand/First Step, Ltd.
891 Main Street
Oxford, ME 04270-9711
(800) 872-9745
Items for children, including food-related
toys and some feeding equipment.

HearthSong
P. O. Box B
Sebastopol, CA 95473-0601
(800) 325-2502
Catalog of wonderful toys, crafts, books,
games, and more.

Hot Potatoes
209 10th Avenue S., Suite 311
Nashville, TN 37203
(615) 255-4055 (9–5 central time)
Nice big rubber stamps with a good
selection of foods and utensils.

Lakeshore® Learning Materials
2695 E. Dominguez Street
P. O. Box 6261
Carson, CA 90749
(800) 421-5354
Play foods (includes foods from various
cultures), kitchen equipment, child-sized
furniture, supplies for classroom cooking
projects, and more.

Lingo
UNICEF
1 Children's Boulevard
P. O. Box 182233
Chattanooga, TN 37422
(800) 553-1200
Bingo-type game in eight languages,
familiarizing children ages 3–10 with
foods around the world.

Music for Little People
P. O. Box 1460
1144 Redway Drive
Redway, CA 95560
(800) 346-4445
Children's audio- and videotapes and
musical instruments. Materials emphasize
multicultural, social, and environmental
awareness.

National School Products
101 East Broadway
Maryville, TN 37804-2498
(800) 251-9124
Stickers, videos, food replicas, computer
software, and many other educational
products. (Ask for the nutrition catalog.)

Noteworthy Creations, Inc.
P. O. Box 335
Delphi, IN 46923
(800) 305-4167
Nutrition education materials for
children.

Yummy Designs
P. O. Box 1851
Walla Walla, WA 99362
(509) 525-2072
Puppets, books, games, and audiotapes.

Miscellaneous

American Heart Association
   44 East 23rd Street
   New York, NY 10010
   Check your telephone directory for a local AHA affiliate. A variety of educational materials are available, including school site health promotion curricula.

Lead Alert Kit
   Francon Enterprises, Inc.
   P. O. Box 300321
   Seattle, WA 98103
   (800) 359-9000
   Tests pottery, toys, metalware, and decorated glassware for leaching of lead.

National Dairy Council® Order Department*
   6300 North River Road
   Rosemont, IL 60018-4233
   (708) 696-1020
   Curriculum packages for children, preschool through high school, and other consumer materials; some available in Spanish.
   *Or check your telephone directory for a local Dairy Council® affiliate near you.

Table Manners for Everyday Use by Handy Vision
   Sybervision Systems, Inc.
   (800) 678-0887
   A humorous instructional video that can be enjoyed by both children and adults.

The Vegetarian Resource Group
   P. O. Box 1463
   Baltimore, MD 21203
   (301) 366-VEGE
   Resource list and many free or low-cost teaching materials about vegetarianism, suitable for preschoolers through teens.

Community Resources, Support Groups, and Information Sources

General Information

Local agencies, including:
   City, county, or state health department
   Cooperative Extension Service
   Women, Infants, and Children (WIC) supplemental food program
   Universities with programs in nutrition, dietetics, or food service management
   Child Care Food Program
   Affiliates of the American Heart Association, American Diabetes Association, American Cancer Society, or Dairy Council®

Help for Children with Special Needs

Nutritionists in state and local health departments

Pediatric nutritionists, occupational therapists, and physical therapists in programs serving children with special needs; for example, genetics treatment centers, diagnostic evaluation centers, and teaching hospitals

Allergies

The Food Allergy Network
   4744 Holly Avenue
   Fairfax, VA 22030-5647
   (703) 691-3179
   (800) 929-4040 (orders)
   National nonprofit organization helps families cope with food allergies and increases public awareness about food allergies and anaphylaxis. Books, videos, supplies, and memberships (including a newsletter) are available.

Infolert
    27068 La Paz, #324
    Laguna Hills, CA 92656
    (714) 454-8809
    Offers neon-colored badges to alert
    caregivers and others to a child's allergy.

Chronic Illness

Children's P.K.U. Network
    (619) 233-3202

Gluten Intolerance Group of
    North America
    P. O. Box 23053
    Seattle, WA 98102-0353
    (206) 325-6980

P.K.U. Parents
    8 Myrtle Lane
    San Anselmo, CA 94960
    (415) 457-4632

Social and Environmental Issues

Center for Urban Education and
    Sustainable Agriculture
    1417 Josephine Street
    Berkeley, CA 94701
    (510) 526-2788
    Resource for information on
    school gardens.

Chefs Collaborative
    Oldways Preservation and Exchange Trust
    25 First Street
    Cambridge, MA 02141
    (617) 621-3000
    Involved in interesting environmental
    projects in schools.

Mothers and Others for a Livable Planet
    National Resources Defense Council
    Dept. D
    40 West 20th Street, 9th floor
    New York, NY 10011
    (212) 242-0010
    Special project dedicated to environ-
    mental problems that especially affect
    children. Publishes *Green Guide*,
    15 issues/year.

National Agriculture in the Classroom Office
    Stop 2291, Room 4309-S
    U.S. Department of Agriculture
    1400 Independence Avenue, SW
    Washington, DC 20250-0991
    (202) 720-7925

Food Safety Questions

EPA Safe Drinking Water Hotline
    (800) 426-4791

Food and Drug Administration
    Center for Food Safety and Applied
    Nutrition
    (800) 332-4010

National Lead Information Center
    (800) 532-3394

USDA Meat and Poultry Hotline
    (800) 535-4555
    10 A.M.–4 P.M. weekdays

Food and Nutrition Hotlines

American Dietetic Association
    (900) 225-5267   Speak to a registered dietitian
                      (Monday–Friday, 9–5 central time)

    (800) 366-1655   Listen to a prerecorded message
                      (Monday–Friday, 8–8 central time)

Baby Food Consumer Information
    Beech-Nut   (800) 523-6633
    Earth's Best   (800) 442-4221
    Gerber   (800) 443-7237
    Heinz   (800) USA-BABY
    Simply Pure   (800) 426-7873

United Soybean Board
    (800) TALK-SOY

Online Resources

American Dietetic Association
    (http://www.eatright.org)

Ask the Dietitian
    (http://www.hoptechno.com/rdindex.htm)

Center for Food Safety and Applied Nutrition
    (http://www.vm.cfsan.fda.gov/list.html)

Dietitian On-Line
    (http://ireland.ioi.ie/~javad/)

Fast Food Facts—Interactive Food Finder
    (http://www.olen.com/food/)

Food and Nutrition Information Center,
    U.S. Department of Agriculture
    (fnic@nalusda.gov)

International Food Information Council
    (http://ificinfo.health.org)

U.S. Soyfoods Directory
    (http://soyfoods.com)

Index

Recipe Index